THE NEXT 20 YEARS OF YOUR LIFE

A PERSONAL GUIDE INTO THE YEAR 2017

RICHARD WORZEL

Stoddart

TORONTO · BUFFALO

Published in 1997 by
Stoddart Publishing Co. Limited

Distributed in Canada by
General Distribution Services Inc.
30 Lesmill Road
Toronto, Canada M3B 2T6
Tel. (416) 445-3333
Fax (416) 445-5967
e-mail Customer.Service@ccmailgw.genpub.com

Distributed in the United States by
General Distribution Services Inc.
85 River Rock Drive, Suite 202
Buffalo, New York 14207
Toll free tel. 1-800-805-1083
Toll free fax 1-800-481-6207
e-mail gdsinc@genpub.com

01 00 99 98 97   1 2 3 4 5

Cataloging in Publication Data

Worzel, Richard, 1950–
The next 20 years of your life: a personal guide
into the year 2017

ISBN 0-7737-3013-3

1. Canada – Forecasting.   2. Twenty-first century – Forecasts.
3. Social prediction – Canada.   4. Economic forecast – Canada.
I. Title.   II. Title: The next twenty years of your life.

HN103.5.W67 1997   303.4971   97-930313-3

Cover design: Bill Douglas @ The Bang
Text design: Tannice Goddard

Printed and bound in Canada

This book is dedicated to all good teachers, past and present, who create a better future by inspiring their students and helping them to understand and fulfil their own potential, and to my own teachers who helped me become who I am. Foremost among them are:

- Miss Englander, my grade 1 teacher, who taught me to read;
- Mrs. Crole, my grade 3 teacher, who taught me how to create an outline and write topic sentences and paragraphs;
- Miss Sharon Smith, my grade 12 social studies teacher, who taught me how to use the library effectively and perform systematic research; and especially
- Dr. Peter A. Lawton, my high school math teacher and friend, who led me to see my potential as a student and worth as a human being at a time when I had serious doubts about both. One of Pete's other students once made a comment about him that I would like to extend to all good teachers:

"You make your living by teaching,
but your profession is humanity."

Contents

Prologue:
The Future Starts Now

Would your life be easier if you knew what to expect during the next 20 years? That's what I'm going to attempt in this book: to help you anticipate what your future will be like, and how you and the world are going to change, between now and the year 2017.

Wherever I go, I find that the future bewilders people; they don't know what to make of what's happening around them or what these events will mean to them. So to start our journey, let me offer you a simple, unifying principle that sums up the changes we will all encounter: the future will offer both more opportunity and less security.

Virtually every trend I see verifies this assumption, and you will better understand the changes that you see if you keep this principle in mind. In this book, I'm going to explore a variety of factors that are going to produce dramatic changes in your life: computers, communications, society, families, jobs, business, management, health care, life expectancy, education, and more. Each offers more freedom (another word for opportunity) coupled with more danger and uncertainty.

The Dominant Theme of Our Time

A while back I was a guest on a television phone-in show. Before we got down to taking calls, the show's producers posed a question for their viewers: "Would you rather live 100 years in the past, or 100 years in the future?" They gave two different numbers to call, depending on how you wanted to answer. When they tallied the replies, we found that almost *two-thirds* of the callers wanted to live in the past. Surprisingly, this show catered to young adults, people in their late teens and early twenties.

I was taken aback at the yearning for what many think of as a simpler, easier past, but not by the widespread anxiety about the future, because I encounter this fear of an uncertain tomorrow all the time. Anxiety and fear have become our society's dominant emotions.

Why Are People Afraid?

Canadians fear the future for several reasons, but the predominant source of worry for many people is job security. In fact, the one question that I am asked more than any other is: where will the jobs be in the future? I hear this question whether I'm talking to high school students or the senior executives of major corporations. Some people ask out of concern for their own careers, but most adults are anxious about whether their children will find work. And young people themselves, even as early as grades 7 and 8, worry about whether they will be able to find a job. Seeing friends, older brothers and sisters, and perhaps their parents out of work, and knowing that even people with solid qualifications and a wealth of experience are sometimes unable to find employment, makes them wonder what they will have to do to succeed.

The reality is that society and the economy are changing at a speed and in ways that we have never experienced before. The old ways of doing things, the reliable patterns by which we once governed our lives, no longer work. This constant barrage of change gives rise to widespread anxiety.

Does this mean we have a gloomy and unhappy future before us? Not at all — because what we will lose in security, we will gain in opportunity.

What Will the Future Be Like?

No one can accurately and consistently predict what will happen in the future. However, it's not necessary to predict all aspects of the future to prosper. Instead, you can plan successfully for the future by using what you know today and having the necessary flexibility to adapt as you go along. Think of a surfer riding a wave. The surfer doesn't expect to be able to predict exactly what the wave is going to do. Instead, she watches for unexpected changes and alters her stance and her tactics in midstream to stay afloat.

This is what we will all need to do in future: watch for developments, plan for possibilities, and change our actions in midstream to adapt. And, like the surfer, we will have to be prepared to start again when we wipe out.

The purpose of this book is to make you aware of some of the changes likely to roll toward you in the next 20 years so that you can think about them and start to prepare. Some of this material I've written in the form of vignettes, little stories told from the perspective of people like you who are living in tomorrow's world. These may seem like predictions, but they're not. Rather, they are projections of what *might* happen.

Indeed, some of these projections may appear to contradict each other. Some are highly optimistic, others deeply pessimistic, and yet others are hard to label. Rather than try to weave a single, internally consistent picture of tomorrow, I'm using these stories to highlight specific developments, and to illustrate the kinds of effects they might have on your life. You can be sure that the future will be different from what is contained in any specific vignette, but their overall purpose is to give you the information and the mental tools to think about how specific developments might affect you.

Those who have read my previous book, *Facing the Future: The Seven Forces Revolutionizing Our Lives*, will notice that this book takes a different approach, but that the two books complement each other. Nevertheless, you can read this book without having read *Facing the Future*, or vice-versa. Each covers subject material not available in the other, although they also intersect at important points and have some themes in common. But *The Next 20 Years of Your Life* is intended to be both more personal and more speculative. It is more personal because people don't just want to know what the future will hold in general; they want to know what it will hold for *them*. It is more speculative because it looks at a specific time period, and attempts to anticipate the events that might occur over the next 20 years. Sometimes I move chronologically from development to development over the 20-year span. Other times I jump to the end and look at the cumulative effects of change.

Whether you find the changes rolling toward us fascinating or frightening, the future has issued you a surfboard, and the curl is most definitely up. You can wait for the waves to crash over you — or you can grab your board, and head out for the ride of your life. The one thing you cannot do is sit on the beach and expect to wait for calmer weather.

Surf's up! Good luck.

1
Your Computer Genie

Tama's computer butler, Alfred, awakens her by gently calling her name, and gradually raising the lighting level in the room. She sits up, rubs her eyes, and calls to him that she's awake. Once she's finished with the washroom, she gets back into bed and puts on her "Looking Glasses," which look like a pair of eyeglasses but have transparent liquid crystal diode (LCD) panels instead of lenses. The Looking Glasses act as her computer monitor and let Alfred display information for her: graphs, pictures, videos, even live images of people she's talking to on the phone. They're also ground to her prescription, so they act as eyeglasses when no data is on display.

In her younger days, Tama shied away from technology, especially from computers. Now at age 58, she still remembers the computers of her school days as behemoths with flashing lights that spoke strange languages like FORTRAN and COBOL and worked in mysterious ways that always made her feel stupid. She also remembers when computers forced their way into her workplace at a big corporation, and the panic she felt when she finally had to confront the beast that had been placed on her desk. She remembers all the talk about the Internet, once it started to become popular in the 1990s, and how it also gave her the feeling of being dumb about something that everyone else was so smart about. And she remembers the disdain she and so many others felt when trendy people started wearing computers after the turn of the century, as if they were flaunting their position among the cyber-elite, plugged in and turned on all the time.

Wearable computers started out as boxes the size of a double deck of playing cards worn on a belt, with displays like oversized, rectangular wristwatches. They quickly evolved into machines small enough to be effectively invisible, with the central processor disappearing into pieces of jewelry, or incorporated into a wristwatch, coupled with an earpiece the size of a hearing aid, a throat microphone, and Looking Glasses.

At first, the people who wore computers were called "tuppies" — "technologically upscale peasants" — and stand-up comics made jokes about brain-dead zombies being operated by their computers. But, gradually, as people became more familiar with the new technologies, and the costs came down to where they were affordable for anyone who was working, more and more people started to discover the advantages of having an electronic slave.

When she thinks about it at all any more, Tama has to admit that things are so much easier now that computers have become almost human, like a pet that can speak, understand, run errands, and make phone calls for you. Although she found it intimidating at first having Alfred with her almost all the time — like having someone constantly looking over her shoulder — she would now find herself almost completely lost without her "computer genie" to take care of the routine details of her life.

Right now, Alfred is reviewing her day's agenda with her. He informs her he's made a hair appointment at 10:00 a.m., as she asked him to do five weeks ago following her last appointment; that she has to finish the next chapter of the book she is writing on the history of English drama if she is to stay on schedule; and that she has a committee report due on child labour before 9 p.m.

Since she has an hour free, Tama asks to speak to her 20-year-old foster daughter. Helen is a street kid whose father left her family when she was three, and whose mother is an alcoholic, prompting Helen to run away from home at age 12. Now Helen is living at the city-sponsored Step Up residence — a converted hospital — while she finishes her high school equivalence.

Alfred makes the contact, and Tama finds that Helen has been up for two hours, delivering free samples of a new antibacterial hand soap. They chat about their plans for Helen's graduation from Step Up's online tutoring centre. Tama asks Alfred to remind her to speak to an old chum who works in admissions at the Sorbonne in Paris. Although Helen couldn't afford to move to Paris, she can still take a degree program through distance learning — if she can pass the International Baccalaureate-administered entrance exam. After chatting about Helen's plans for a while, the two women bless each other and clear.

A New Way of Thinking About and Using Computers

We're used to thinking of computers as distinct pieces of equipment, boxes with monitor screens that are housed in special rooms in an office, or personal computers that sit on our desks. That is all about to change.

As computers continue to get smaller and faster, they will soon reach the stage where we'll be able to pack a really powerful computer into a very small, lightweight package. In this vignette, Tama's computer, which she calls Alfred, acts as her assistant and gofer, yet is compact and light enough that we would not notice it if we were in the same room with her. Her central home computer with most of her permanently archived files, which is secured in an unobtrusive place in her office, communicates with her by infrared, low-power FM radio, or telephone (about which more later). She wears the local node of her computer network in a lightweight bracelet.

Tama instructs Alfred by voice, speaking what seems to be ordinary English (or French, Spanish, Italian, or whatever her language of choice might be), but is actually a well-defined language structure worked out between her and Alfred over a period of time. Right out of the box, Alfred was able to speak and understand a simplified version of English. Over time, as Tama used expressions, words, or grammatical constructs that Alfred did not understand, he asked her for clarification, then stored the information for future use. When he received a command for a significant action that could not easily be undone or corrected, he always repeated back to her his understanding of what she wanted, and asked her to confirm that he had it right. This gradual and careful structuring of Alfred's language recognition programming eventually gave him the ability to understand most of what Tama said without further explanation.

Moreover, without even realizing she was doing so, Tama came to avoid those complicated sentence structures that gave Alfred the most difficulty, learning from him even as he learned from her. In this way, over a period of weeks and months, Tama and Alfred reached a high level of mutual understanding, allowing her merely to speak her wishes and be confident that Alfred would understand and interpret them correctly.

Today's computers can already "recognize" human speech. The hardware and software currently exist to take a specific sound, which we would recognize as a particular word, for example "open," and convert it into the combination of letters, "o-p-e-n," that corresponds to the sound. As a result, it is now possible to give verbal commands to computers, and to dictate memos and other documents, at speeds of up to 80 words a minute or more, once the speaker has become adept at using a computer in this way. But there is a still quite a bit of daylight between recognizing a sound as corresponding to a particular combination of letters, and understanding the meaning of a sentence. While computers may never truly "understand" human speech, with all of its subtle emotional and other connotations, the ability of a computer genie to interpret correctly fairly complex verbal commands is a virtual certainty within the next 20 years.

Tama's microphone for speaking to Alfred could be a small disk, perhaps the size of a dime, either taped to her throat under an adhesive bandage, or worn as a necklace. In her home, she might have a low-powered radio receiver pick up the signal from the microphone and transmit it to her main computer. On the road, or outside her home, she might wear a transceiver on a belt, button, or hair band, whatever was simplest and least cumbersome. Alfred would reply to Tama through an earpiece of the sort that come with the portable tape players now used by joggers, or perhaps even through a surgical implant in her ear.

Even in early 1996 it was possible to buy special-use wearable computers — such as the System Six Wearable Computer from Intervision Systems Inc. — for such applications as fire fighting, process control, field and plant surveys, and military use. These computers had 25-MHz Intel 486 processors, with 105 megabyte removable hard drives, and a head-mounted display worn on a hard hat or helmet. This computer was voice-activated and had a 500-word vocabulary of continuous speech. In 1996, computers like this weighed about 1.5 kilograms, and cost less than US$10,000. Such computers will get progressively lighter, cheaper, and more powerful. Within 20 years, virtually everyone will depend on them.

Desktop computers and even mainframes will continue to exist in the short run because they offer power and resources hard to duplicate in a lightweight, wearable computer. However, the steady march of smaller, cheaper, and faster computers, combined with other radical changes about to hit the field of communications, may eventually banish larger computers entirely.

6

What Will Computer Genies Mean to Your Life?

The "downstream" effects of a technological development are usually the most important and the hardest to anticipate. One of the classic examples of unforeseen effects is the impact of electronic communication. The primary effect of the invention of electronic communication, starting with the telegraph, was the ability to transmit information over long distances. One of the secondary, or downstream, effects was that electronic communication increased trade, because people could coordinate their efforts over longer distances. Another secondary effect was the growth of the mass entertainment industry, starting with performers on the "wireless," or radio, and leading to today's global distribution of popular entertainment in the form of television, videos, and CDs. The tertiary effects of electronic communication include the emergence of a global economy, which is displacing people in low-skilled jobs in the developed world, and the erosion of the need for people to come together to be entertained. This results in social isolation and a declining interest in formerly shared community values. In the end, the social and economic shifts created by electronic communication are more important than its ability to transmit information over long distances.

What downstream effects of having a computer genie like Alfred will you experience 20 years from now? A high-capacity computer dedicated to serving you 24 hours a day, every day of your life, would come to know you very well indeed. Moreover, such computers will be able to *learn* — that is, add to their stock of information and adapt their behaviour according to situations they have experienced before. They will be able to monitor scores of routine functions in your daily life: keep your appointment calendar; watch your bank balance and trigger payments for bills at the appropriate times; store your telephone directory and address books; and manage the logistics of housekeeping, like controlling temperature and ordering groceries. But this is just the beginning of their potential.

Watching Your Health

As Tama works through the day, Alfred starts to notice that her heartbeat is faster than it should be for the time of day and for her current level of exertion. Her galvanic skin response indicates that she is starting to experience unusual stress, even though she hasn't yet become consciously aware of it. As Alfred monitors the fine movements of her muscles, he notices that she is tense and uncomfortable. Finally, her body temperature starts to rise slightly, and this triggers Alfred to call Aesculapius, the provincial health diagnostic service genie.

Aesculapius maintains a database of all current diseases and health disruptions in Tama's area, as well as all new medical research findings. It is the first agency that people who are covered by provincial health insurance consult when they are having health problems.

In Tama's case, Aesculapius estimates that there is a 54 percent probability that Tama is coming down with a virus that is currently making the rounds in southern B.C. It forwards this diagnosis, along with less likely possibilities, to both Alfred, and to Tama's doctor's genie.

Tama first finds out about any of this when Alfred interrupts what she is doing to tell her she is probably getting sick, and to inform her that she has an appointment to speak with her doctor by videophone in 17 minutes. He suggests that she goes back to bed. This has all happened in accordance with a procedure that Tama, Alfred, the provincial health service, and her doctor worked out years earlier, when Alfred first started serving

Tama. As part of this procedure, Tama instructed Alfred not to disturb her unless there was a significant possibility that she was getting sick, which now exists.

A wearable computer that is with you all the time will be able to gauge your health on a second-by-second basis. This capability has many downstream implications. The first and most obvious is that genies will be able to save lives. Most people who have heart attacks, for instance, either do not recognize the symptoms, or refuse to accept that it is happening to them. But the survival rate for people who receive treatment within two hours of the onset of an attack is substantially higher than for those who do not. With a computer genie, there will be a much higher level of certainty, as the genie will be able to quickly assess all of the early warning symptoms and verify that they are consistent with those of a heart attack. The same will be true for people going into insulin shock, or trauma shock, or experiencing the onset of a rapidly developing disease.

When this computerized diagnostic capability is combined with the timely attention of a human doctor, medical conditions will be identified much more quickly, treated more effectively, the results of treatment will be monitored more carefully, and the details of such treatment available in much greater detail than ever before. I'll talk about this more in chapter 9. If patients are willing to share the information collected on their responses to treatment, physicians and pharmaceutical companies will be able to refine treatments and hone in on improved procedures with astonishing rapidity, which will save more lives and money.

But this kind of health monitoring is a two-edged sword, for it will also make it much easier for governments, insurers, and other outside agencies to intrude on your privacy. Suppose, for instance, that provincial health insurance in future is based partly on the kind of lifestyle you lead. If you live right, exercise, eat properly, keep your weight down, avoid smoking and excessive use of recreational chemicals, and are willing to have your genie share this information with your medical insurer, you will get the lowest possible life insurance and health insurance premiums. If you don't exercise enough, or you eat too much, then your premiums will start to rise according to a statistical scale of how likely you are to have health problems. And if you refuse to share this information, you will get either the worst available rate, or the most pessimistic rate for someone of your age, sex, and background.

But wouldn't such an intrusion be prohibited as discriminatory? Well, maybe — but if our current problems in funding health services continue (and I expect they will get worse), there will be increasing pressure on individuals to take responsibility for managing their own health.

Screening Incoming Information

A computer genie could handily manage the flood of information that flows in and around your life. One of the problems of the information age is information overload: it's hard to know what to pay attention to and what to ignore.

Imagine that your genie could answer calls for you, then decide whether to let the call through or not, whether to take a message or not, or whether to refuse calls from a particular individual, or kind of caller. Your genie could, for instance, check the number of an incoming call against your databank of previous calls. If the caller had phoned earlier, you will have given instructions for subsequent calls from that person, which the genie would then follow. If the call was from someone you didn't want to talk to, the call would be shuttled to your answering machine. If it was from someone you desperately wanted to talk to, your genie could track you down, using a list of previously stored numbers or locations where you might be found (assuming you didn't wear your phone all the time).

If you weren't taking calls at the moment, and someone tried to call you, your genie would simply record a message, then hangup. If you were taking calls, but a call was from a number not listed in the genie's database, then your genie would check to see if it was from a business phone, or from a personal phone. If it was from a business phone, your genie could ask why the caller was phoning, record the answer, put the caller on hold, contact you, play the recording, and ask if you wanted to accept the call. If not, the genie would relay that message to the caller and hang up. Among other things, this would prevent telemarketers from interrupting your dinner. If you were trying to prevent a specific individual from getting through to you, you would be protected even when they called from a different phone. Your genie could record and file their voice print, and check it against incoming callers. If the genie found a match, it could refuse the call.

Filtering phone calls this way will have the downstream effect of making it easier for people to shut themselves off from each other. If we start substituting videophones and telepresence for direct human contact, and if genies become gatekeepers for all such communications, human beings may become less gregarious, less tolerant, and less understanding of each other.

Likewise, your genie will start to sift through the huge volume of news that comes your way electronically each day. You'll start by letting your genie know when you read something you find interesting, and when you read something you find a waste of time. Soon your genie would start to be able to predict whether you will find a particular article of interest and ensure that it came to your attention.

You could, for example, instruct your genie that you never wanted to view another story about Madonna or O.J. Simpson. It could then weed out such articles from your daily news stream. You could also tell it that you wanted to hear — immediately — any news about developments that might affect your business.

Much of the technology for this is under development right now. Some of it, such as neural network software, which mimics the techniques the brain uses to process information, has been around for some time, and is only now becoming powerful and refined enough to be of use. Along with other developments, including a brand-new category of software described as "adaptive" or "data-driven" programming, these techniques have the potential to solve problems that defy even human ingenuity. Accordingly, all of the technology needed for a genie capable of the filtering described above is available today. It will revolutionize the direct marketing business, a subject I explore in more depth in chapter 7. It will, however, take time for these techniques to be refined and become commercially available.

This is all fine, but suppose, for instance, that you've told your genie to screen out all mention of flying saucers — and one lands in your city. You would want to hear about it, even though you were previously uninterested in the subject. Some kind of browsing ability will need to be built into the system to allow your genie to scan for news of universal interest.

One of the most profound effects on society as a whole will be that computer screening may destroy our sense of shared destiny and community. If each person gets a personally edited newspaper, and views only those things of particular interest to him, and these choices are completely different from his neighbours', what does that do to the fabric of society?

If we don't experience the same information and ideas, discuss subjects of mutual interest, and share assumptions about what is good and bad, then we will surely drift apart from each other, defining ourselves less and less as "we," and more and more in terms of "me." This trend is evident even today in the gap between what is reported about Quebec and related constitutional issues in the English-language media and the French-language media, or even in the central Canadian newspapers, and those of Atlantic Canada and western Canada. So if, in future, you tell your genie to screen out all discussion about renewed federalism, the separation of

Quebec, and the actions of the Bloc Québécois and the Parti Québécois, you run the risk of waking up one morning to the news that Quebec has separated. Worse, you may no longer care, because you will have no sense of Canada as a nation or of Canadians as a people.

> Three days later, Tama sits down to work on the text she's authoring on the history of English drama. She reviews her research to date, and finds that she's up to Shakespeare. Tama calls up her existing notes and tells Alfred to access the Net for information relating to the question of whether Shakespeare wrote his plays or someone else did. She finds most of what she needs, but wants the current phase of this neverending debate, and asks for a summary of an online discussion held two days ago that was hosted by the University of Belfast, in Gaelic. Alfred provides a translation of the Gaelic commentary.
>
> A comment by one of the debaters, who participated by telepresence from India, catches Tama's attention, and she decides to follow it up. Tama asks Alfred to contact that person. He informs her that it's 1:00 a.m. in India (it's 11:30 a.m. PST), so Tama instructs Alfred to call the scholar's genie and request an appointment for 7:30 PST the next morning (9 p.m. in India). The conversation will be in English and Hindi, and will be translated by each person's genie.
>
> Going back to the text, Tama dictates the points she wants to cover, then uses her finger as a cursor to arrange the points in the desired order on the flat screen above her desk. Tama then uses a wireless keyboard to type the outline of the chapter. Alfred takes the outline and Tama's oral and typed notes, and produces a rough first draft, using previous examples of her writing style to guide his choice of words. Tama reads through the draft, making the changes she wants on her keyboard, or instructing Alfred on what changes to make. Alfred automatically adds

footnotes and bibliographic annotations.

Tama then instructs Alfred to source and buy the rights to use an illustration of the original Globe Theatre, portraits of Shakespeare and Sir Francis Bacon, a photograph of the Globe Theatre rebuilt in London in the late 1900s, and a video clip of A Midsummer Night's Dream being performed before a live audience there. Alfred arranges these on her screen for Tama to review and edit.

She's unhappy with the overall appearance of the document and asks Alfred to forward it to her favourite graphic artist for suggestions and sprucing up. Alfred makes the contact, negotiates a price for the work, and receives a completion date, based on arrangements Tama's made for such work in the past. Tama pushes away from her desk, satisfied with her morning's efforts.

Within the next 20 years, virtually all of the world's knowledge will be available electronically. Most books will have been transferred into electronic form, and whole libraries will be available either online or on compact disc. As the data capacity of compact discs continues to expand, some enterprising companies will start to translate books that are out of copyright into electronic form, and sell them online and on CD-ROM. Given that the developers of consumer electronics expect to be able to cram about 17 gigabytes on a CD-ROM within the next decade, it will be possible to have a massive collection of English literature on a single disc. Without graphics or multimedia, a single CD-ROM could hold the text of roughly 28,000 books — an entire library on a single, silvery disc.

Moreover, as the Internet continues to grow, and as people around the world continue to make resources available online, most of the works of humanity will become available. You won't be limited to works in English, either, because computers will be able to perform passable translations of other languages on demand.

But how will you be able, practically speaking, to use all the knowledge available? How can you drink an ocean, even if it's held to your lips? The simple answer is: you can't.

Anyone who has tried to find a specific piece of information on the Internet knows how frustrating the experience can be. You know it's out there, but you just can't find it. Now imagine an Internet that has matured into a truly global network, to which most people have immediate access, and on which everybody stores everything that they want to share or sell. Clearly, the organization of information and the ability to search intelligently will become crucial so that we don't drown in our own wealth. And this is where genies will come in again. Based on its understanding of the kind of work you do, and the information you have asked for and found useful in the past, your genie will wade through the global haystack of knowledge and find the needles of pertinent information you are seeking.

Some of the biggest financial winners in the technology race will be those who design efficient and easy-to-use search and cataloguing systems. Even a high-speed computer genie will need such information-management tools as indices, catalogues, and guides to published literature.

Current technology makes it plain that within the next 20 years it will be possible to send your genie off to ferret out highly specific information, and have it return promptly with what you want. Given that most of the work we will do in the future will be based on information, the speed at which we learn to access relevant information is going to be a major factor in how successful we are as individuals.

Imagine the incalculable riches that will be available to you in your own home! If used wisely, this will be wealth that our ancestors could not have dreamed of. If used poorly, or with evil intent — such as teaching others how to build bombs or commit acts of terrorism — this will unleash destructive powers we can barely imagine, and against which there may be no defence.

2
Whenever, Wherever Communications

The communications industry is going to experience more radical and more rapid changes than any other major industry in the world during the next 20 years, making it a rapidly moving target, hard to hit, and hard to evaluate at any given moment. Moreover, the older you are, the more confusing and chaotic you are likely to find the successive waves of new developments that will wash over you.

Why does age have anything to do with it? In my experience, older people are less intrigued by technology, and more irritated and intimidated by it. I'm not sure if this attitude is related solely to age so that today's young people will have just as hard a time with new developments when they are older, or whether it's a fundamental difference between the pre-wired and post-wired generations. Nevertheless, if you are now over 45 or thereabouts, you may find the changes to come frustrating. No sooner will you adjust to one new service, and one new set of ways of using communications, than a newer one will come along, forcing you to learn everything all over again.

Think, for example, of your present experiences with long-distance service providers. You're sitting at dinner when the phone rings, and this unnaturally cheerful voice asks you how you are today, and whether you'd like to save money on your long-distance calls? All you really want to do is get back to your dinner, but you feel pretty stupid saying you don't want to save money, and so you let your dinner get cold while you listen to yet another sales spiel. Now imagine if you had perhaps a dozen or more different kinds of new communications services available to you, all of which you feel you must understand, evaluate and learn how to use, and all of them competing desperately for your business. That's how the communications field is going to be, like it or not.

Here's how telecommunications might look through the eyes of an adept user 20 years from now, after most of the dust has settled in the Comm Wars to come.

Marc is late, he hasn't been able to find a parking space near his appointment, and he has to walk through one of the seedier, more dangerous parts of town to get to his appointment. Even though his concern about the interview ahead occupies most of his thoughts, he also has niggling doubts about his safety on the mean streets of Toronto's inner city.

Marc is a 35-year-old software engineer specializing in adaptive computing software. He was a technologically sophisticated teenager, keen on the latest computers and an avid Net surfer even back in the communications Stone Age of the 1990s. As a result, he has eagerly and nimbly shifted from change to change as new communication technologies have appeared, and as companies have come and gone in the industry. He now prepares to use this skill to protect himself from potential danger.

"Shields up, Mr. Sulu," Marc mumbles to his genie, whom he has named after a character in the classic 1960s television space opera "Star Trek." The "shields up" command triggers a sequence of events. First, Mr. Sulu pinpoints Marc's exact geographic position using the Global Positioning Network of satellites. Next, Mr. Sulu contacts Marc's security provider,

16

Minders Inc., alerting the monitoring genie that Marc is currently safe, but has concerns about his welfare. This commlink will remain continuously open during the shields up alert, and if trouble arises, or if the link is cut, Minders' genie will immediately call the police and give Marc's last known location.

Finally, Mr. Sulu turns his attention to monitoring Marc's surroundings. Tapping into the satellite network again, Mr. Sulu calls for a live video picture of Toronto, tightly focused on the area immediately around Marc. This is relatively expensive — it will probably cost Marc four or five dollars for the ten minutes he will use it — but it gives Mr. Sulu the opportunity to examine all the buildings and people around Marc, and to warn Marc of potentially dangerous situations or ominous groupings of people.

"Cross the street here," Mr. Sulu says to Marc. "There's a group of five people in the alley on your right up ahead, and only one of them has a phone address. From their dress and size, I would guess they are street kids. Move to the far side of the sidewalk opposite, and put some other pedestrians between you and them." Marc does as suggested. Sure enough, as a woman walks by the alley, the group emerges and starts to hassle her under the guise of asking for spare change.

"Video feed to the police," Marc instructs. He has ordered Mr. Sulu to forward the satellite image of the group, along with his own video images captured by his LCD Looking Glasses as he walked by, to the police.

Thirty seconds later, a police cruiser and van pull up, and two officers get out while their drivers watch alertly, hands on riot control weapons. The police don't arrest the loitering kids, but they leave, muttering about invasions of privacy, and casting about angry looks as they try to determine who might have called the cops.

"Try to sell the images," Marc tells Mr. Sulu, even as he hurries away from the scene. Local news retailers are not interested in an assault that didn't happen, but a sociology professor in Wichita, Kansas, who is researching street youth offers to reimburse Marc for his costs for the clip. After a brief negotiation, Mr. Sulu accepts the offer, and the credit transfer is made.

Marc arrives at his appointment in time to catch his breath and cancel the shields up alert before being ushered into the interview. As the conversation between Marc and the interviewers goes back and forth, Mr. Sulu reminds Marc of the things he has said in his proposal to this group, of the committee's statements about what they are seeking in a candidate, and something of the backgrounds of each of the interviewers. The interviewers hear and see nothing of the information Mr. Sulu is feeding Marc, and Marc gives nothing away by his demeanour. However, the interviewers know exactly what Mr. Sulu is doing for Marc, because each of them is getting the same kind of information from their own genies.

At a critical point in the interview, Mr. Sulu tells Marc that the company interviewing him has just issued a press release announcing the signing of a contract in Venezuela. The services they are to provide to the Venezuelan government are dependent on exactly the kinds of skills Marc has. Mr. Sulu estimates that the company will need either him, or someone very much like him, and quickly. Based on this information, Marc makes a calculated gamble, and toughens his negotiating posture, asking for a lower base fee plus a share of the profits, rather than a flat fee for the entire project. Realizing that his genie has tipped Marc off, the interviewers quickly agree before Marc has a chance to make any further evaluation and up his demands.

There are handshakes most of the way around. However, the personal health profiles each person's genie transmits to every other genie indicate that there are slight but measurable health risks between Marc and one of the interviewers if they come into direct physical contact. Accordingly, on the instructions of both genies, they merely nod in a friendly way. No offence is taken by either party; this is a common social occurrence that carries no stigma.

Marc leaves, satisfied that he has an entry into a major new contract, and has started to build a useful new relationship. Feeling cocky and preoccupied with his good fortune, he has to be reminded by Mr. Sulu to call for a shields up alert again for his walk back to the car.

This vignette indicates the kind of widespread use of communications that will become commonplace within the next 20 years. Note that the retrieving and delivering of information was funneled seamlessly through a single agency: his computer genie. Having an "intelligent" personal computer assistant will mean that you won't have to think about whether to use the telephone, the Internet, a library, a road map, or broadcast media. Rather than having a range of different communications and information devices for different applications, your genie will serve as your "information appliance," managing your computing, reference, directory, and information needs without requiring instructions from you beyond initial programming.

The seamless management of a wide spectrum of communications media is a necessary adjunct to the inevitable proliferation of services. Without it, we will be surrounded by an incredible clutter of equipment, and frustrated by the need to remember how to use it all. For instance, at the moment I have eight telephones in my home, including a wireless phone, a cellular phone, a Northern Telecom Vista 350 with a built-in computer display screen, plus three rotary dial phones, and a fax/data modem. I also use three different long-distance services, depending on what I'm doing. Each kind of phone or service requires me to have different equipment and remember different procedures. This isn't difficult but it's unnecessarily complicated given that I'm basically performing one simple task — making and receiving phone calls — with all of them. What would it be like if I were using as many different services as Marc, and had no genie to manage them all? The transition period between the proliferation of electronic communications services and the development of intelligent services is likely to be messy.

There are three major forces that are going to produce the barrage of change over the next 20 years: the conversion from analog to digital communication; the emergence of new communications technologies; and a dramatic increase in competition.

The Advantages of Being Digital

Until recently the vast majority of human communication has been analog. This is communication by comparison or by example, pointing at something and saying "the message is like this." An analog clock is one where the hands "point" to the numbers. They don't actually "tell" the time, but they make an image that we have all agreed to interpret the same way. An analog radio broadcast mimics the sounds of a singer by overlaying the patterns of the sound waves onto a radio carrier wave, which your radio receiver interprets and converts back into sound.

Analog communication has many virtues, first among them that it comes naturally to human beings. People use analogies all the time to communicate. If you had never seen a fire, someone would probably describe it to you by analogy: "It's kind of like a bright red flower, but it moves like water" would give you some idea of the appearance of fire.

But analog communication requires you to preserve the structure of the analogy. If someone inaccurately repeated the description of fire by saying, "Fire looks like flowers and water," the analogy would create more confusion than it would dispel. Anything that distorts the structure of an analogy distorts the communication. That means that analog communication is not easy to compress into a compact form. It is also subject to natural distortions during transmission.

This is one reason why we get static on radio broadcasts, and "snow" on our TV screens.

Digital communication translates the original message into a formal and artificial descriptive code based on 0's and 1's rather than on comparisons or analogies. Digital communication has two great advantages. First, it can be compressed into compact form. Repetitive patterns, such as a section of a TV image that is a blue sky, can be sent as a description saying: "536 dots of blue" rather than "blue dot, blue dot, blue dot, blue dot, blue dot, blue dot ..." repeated 536 times. Second, distortion doesn't interfere with the clarity of the final message. Digital communication has built-in quality assurance checks to make sure it has not been distorted. If the receiver notes that a message has failed this check, it either requests a retransmission, or it kills that portion of the message. Hence, a digital message is generally either received perfectly, or not at all. This means that a digital TV image will be much clearer, and will never show snow; a digital radio transmission will be as clear as a CD-ROM played in your own home, with no static.

Up until now, our ability to communicate has been limited by the scarcity of our communications resources. A telephone wire, called a "twisted pair" because it is formed by a pair of wires, can only handle so much analog information and no more. Broadcast frequencies have distinct physical limitations on the quantity of analog information that can be sent over them, so that a television broadcast which relays both sound and visual content requires vastly more frequency spectrum than a radio program. The amount of information that can be sent per second over a given medium is called "bandwidth." Bandwidth has been likened to the diameter of a hose, which determines the amount of water that can be pumped through it. In an analog world, bandwidth is normally fixed; when you've used it up, it's gone and there ain't no more.

In a digital world, though, this is no longer true. As data compression strategies improve, and as computers code and decode compressed data at ever faster rates, the capacity of, say, an ordinary twisted pair will steadily rise until we finally reach the limits of digital compression. Moreover, data transmission doesn't usually happen in an even flow, but with bursts of activity intermixed with lulls. Digital transmission allows for multiplexing — sending more than one digital signal through a given channel simultaneously — which is not normally possible with analog transmission. Multiplexing allows one sender to take advantage of a lull in another's transmission to send a burst of his own. Data compression and multiplexing will expand enormously the capacity of our communications media as we switch from analog to digital communications. And, as usually happens in supply-and-demand equations, as capacity multiplies, prices will drop. But that's not all, because new communication capacity is about to come thundering into the marketplace.

New Technology Means New Choices

Once a telephone conversation is converted to 0's and 1's in digital form, it looks the same as the transmission of data over the Internet, which looks the same as a digital radio or television signal, which looks the same as a digitized graphic illustration or photograph. The only difference between one form of communication and another is that one may require more information per second to appear responsive to the wishes of the user. As anyone who has waited to download a photograph or a video clip from the Internet can tell you, having too little bandwidth for the task is infuriatingly slow, rather like trying to drain a bath tub through a drinking straw.

The growing trend to transmit different kinds of information digitally will have a couple of important consequences over the next 20 years. First, there will be a precipitous drop in the cost of telephone usage. Consider that right now basic telephone service costs about $30 a month. The price is substantially higher for a digital phone line, but let's stick with the lower analog price for now. For approximately $60 a month, you might be able to get a two-way cable hook-up for data communications (if your cable company offered this service, a question we'll come to in a minute). The difference is that an analog telephone line transmits about 28.8 kilobits a second (a "bit" is a single 0 or 1 in a data stream), whereas a cable modem has the capacity to transmit about 30 megabits a second, or about a thousand times more than a conventional phone line. This means that once we switch to digital transmission, and once competition smoothes out the lumps in the different communications media, the cost of being able to transmit 1 kilobit per second will drop from $1.04 to $0.002, which is the difference in cost-per-capacity of a contemporary analog phone line compared with a digital cable hook-up.

Now, in a digital world where a telephone conversation looks exactly the same as a video signal or a picture of your mom, would you rather pay a dollar or two-tenths of a cent for the ability to communicate any of them from one place to another? This is not an apples-to-apples comparison because it ignores developments like digital phone lines and asynchronous transfer modes, and it assumes that the telephone companies aren't going to do anything to stay competitive. But it does illustrate the levels of competition that the communications industry is going to be facing in the next several years.

Several new kinds of communications technologies will become available over the next 20 years, and since they are all going to be digital, they are all going to compete with each other — and with all other existing forms of communications. To envision how the communications market might unfold over the next two decades, let's start with a brief review of the recent past, and then move on to what future developments may mean to you.

Where We've Come From and Where We Are

During the 1960s, consumers were allowed to buy or rent telephones from someone other than their telephone company for the first

time, and to hook that equipment to the telephone network. Today this change seems trivial, but at the time it marked a dramatic change in the relationship between consumers and phone companies. The next significant change was the introduction of the cellular telephone, which happened in 1984. Here was a new way to provide telephone service that didn't come from the traditional cord-from-the-wall telephone. Cellular phones weren't direct competition for the conventional telephone, though, because they were distinctly more expensive. However, in developing countries, where telephone service has yet to become universal, cellular phones are being supplied to communication-hungry consumers who don't want to wait for the phone company to get around to stringing wires. They are, in effect, leap-frogging the old technology with new.

North America and most other developed countries introduced cellular service with limited competition. The wireline, or traditional, telephone company was automatically granted one license, and a second license was granted to a new company or group of companies. In the United States, the second licensee varied from market to market. In Canada, the federal government granted a nationwide license to a single company — Cantel — in competition with the wireline phone companies. One competitor was deemed to be enough, so the competition, although real, was distinctly limited, especially as the two suppliers in each market tend to mimic one another in most respects, matching prices and services.

In the early 1990s competition was taken a step further when the federal government permitted companies other than traditional phone companies to provide long-distance service. For the first time, actual wireline phone service was being provided by someone other than your traditional phone company. Moreover, long-

distance is the single most profitable service for the phone companies, and the new competitors threaten the core of their business.

Competitors charged into the long-distance business, convinced
that the Canadian phone companies were going to be slow to
respond, just as the American phone companies were, leaving fat
profits on the table for the new entrants. However, the Canadian
phone companies had watched what had happened in the United
States, and came out swinging, with the net result that long-distance competitors got off to a much slower start than they expected,
and they've been hard pressed to make money. This may not prove
to be to the long-term advantage of the Canadian phone companies,
though, as the principal competition for long-distance service is
now in the hands of two American-backed companies — Sprint
Canada and AT&T Canada — that have deep pockets and a high
level of consumer name recognition.

In all three instances — allowing outside hardware to be hooked
up to the telephone system, the introduction of cellular service, and
the introduction of competition for long-distance service — Canada
has followed the trends established in the United States, although
with two differences. First, we have followed along behind, often
several years behind, the United States, which means that we can
watch what happens as they deregulate the communications business and perhaps avoid some of the problems that they encounter. It
also means, though, that the price of our communications services
will not drop as fast as theirs, which may put those of our industries
that are heavy users of communications at a competitive disadvantage relative to their American counterparts. This may or may not
be significant if the difference in cost is relatively small.

The second difference is that our market is much shallower than
the American market, and our phone companies are, relative to the
size of our market, much bigger. This means that it is going to be
tougher for new competitors to battle against Canadian phone
companies. It also means that global-scale telecom companies

like AT&T and BT (formerly British Telecom) will find our more homogeneous market an attractive place to compete.

The stage is now set for the next moves, which will start with competition for local telephone service, for the provision of services that compete with cable television services, and for wireless communications services — plus competition between all of these service providers and several other kinds of companies as well.

One Possible Communications Future

The ultimate objective of communications users is to be able to send and receive the signal requiring the largest bandwidth at the lowest possible cost. At the moment, television or video requires the greatest quantity of bandwidth, so the immediate objective is to be able to send a live, full-colour, two-way television picture from any place — a home, office, or studio — to any other place.

At present, we can do this only with expensive equipment, typically owned by broadcasters and a few major corporations, and with a significant amount of preparation. Over the next five years, producing live, two-way, full-motion, full-colour video is going to be possible for an ordinary consumer, although it will still be quite expensive. Within ten years, it may no longer be any more expensive than current consumer electronic products — and that will change everything.

The next stage in the development of that future has already started. It will change the entire complexion of the Canadian telephone market, and will lead to big changes in other aspects of communications as well. Early in 1996, Industry Canada issued four licenses for Personal Communications Service (PCS), a technology that has been called "son of cellular." PCS is a wireless telephone service, like cellular, and works on the same basic principles as cellular, but there are two major differences.

First, PCS is completely digital, which means that its capacity is expandable, whereas cellular is largely analog, which means its capacity is distinctly limited (unless and until the cellular providers change their customers to digital phones). Second, PCS is coming into the marketplace almost 15 years after cellular, with 15 years of technological development working in its favour.

Moreover, partly owing to the frequencies at which it will operate, and partly because PCS companies are aiming to provide service at a distinctly cheaper price than cellular, it is expected that PCS will not be quite as good or reliable at serving rapidly moving subscribers, say in a car. As a result, after an initial stage of providing mobile telephone service, PCS will seek subscribers in homes and offices, where phones do not move or move very slowly. In effect, PCS will provide competition for wireline telephone companies for local telephone service. This should happen before 2000.

Once again, though, the federal government seems to have hobbled the competition in favour of traditional Canadian communications companies. From the outset, the federal government excluded two companies that might have provided rapid and muscular competition for local phone service. The first, TeleZone Corp., had already spent millions of dollars preparing for a fast start with its PCS service, and had already begun to create a market presence. The second unsuccessful applicant was backed by AT&T. Given that AT&T operates a Canadian long-distance carrier, a PCS license would have given AT&T a complete phone system from coast to coast to compete head to head with existing Canadian phone companies. Since AT&T is a company with deep pockets, enormous experience and expertise, and an established consumer presence and name in Canada, it would have made a formidable competitor for the Canadian telephone companies. Indeed, I doubt that AT&T will allow itself to be shut out indefinitely. Instead, it will work its way into PCS through one or more deals with Rogers Cantel.

Secondly, although Industry Canada originally said they were going to issue six PCS licenses, they issued only *four*, including licenses for the two existing cellular licensees (which it would likely have granted anyway). In effect, after saying it was going to allow competition from four new PCS companies, it permitted only two new entrants — and may have deliberately avoided choosing the strongest competitors. This may not be a bad thing. The communications business will definitely undergo turbulent change in the next decade. By throwing up roadblocks to change, the federal government, through Industry Canada and the CRTC, may be trying to manage this change, watching and learning from the mistakes made in the United States. However, I suspect there is more than just a little favouritism at work here as well, with the government fattening up existing companies at the expense of consumers. In any case, the federal government can only delay change; it cannot stop it.

Beyond the year 2000, the cable companies will pose the next major challenge for the phone companies. The wire that cable companies run into homes and offices has substantially more bandwidth than the twisted pair that the phone companies supply to most Canadian homes and offices. The coaxial cable used by cable companies has the capability to carry at least a couple of hundred video signals. With the right data compression protocol, this could be expanded to roughly 6,000 video signals — or an equivalent amount of (digital) telephone traffic. Some of the more advanced cable companies, and Rogers Cablesystems in particular, are working very hard to get ready for the future. They are taking a segment of their capacity and turning it into a conduit for information to flow out of the home, which is necessary to make cable a two-way medium. Moreover, the major cable companies, and again, especially Rogers, have been furiously building optical fibre networks across their major service areas, financed by cable subscribers under the pretense of providing traditional cable service.

Now, cable systems were designed primarily as a means of distributing large quantities of information in one direction: from the cable company to the home. Accordingly, cable systems require a major redesign and overhaul to become completely switchable, two-way systems. Add the patchwork effect of having regional cable monopolies owned by different companies, compared with the province-wide coverage of most Canadian telephone companies, and it will be a daunting task for the cable companies to jump into head-to-head competition with the well-entrenched phone companies.

29

Nor are the cable companies eager to compete. They know that competition with the telephone companies is going to be a tough, bruising affair, far more difficult and uncertain than their current, cozy, revenue-churning, regional monopolies. Worse, the cable companies generally have much weaker balance sheets, and may not be able to sustain as many knocks and bruises as the telephone companies. But they won't have a choice.

The telephone companies, seeing the way things are going, and again trying to pre-empt damaging competition, are running full speed to provide a dial-up service for video-on-demand. This would allow them to compete directly with the cable companies by providing video signals to the home by telephone. But the phone companies face two problems. First, they have limited capacity owing to a lack of bandwidth, and second, they have no video signals to offer subscribers, whereas video is the *raison d'être* of the cable companies. At the moment there's a standoff while both sides scramble to get their technologies lined up for the coming battle, but it won't last long.

Coming back to PCS, remember that both the traditional telephone companies and Rogers Cantel have been granted PCS licenses. This means that the phone companies will be able to provide a much higher capacity service by using a PCS link to the home to augment the twisted pair they already have, without having to change all the wires strung to every house in the land. It also means that Ted Rogers, the president and CEO of Rogers Communications Inc., has a distinct advantage over his cable company peers — and will undoubtedly try to parlay that into some kind of competitive edge in an age of two-way broadband communication.

What Does All This Mean to You?

For starters, it means inexpensive two-way videophones within the next five years. If you have a digital (ISDN) phone line today, you can buy the hardware and software to hook up to your computer that will give you a slightly jerky, black-and-white videophone for about $200. Within five years, you'll get slightly jerky, full-colour video over your normal phone line to your computer. For a stand-alone videophone you will need a phone that has a video screen, a video camera, and a microprocessor to perform the data compression — in effect, a computer designed to work as a phone. It may be pricy at first, but those who want it will be able to buy it off the shelf.

Sometime within the next ten years, we should see an explosion of videophones comparable to the sudden and unexpected boom in fax machine popularity in the mid-1980s. They will be relatively cheap, on the order of $200, and the image quality will be good (as long as the screen size isn't terribly big). There will likely be the kinds of giveaways and purchase subsidies now taking place with cellular phones as telephone companies, cable companies, and PCS suppliers struggle for market share.

The widespread use of videophones will usher in a new form of communications, which has tentatively been labelled "telepresence." It will become possible to visit with friends and family over long distances in a more emotionally intimate and satisfying way than merely by voice. Business "meetings" will be held by videophone, which will cut down on airline travel and time away from home. Since most interpersonal communication is nonverbal, we will get a better idea of what message is really being communicated by seeing the people we are speaking to. But we'll probably think twice before answering in our pyjamas or doodling while talking.

Messages from On High

In my earlier example with Marc and Mr. Sulu, I illustrated two kinds of satellite communications services. Mr. Sulu used a satellite system to fix Marc's precise location on Earth. Such a system already exists; it's called the Global Positioning System (GPS). It was created by the U.S. military for the positioning and guidance of missiles, and to allow its forces to get to where they want to go with a high degree of navigational accuracy. It has, over the past several years, come to be widely used for civilian applications, as in the shipping industry.

One of the applications of satellite communications that will make a difference to the average person is guidance systems for cars, in which on-board computers, hooked to the GPS and digitized maps, will provide detailed instructions to get to a desired destination. Such systems are already beginning to appear in rental cars in selected U.S. cities, were featured widely in Atlanta during the 1996 Summer Olympics, and are now becoming available as optional equipment in luxury cars. By 2005 they will filter down as options on moderately priced cars until they become as widely available as air bags or anti-lock braking systems.

Meanwhile, businesses are somewhat nervous about relying on a single supplier, the U.S. Defense Department, that can arbitrarily change the accuracy or availability of the GPS at any time. Accordingly, there is at least one additional satellite service in the works, sponsored by the Russians, and the French are talking about getting into the business as well.

Moreover, we don't have to wait for the future for satellite communications to enter our homes, because they're already here if we want them. The existence of so-called death star communication satellites already makes it possible to receive video signals direct to the home. Introduced first by DirecTV Inc., a unit of Hughes Electronics Corp., these satellites offer direct-to-home (DTH) broadcast of hundreds of video channels, many more than traditional cable television systems, with superior picture and sound quality because transmissions are digital. To receive these signals the consumer needs a satellite dish about the size of a large pizza, and a decoder. Because these signals are digital in nature, the steadily rising number of channels available will be an ever-present threat to both cable television systems and traditional broadcasters. DTH satellite broadcasting also represents a threat to Canadian cultural industries, because such satellite signals are not subject to the Canadian content rules of the Canadian Radio, Television and Telecommunications Commission (the CRTC).

The CRTC seems bent on deliberately frustrating Canadian consumers' ability to receive such satellite signals, first by outlawing the sale of U.S. services in Canada, and secondly, by setting rules that are seemingly unworkable for Canadian satellite service providers. The purpose of these actions is to protect Canadian broadcasters and cable companies by preventing foreign (mainly U.S.) signals from making further inroads into the Canadian market. Good intentions notwithstanding, the CRTC is fighting a rear-guard action that it will eventually lose. It is also curtailing the choices available to Canadian consumers, while simultaneously encouraging Canadian content providers to assume they are safe from fierce foreign competition when they are not. This strategy can only work in the short run, while satellite direct-to-home television service is more expensive than cable and more difficult to procure.

A related satellite service already available is direct-to-home data communications, typically used for things like Internet access. Since the vast bulk of the information in a typical Internet connection flows into the home and not out of it, a subscriber will be able to download information, say from a World Wide Web site by satellite, and send his requests back to a central server by telephone cable. The speed of such downloading will be many times greater than that available through even the fastest of telephone data modems, and rivals the speeds being talked about for data modems available experimentally on cable television systems. As these satellite systems become more accessible, they pose a new threat to traditional telephone and cable companies alike.

The second satellite service Marc uses in my illustration is an "eye in the sky" — a live video picture of his surroundings. This technology has, until now, been the exclusive province of the major national spy networks, notably those belonging to the U.S. government. To date I have heard only vague rumblings about this kind of satellite service, but I suspect that it may come about as part of a satellite-based, global telephone service.

At one time there were at least eight competing satellite telephony systems in various stages of design and implementation. One of the most ambitious systems is the Iridium system, which is being backed by Motorola. The Iridium consortium, in which Bell Canada is the principal shareholder in Canada, began launching a total of 72 LEO (Low Earth Orbit) satellites in six different polar orbits, at the end of 1996. It is expected that by late 1997 or sometime in the first half of 1998, any point on Earth will have a minimum of three satellites in sight at all times, and most places in the temperate zones will have five or six. This will give anyone with the right equipment the ability to make a phone call from anywhere on Earth to anywhere else on Earth. It will be almost as easy to phone the middle of the Amazon rain forest from Antarctica as it is to phone from your home to the local pizza delivery service.

The cost of satellite telephony is currently projected at about $3 a minute, plus ground station charges. However, the actual customer cost will probably be lower. Take the Iridium system, for instance. Because of the way it is designed, it will only be fully functional when the entire system of 66 satellites (plus six spares) is online and available. Consequently, when it is first switched on, it will have 100 percent of its capacity available for use — and no revenues. This would be analogous to wiring up all of North America for telephones, but waiting until the entire network was finished before starting your sales effort. As a result, I suspect Iridium — and its satellite competitors — will wind up selling their services for less than the projected cost until their networks start to approach capacity. After all, it's better to have some revenue than none, especially when your fixed costs are the same no matter how many subscribers you have.

As time goes on, each form of communications service will start to be integrated with all the others. Hardware suppliers, such as Motorola and Northern Telecom, are already starting to manufacture phones that will switch seamlessly between your wireless conventional phone when you use it in your home, to cellular or PCS service when you are away from home. As satellite systems come into existence and start being used more regularly — say, by 2006 — they, too, will be integrated into your phone service. This integration will make your phone just that: yours. You will eventually have one phone number for any kind of service, and it will follow you wherever you go. Indeed, in the long run, your telephone number may become your universal identification number, perhaps replacing your Social Insurance Number, your driver's identification number, and your passport number.

There will be a range of companies from which to choose each piece of the communications mosaic, and their services will all work with whatever equipment you buy. For instance, your local phone service may be provided by your traditional telephone company, your present cable television company, a new PCS competitor, or some other company using a different technology. You may even have accounts with more than one supplier for each part of the service. Within the next five to seven years, I expect that your communications equipment will start to select the least expensive and most reliable form of communications, even before computer genies emerge to manage your information flow. Indeed, it is quite possible that genies will come into widespread use through their initial management of your phone communications.

Once a broad range of satellite services is widely available for individual use, people will start to think about other things they could do with the systems that are up there. One might be to transmit television pictures from orbit. With every spot on Earth within line of sight of at least three satellites at all times, at least one satellite will be in position to provide a decent picture of any given location at all times. Such a service would be a boon to many. Shipping companies could keep track of their ships, planes, and trucks. Cities could monitor traffic flow and identify developing problems quickly. News agencies could watch events anywhere in the world, with or without the consent of a national government or police. Farmers could gauge the status of fields in their region or in other countries, and decide whether to sell their crops early or late. And, of course, people could abuse it, say, by watching their neighbours sunbathing in the privacy of their back yard, or peering in on a nudist colony. Indeed, there will be public concerns about governments, corporations, and other organizations (such as white supremacists) watching specific individuals or groups. We will be forced to come up with a new set of rules about who is allowed to watch what, and under what circumstances. Governments will get pretty touchy about private companies going into competition with them in the cloak-and-dagger business, but once people start to think about what else we could do with widely accessible, space-based communications, new, unconventional, and uncomfortable answers will start cropping up.

New Technologies

One of the most important new technologies to evolve over the next decade will be a video data compression method called MPEG2, which was ratified internationally in September 1995. MPEG stands for Moving Picture Expert Group, and the "2" signifies that this is the second version adopted. MPEG2 is an agreement on how video signals will be compressed and decompressed, and it is significant because it holds the potential to allow the transmission of full-colour, full-motion video through a wire that has not much more capacity than an ordinary telephone line. As the MPEG2 protocol starts to be used more widely, and to be coded into microchips, we are going to move closer to video-on-demand and two-way video.

If MPEG2 can enable phone companies to transmit a video signal on an ordinary telephone line, then they will be able to go into direct competition with the cable companies. Moreover, the phone companies will have a more elaborate and flexible network that has been designed to deliver unique signals from one place to another, rather than delivering a broadcast signal from a few programmers to large numbers of receivers as cable systems do.

Industry Canada has just licensed three new groups for another new technology called Local Multipoint Communications Service (LMCS). LMCS operates at extraordinarily high frequencies — in the range of 28 gigahertz — coupled with the small-cell broadcasting technology developed for cellular telephony to send data, phone calls, and two-way video signals. LMCS, although mainly experimental, will be used to establish new communications networks of tremendous bandwidth, primarily in urban Canada, in direct competition with the telephone companies, cable companies, radio and television broadcasters, Internet service providers, and anyone else in the business of transmitting information from one place to another. Western International Communications Ltd. has been experimenting with a version of LMCS called CellularVision, and sees it as a new way of transmitting almost any kind of information. WIC views itself as a carrier, rather than the originator, of the signals, much as a telephone company carries voice and data traffic but doesn't produce it.

LMCS illustrates a basic trend in communications that will have profound implications for the future. It's very expensive in both human labour and materials to string wires from one place to another, but it is becoming progressively cheaper to put up radio transmitters to send information by wireless technology. Accordingly, the telephone and cable companies, which rely on the revenues produced by the use of their wired networks, are going to find themselves at a steadily worsening disadvantage as time goes on. Eventually they are going to be forced to switch to wireless services for new capacity.

The physics of wireless communications just happens to favour this trend. As the lower frequencies are used up, companies are moving higher and higher in the radio frequency spectrum. Higher radio frequencies have different characteristics than low frequencies. A low-frequency transmission can be picked up over a very long distance, but cannot carry much information. A high-frequency transmission can be received only over a very short distance, but can carry an enormous amount of information. In an earlier day, lower frequencies were more valuable because equipment was very expensive, and there weren't many people who wanted to use broadcast frequencies. Today, the situation is reversed. Lots of people want a slice of radio frequencies for wireless applications, and equipment has fallen dramatically in price. This makes a small broadcast area an advantage, because you can then reuse a frequency in another location without creating interference. This is the basic principle behind cellular telephony: reusing frequencies over and over again in different cells, without having one conversation interfere with another.

Within the next 20 years new competitors are going to provide enormous quantities of bandwidth (and hence communications capacity) by setting up millions of very-short-range broadcast antennas, say on top of telephone poles, houses, or buildings. They will offer transmission capacity to homes and businesses within a radius of perhaps 100 metres of the transmitter at the lowest possible data transmission cost. The companies that create this new communication backbone will tie these short-range transmitters together with other wireless services, or coaxial cable, or fibre optics, or any other means that comes to hand, depending on where they can buy at the best wholesale rate. Everything will drive toward minimum cost, and there will be no differentiation in service. The resulting stream of data will be interpreted by the smart electronic equipment you install at your end of the transmission.

While new communications systems like LMCS slowly emerge, the development of fibre-optic networks will continue to grow, expanding available bandwidth as they do. There are a number of companies, principally telecommunications companies, investing billions of dollars in laying optical fibre networks. This has major long-term implications for communications, because fibre-optic networks have no theoretical limit to their carrying capacity, and we don't know how high the practical limits are, either.

Even using conventional electronics, fibre-optic cables have enormous potential. However, if the newly emerging optical processing technologies start to become practical, the capacity is almost infinite. Using optical processing, a single strand of optical fibre could, at least in theory, substantially duplicate the carrying capacity of most of the frequency spectrum of conventional wireless communications now used for analog communications, including television and radio.

The enormous potential of both wireless communications and fibre-optic networks spells trouble — and opportunity — for anyone in the communications business. The logical end result of these trends is that there will be no more phone companies, no more television broadcasters, no more cable companies, no more radio stations: just companies that will convey a data stream from one location to another at the request of an end user, and companies that provide a message to be conveyed. And the target of all of this activity will be you, the communications consumer.

Who Delivers the Envelopes and Who Puts Stuff in the Envelopes

There is so much going on in the field of communications, in so many places, and it is all happening so rapidly that it's difficult to understand who's doing what, or what it will all eventually mean. But, for the moment, let me give an overview of what's happening, and of some of the primary effects of the communications revolution, before moving on to describe how it will change your life.

The communications field is experiencing what commentators have taken to calling "convergence." This means that companies in what used to be different industries will start competing with each other. For example, Microsoft, a software company, is involved in the development of a LEO satellite communication system that is even more ambitious than Motorola's Iridium system. It is also creating software that will allow people to use the Internet reliably for long-distance telephone calls — the so-called Net Phone — in competition with your telephone company.

In one way or another, all of the carriers of communications are going to start competing, directly or indirectly, with all of the other carriers. This is going to break down all the neat little divisions between industries and, as a result, the communications industry as a whole will shake down into two major groups: people who deliver envelopes, and people who prepare the content to put into envelopes. Those who deliver envelopes, such as the telephone companies, will find that their service will be viewed as a commodity, like any other, and that the price people are willing to pay for it will decline steadily. Those who prepare the messages contained in the envelopes, such as the people who produce television shows, are going to find that there are dozens of choices of delivery systems. As a result, there is going to be a steadily rising demand for content, plus a dramatic increase in the supply of content, which will increase competition. There will also be some overlap between envelope delivery and content creation. Television broadcasters, for instance, both provide content and deliver a signal.

In financial terms, this combination of digital communications, new technologies, and new sources of competition is going to foster a dramatic decline in the cost of communications. The cost of long-distance communications, for instance, could drop to less than one percent of the current cost over the next ten years. This will to lead to major corporate casualties in the communications field, huge losses in the value of communications companies now traded on the world's stock markets, and a new crop of billionaires among those who find ways to exploit the communications revolution.

Two major questions remain. What are we going to communicate and what will all this change mean to you?

3
Television Is Dead;
Long Live Television!

Sixty-five-year-old Terri Galwan had hoped to be famous when she was young, but had never wanted to be remembered for the manner of her death.

Terri lived in London, Ontario. She was driving along Highway 401 to visit her grandchildren in Windsor on an ominous, overcast day that threatened thunderstorms when she noticed a strangely shaped cloud seeming to dip down from the sky. Remembering the storms that had ripped through southern Ontario 30 years ago, Terri knew immediately that it was a tornado about to touch down, and it was right in her path. She instructed her genie, Topper, to start recording the storm through her Looking Glasses and to see if the images could be sold to a news service. She then instructed her car to reverse direction. It refused because the 401 is a superhighway and she wasn't near an exit. It was illegal to go east on the westbound lanes, or to use the turnaround ramps set aside for official vehicles only. After trying to argue with her car for several moments, Terri shut off the auto pilot, resumed manual control, and cut across the grass median to reverse directions.

In the process, she hit a drainage ditch, blew her right front tire, and damaged the axle before skidding to a stop. Panicking, she got out of the car and started to run away from the tornado, glancing back over her shoulder now and then. Each time she looked back, the evil-looking yellow-grey funnel had grown bigger.

She darted off to the north, climbing a farmer's fence and running through the narrow corn rows, praying that the tornado would turn south. It didn't. Swaying back and forth, the funnel sucked Terri into the air, tossing her about, along with the pieces of wood, metal, and other debris it had collected. Terri died very shortly thereafter — but her genie, Topper, being less fragile than his mistress, continued to record the scene, which news agents around the world broadcast live on their news services.

Only when the tornado finally died out did Terri and Topper fall back to Earth. He continued to broadcast his now stationary view of a patch of grass and mud, all the while calling for emergency help for his mistress.

Terri's last moments were sold all over the world. The scenes of terror she experienced, complete with Topper's recording of her heartbeat and other vital signs, were later incorporated in an interactive game and copied by story-sellers for use in their work. The tragic death of this shy, unassuming grandmother touched the hearts of billions, and made her mourning children and grandchildren wealthy.

In a world of seamless communications, where computers manage our access to information that flows effortlessly and almost instantaneously around the globe, such a scenario is not far-fetched. The ability to record such a scene from the middle of a tornado becomes unremarkable. Moreover, anyone will be able to record and offer for sale any image from anywhere at any time.

When this is possible, what happens to television stations? TV stations work on the principle that only a few select people — station owners and their staffs — backed with significant resources, can distribute images to the larger population. This prompts the question, what will happen when any ordinary person has that ability?

The End of Television

Most television shows today are created by someone other than the television station that supplies them to you. Television broadcasts generally have a limited geographic reach, so program producers sell the broadcast rights to different television stations around the world if they can. But this process will change completely if all video images can be made available to everyone in the world, simultaneously, and from one location. This model is already apparent in the operation of CNN, which works as a one-source broadcaster for interested viewers from Detroit to Dhaka.

If your local television station could broadcast only those shows that it produced, you wouldn't see the vast majority of the costly programs it now shows, such as sitcoms, soap operas, sporting events, national news programs, and mini-series. Using the new technologies I've described, the producers who own the copyrights to these shows would be able to make such programs available directly to viewers, instead of filtering them through a network of local broadcasters. What would your local TV station — or even Canada's major TV networks — have left to show? For starters, it would be almost solely Canadian content. That's ironic, because now Canadian television stations think of Canadian content as a necessary evil, a toll they have to pay to broadcast the popular U.S. programs that draw the enormous audiences that advertisers pay big bucks to reach. But what happens when Fox or Paramount or Disney don't need CFTO, CFCN, or CKVU to distribute their images to the good viewers of Toronto, Calgary, or Vancouver? Then these, and all the other stations in the world, will be able to show only those programs that they either originate themselves or coproduce. I doubt that many current television stations will be able to survive if they are only able to offer the nightly local news, the local cooking show, the local talk show, the local game show, and so on.

The line between producer and broadcaster is going to disappear once two-way video-on-demand appears. Anyone who is in the production business, and can sell what the entertainment market wants, will be able to make themselves into a media company, much as anyone today who can create a World Wide Web site can become an Internet star. While this inevitable shift threatens the supremacy of traditional broadcasters like the CBC or Global, it opens up opportunities for many other people.

Karen Littorelli is a 21-year-old journalism student who looks at her professors and decides she would do better on her own than listening to them theorize about how the world works. Accordingly, in the December before graduation, she sets herself up as a news agent specializing in selling information for senior citizens.

There are lots of seniors' channels in 2017, but most of them use mature newscasters. After talking to her grandmother, Karen realizes that many seniors find a steady diet of watching and listening to older people depressing. In their hearts, they don't believe that they are old, and they get tired of being around old people. At the same time, the issues that young people tend to talk about are alien to seniors. Still, they miss having younger people in their lives.

Karen recruits some of her friends to work part-time at minimum wage. She makes sure she hires kids who look fresh, attractive, perky, slightly sexy, but basically wholesome. Then, using the remaining tuition money her grandparents had put aside for college, plus money saved from summer jobs, she hires freelance story advisors who are professional newscasters and news editors nearing retirement, and who want to slow down but not stop. They like her, think that what she's doing is cute, and lower their rates to the point where she can afford them.

Her first "studio" is in her parents' basement. She puts sound-deadening tiles on the walls, and pins up a chromakey blue sheet as a backdrop for her reporters. She then works a one-time royalty deal with a struggling local television station that allows her to video their news studio without any people in the scene. Working with ImageMaker computer software, she creates and drops in moving images of people of all ages to the scene. She adds appropriate background sounds, and the final results are an environmental backdrop that looks and sounds just like a professional news studio but doesn't exist outside her computer.

Her advisors make sure she has information, news, features, and interviews on subjects that are interesting to seniors. Karen then writes the stories herself, submitting them to her more experienced advisors for editing, so that the stories are presented the way a teenaged grandchild would describe an event they wanted to share with a much-loved grandparent.

Karen's combination of sunny, bright, wholesome young people and news and information tailored to the mature market comes to the attention of seniors' genies very quickly. It's an instant hit with viewers — and advertisers follow right behind. At first, other news agents pooh-pooh her efforts as amateurish, but seniors love her show. Karen then adds a twist to the formula for call-in shows by presenting problems that kids encounter and asking seniors to call in to give advice. The ratings hit the roof and keep going. By the time more established news agents twig that "The Grandkids' Network" is for real, Karen has a lock on the market. Her fondness for her own grandparents, and her empathy with their friends, gives her a sincerity that the professionals can't touch. Karen becomes one of the most successful niche news marketers in North America — and a multi-millionaire before she's 30.

Right now the idea of establishing a television network in your basement is ridiculous. Within 20 years, it won't even be news.

Of course, professional broadcast organizations start out with some huge advantages. They already have an established relationship with viewers — a franchise, if you will — and a well-oiled machine for dealing with programming and with the daily flood of information that has to be filtered, edited, and organized. As well, their production values — the "look" that goes on the screen — will remain far superior to that offered by amateurs for some time to come, although computer software, like the fictional ImageMaker described above, will eventually level the field. But over time these advantages will fade, and if broadcasters do not adapt to the new realities, and insist instead that what has worked in the past will always work in the future, they will experience a rash of bankruptcies, collapses, rescues, and takeovers. Whatever happens, the broadcast industry will never be the same.

All the News — Period.

So if the 100-channel universe is going to give way to the 500-channel universe, and eventually to an unlimited-channel universe, where will the content come from to fill all these channels? Will you have 50,000 channels and still find nothing worth watching?

First of all, a "channel" or video source will not have to "broadcast" 24 hours a day. It won't even have to have regular broadcast hours. Instead, programs will be stored online, and you'll be able to download them whenever you want, just as Web pages can be downloaded on the Internet today. Hence, when a news agent, or a story-seller, or anyone with a message completes a program segment or "show," they will post it for you to pick up whenever you like. Imagine being able to watch the latest episode of *Coronation Street*, or *Seinfeld* or *Mystery!* seconds after it's finished, and being able to backtrack through old episodes at will.

If you look at the enormous range of use groups and news groups on the Internet, you get some idea of what the future of video will be. It will, in short, include just about anything and everything you can imagine — and probably things that few of us would want to imagine. This glut of content will eventually become a problem. As it becomes apparent that there are fortunes to be made from grabbing even a minuscule percentage of humanity's attention, people will do almost anything to attract an audience, sell pay-per-view rights, or win advertising sponsorship. What might this include? I would not be surprised to see offerings that included any and every kind of pornography, up to and including live "snuff" shows; elaborate suicide competitions, perhaps with cash prizes going to support the families of the "winners"; recreations of the kinds of bloodthirsty "circuses" of the Roman Empire, including gladiator matches; and just about every other perversion that might attract attention and revenue.

That decent jurisdictions might outlaw such "entertainments" may be largely irrelevant. Operators could merely relocate to jurisdictions that condoned such things for the tax revenues they produced, or jurisdictions where enforcement agencies turned a blind eye for a consideration. In an interconnected world, it won't matter where such abominations originate, and I see no practical way of imposing effective legal sanctions to stop them.

Of course, the same technology will also allow for a blossoming of the arts and other edifying forms of entertainment. When anyone can be a broadcaster, then every ballet and every opera company will be able to televise their performances, and every singer or musician will be able to offer his art to the world. With all the world to draw on, forms of artistic expression whose audiences tend to be small, like experimental theatre companies and avant-garde poets, may finally be able to attract sufficient numbers of people worldwide to make their work financially viable. But the competition will be intense. If every ballet and opera company can make its programming available, why would you watch the local company instead of one in Vienna, say, or New York? Still, smaller arts groups will at least have potential access to audiences now reserved for famous international companies.

Since becoming famous will be a shortcut to the soft life, everyone will want to try his hand at it, but the vast majority will be ignored in the tidal wave of competition. Viewers will tend to rely on proven sources for programming, in the same way that travellers stop at a McDonald's restaurant rather than at Joe's Burgers because they know what to expect. The providers of reliably good programming of international interest will become the media moguls of the future, and these will likely include those organizations — Disney comes to mind — that have a strong consumer franchise and reputation, and are innovative enough to stay abreast of change.

Radio in the Twenty-first Century

Radio will experience a different future from that of TV. First, there are already too many radio stations for all to survive. But this surfeit is patterned on our current concept of broadcasting, wherein entertainment is pumped out for the largest possible audience, and advertisers pay for it. It's tough for radio stations to make money outside the rush-hour slots because most of us listen to the radio in our cars, and far fewer listen in our homes.

Converting radio to digital format will be costly. Right now, and for the next decade at least, digital radio broadcast equipment will be dramatically more expensive than analog broadcast equipment. Digital radio conversion will also require a completely new stock of digital radio receivers. Unlike digital television, which will go through a transition period making use of converters to turn digital TV signals into analog signals for older sets, a digital radio converter makes no sense because it would probably cost as much as a brand-new digital radio. Accordingly, the conversion to digital radio will be messier than for digital television, because for many years analog and digital networks will run in parallel. Eventually, though, all radio will go digital because of bandwidth considerations (with analog hogging too much of a highly desirable portion of the broadcast spectrum), and that will force broadcasters to alter the way they do business. Like television, radio will have to reinvent itself.

Right now, commercial radio stations believe they are in the business of providing us with entertainment to attract advertisers. However, radio stations are really in the business of charging for a defined flow of information. Most of that information currently is entertainment, mixed with news and talk shows. Only one group — advertisers — pays for the full cost of conveying all the information. In future, I suspect both the people sending information and the people receiving the information will pay for the privilege.

In the vignette at the beginning of chapter 2, Marc receives information about the surrounding streets of Toronto via digital radio. When we have "smart" cars, the genie that monitors or even drives your car will likely buy access to construction and traffic information from such a digital broadcast to work out the best route to your destination. Such broadcasts might be made available by the municipality, or by a private concern, but each city will have at least one, and will sell the information both to residents and to visitors.

Once computer genies appear on the scene, and once anyone can convey any kind of signal from any place to any other place, broadcast radio will become just another means of conveying information. It will also be considerably less flexible than, say, Personal Communications services. PCS, which is also wireless, will allow listeners to tap into the wired universe, and dial up any signal, including sound only (which we now think of as "radio"), then deliver it by wireless means. Accordingly, radio as a broadcast medium will survive for the next two decades, but will gradually change from its present form into something very different — and may eventually disappear altogether as a distinct form of communications.

This doesn't mean that the programs now conveyed by radio will disappear. Quite the contrary; they may become independent of the radio stations that broadcast them. Any show that can create its own following will be able to reach its listeners, much as Canadian television host Pamela Wallin has created her own news magazine franchise and has CBC Newsworld deliver it. Accordingly, while radio may eventually disappear, all Canadians will be able to enjoy Joe Easingwood from Victoria, *The World Tonight* from Vancouver, *The Calgary Eye-Opener*, or *Metro Morning* from Toronto, and enjoy them from anywhere in the world. The difference is that you won't have to "touch that dial." Just ask your genie.

And who knows? Maybe the venerable CBC *Morningside* host Peter Gzowski will come back 20 years from now and start his own network.

New Media

New communications technology and a dramatic decline in the cost of communications will lead to the invention of new media as well as revolutions in the old. Here are a couple of possibilities.

• Interactive programming

This would be kind of a cross-fertilization of interactive computer games, talk shows, and soap operas. Let's use a soap opera format to illustrate how it might work.

> You're relaxing at home, experiencing your favourite soap opera. Wearing your virtual reality gloves and body suit, and sitting in the VR corner of your recreation room, you've once again chosen to play the role of Dr. Timus on "Days of Our Children's Hospital Romance Lives." The other characters all come from the scriptwriters' minds (at least, that's what you think, although you're never really sure), but your character is under your control — at least in your home. You choose the actions you want to take: you become hero or villain, you kiss the romantic

lead (male or female, or sometimes male and female).

Your genie, working with the software and plot outline provided by the writers, plus live, two-way interaction with the show's computer, presents the episode to you, keeping you abreast of things that happen outside your presence, and waiting for you to react to the machinations of the plot as it unfolds.

You've really been getting into the episodes of late and have developed your character into a malicious, spiteful, evil person after being jilted by your latest lover. You find yourself playing the role to the hilt, and having a ball. You're surprised when you get a call from the show's producer at the end of today's episode, asking if you'd be willing to play the role of Dr. Timus for the next month. They'll pay you their standard rates — but, of course, the show has the right to cancel you at any time if they don't like your work. They also have the right to extend your contract if you keep up the good work. They'll ask you to tune in two hours early to act out the episode that they will then broadcast to the rest of the world.

It turns out that all the characters on "Days of Our Children's Hospital Romance Lives" are played by members of the audience, and that the show's producers are constantly monitoring audience participation for new talent. Each on-screen character is actually a computer construct that looks the same from episode to episode, but the character's behaviour comes from an actor/viewer like you. The actor playing a character can be replaced suddenly without the other viewers ever knowing.

The soap opera story, far from being tightly scripted by the show's writers, has become kind of a consensual fantasy concocted by the viewers themselves, with random events thrown in by the writers every once in a while to spice things up.

- **Multi-dimensional media**

These are much more than multimedia, which is the use of several different kinds of media — text, pictures, graphics, video, and so on — in the creation of a document. Multi-dimensional media use several different kinds of media to allow users to experience content, such as a television broadcast, in different ways, and at differing speeds. Let's consider multi-dimensional media as used in a future news broadcast.

It's 6:47 in the evening, and you're knocking off work for the day. While your supper is cooking, you decide to catch up on the news. You ask your genie for your personally edited news program.

You sit back and watch the news anchor go through the stories, each lasting about 30 seconds, but none really catches your interest. Following each story is a two-second "spacer," which allows your genie to select the next story for presentation, and which also allows the news agent to sell two-second commercials to advertisers who want to reach you, specifically, with a message. You could, if you wanted, ask your genie to download more information from any of the advertisers about the products and services presented on the spacers, but none of them appeals to you today.

Then a story comes on about street kids, and you recognize one of the kids from the Frontier College street literacy program that you work with as a volunteer. You tell your genie to call up more detail on that story. The news story currently playing on your screen is interrupted part way through, and your genie displays a magazine feature story with a much more in-depth description of the new joint public-private sector project on literacy, for which Frontier College is serving as the host institution.

The initial story was delivered by a universal broadcast signal, and the stories of interest were recorded by your genie until you were ready to look at them. When you asked to see the news, your genie started showing you the opening credits and the general headlines, while simultaneously dialing up the news agent by phone to download any updates to the stories it was about to show you. When you asked for more information, your genie again contacted the news agent by phone and downloaded the in-depth magazine coverage of the story.

After you've finished viewing the magazine coverage, the news agent offers you a number of additional options. You choose to participate in a phone-in discussion, hosted by the reporter who wrote the magazine story. The news agent initiated this discussion when enough people requested the magazine to indicate a sufficient level of interest. The president of Frontier College and some of the street kids involved in the literacy program have been brought in, online, for the discussion. As you join the live discussion, it's been going on for about 17 minutes, and has become heated. To understand what's been said so far, you ask for a summary, which is also downloaded by the news agent. You listen to the discussion while you scan the summary text on the screen. Once you think you understand what people are discussing right now, you kill the text summary and go back to the discussion.

You join in for a while, participating in the debate over whether public money should go to a non-governmental organization (NGO) like Frontier College. Because you are a tutor for the program, you get a request from a member of the audience for a one-to-one conversation. Muting the discussion, and putting up a signal that you are "off the air" to other participants, you talk with a woman who wants to know more about the program and how you got involved in it. You instruct your genie to forward information to her about Frontier College and the Beat the Street program while you describe your part in the project. When you've finished answering her questions, ending with a suggestion that she might want to become a tutor herself, you rejoin the discussion.

While you were out of the loop, the news agent found a similar discussion about NGOs in education going on in a class in Stanford University in California, and invited the professor and her class to merge into the discussion. The network has also opened a window on the screen displaying cost-benefit studies done by the United Nations on NGO participation in education, along with graphs on literacy in Canada and its major trading partners, which you can select and have enlarged for your perusal. Meanwhile, the discussion continues, although it is going off on an academic tangent that you find less engaging. You lose interest, and tell your genie to take note of the professor's e-mail address for one-to-one contact tomorrow, then instruct it to go back to your original news program.

The genie cuts you out of the discussion, then restarts the news scanning program, picking up with the story you had interrupted earlier after your genie checks again for any updates to the stories not yet shown.

The news agent has delivered stories to you by over-the-air broadcast, much as a news broadcast occurs today. Your genie records selected stories for your later viewing. The broadcast, watched live, is free as long as the two-second spacers are shown along with the news stories. The news agent considers its news broadcast a vehicle to attract interest in its collateral information services. Recording the stories results in a small fee, less than one cent per story saved, and you retrieve them from your own local storage. The news magazine story you requested was delivered by the Net — wireless transmission from the news agents' studios to the switch closest to their offices, optical fibre to the local switch nearest to your home, then wireless PCS to your screen. It cost you a few cents. The discussion went back and forth between the homes of the participants and the news agents' studios by coaxial cable it reached your home through your cable modem. The discussion cost about three cents a minute. Your side conversation took place by normal phone — although, since the woman who wanted to speak to you lived in the far North, her end of the conversation was delivered to her by satellite. The news agent took a five-cent "matchmaker's fee" from the woman, and a similar fee from you for the professor's e-mail address, but otherwise the cost to you was too small for anyone but your phone service to worry about.

You noticed none of these transactions, although you knew that they were happening in the background. The process just unfolded as you wanted it to and without your attention. You could have expanded the experience further by accessing databases for more information on the subject; sponsoring a second discussion group that took the discussion off in a different direction; publishing a taped program with your own commentary using some of the material from the online discussion; or almost anything else you could imagine, unconstrained by what other people did or were interested in. Multi-dimensional media will allow people to go in any direction and every direction, as a group or on their own.

More Downstream Effects of the Communications Revolution

- **Loss of privacy**. When anyone, anywhere can operate a broadcast station, and anyone with a video camera can sell footage to news agencies, media reporting will become universal, and your actions at any time may come under public scrutiny. Some people will choose to grandstand on the off-chance that they will stumble into their 15 minutes of fame. Others will hide behind walls and doors and shutting themselves off from potentially prying eyes.

  Because you will purchase information, products, and services to a great extent through a computer-assisted network, marketers will be able to develop much more detailed files on you than they do today. These files will start to show frighteningly accurate profiles of your behaviour, your likes and dislikes, and will probably be available to any commercial enterprise willing to buy or trade this kind of information. I'll talk more about this in chapter 7.

- **The ability to search for useful information may become more valuable than the information itself.** One comment made about the Internet that will be true in spades for the world of seamless communications is that while there will be more needles to be found — that is, pieces of valuable information — there will be one hell of a lot more haystacks in which to find them. This will place a premium on the ability to research, organize, sort, index, and catalogue information. All of these activities will be high-paying enterprises for those who can determine how to manage both the search capabilities and the marketing of their services.

- **The free flow of information will cause creative people to become more secretive.** Once you make content available on a global communications network, it becomes impossible to control its reproduction, and hence, to profit from it. This inability to monitor and enforce copyright has been coming for some time, especially since the development of the photocopier, but soon a book, a poem, a piece of art or music, or a scientific discovery could become instantly available to everyone, whether they pay the appropriate toll for using it or not.

  The current crisis surrounding the protection of intellectual property — copyrights, patents, and trademarks — has no resolution that will protect innovators, even though some lawyers who specialize in this area are proclaiming that all is well. Accordingly, there are only two major strategies available to creators: either find a way of making it profitable to give your work away, or make it available only to a tightly controlled group that pays a subscription for access to it. The latter harks back to the model used during the Industrial Revolution in Great Britain, when all innovations were closely guarded, rather than to the more recent model of successful patent and copyright protection. There will be a distinct drag on economic development as a result — unless some clever person can invent a way of tagging and billing for every individual byte of information sent across the Net and by other means. The Xanadu Project in California claims to have developed just such an algorithm. Ironically, they have kept their process supersecret, being unwilling to license or share it with anyone else. Meanwhile, they have not been able to make a commercial success of their own efforts, having reportedly burned through the money of several frustrated investors.

- **The speed of scientific discovery will *decrease* as researchers become more possessive of their findings**. The free interchange of scientific information has created much of the progress of the last century, as one person's discoveries could piggyback another's. Now, however, with some kinds of information becoming immensely valuable, and with our diminishing ability to protect intellectual property, researchers are hoarding information rather than sharing it. As this trend escalates, scientific research will slow perceptibly.

  This phenomenon is particularly evident in genetic engineering, where even the internationally sponsored Human Genome Project is falling prey to bickering over who has the right to patent which discoveries. As large salaries and stock options lure more geneticists into private corporate laboratories, the pace of genetic research will dwindle.

- **Business travel will fall dramatically**. A friend who works for a telecommunications company used to fly from Toronto to Ottawa several times a month and sometimes several times a week. However, since his working group established easily accessible video-conferencing between their Toronto and Ottawa offices, he has gone for more than two and a half years without flying between the two cities.

Staying put will make good business sense as video-phones become cheaper and widely accessible. Over the next five years, the quality is going to improve, access to digital transmission media is going to become more widespread, and the ability to accomplish the same result over an analog phone line will improve. It is cheaper, even at today's long-distance rates, to hold a two-hour video conference than it is to travel from one city to another. When the cost of video conferencing, telepresence, and data transmission falls even farther, the comparative cost of travel will skyrocket and the benefits will decline.

This does not mean that business travel will cease. Not all the information that flows between two people is visual, and not all the value of human interaction can be scripted and scheduled. For instance, I speak at dozens of conferences a year. It is obvious to anyone who attends conferences that some of the most valuable interactions happen outside the formal proceedings. The hallway conversations, the chance meetings, and the social schmoozing are all invaluable parts of the conference.

So there will still be business travel, but the need for much of it will decline, and the decline will be cumulative as time goes on and people become more comfortable doing business by video rather than in person. Airline shareholders take note!

4
The Prospects for
Secure Employment

I speak to about 10,000 people a year at various corporate and industry association functions, and one question comes up almost every time: How can my kids get a secure job, preferably one that will last them through their working lives? There is also a second, unvoiced question lurking in the background: How can I stay employed until I retire? Both questions inspire a tremendous amount of anxiety.

A career-spanning job has become the Holy Grail of our time. Psychologically, the wish for this treasure expresses our yearning to return to what seems, in soft-edged memory, to be a simpler, more secure time. Although most people never think of it in such blatant terms, what they want for themselves and their children is a job that offers secure employment, regardless of economic climate or their own individual performance. This is, in effect, a time-server's job, a conveyor belt to carry you from the end of your school years to the beginning of your retirement. But the market and the world have changed, and "job security" no longer exists.

George looks at the cheap Christmas decorations hung up around the drop-in centre with a mixture of disgust and despair.

Much as he hates the ugliness and cheap sentimentality of the barren hall tarted up for the Christmas holidays, there is nowhere else he can go. He dreads yet another turkey dinner being served up by excessively cheery volunteers, "doing their bit" for the poor unfortunates who are homeless over the holidays. He appreciates what they are trying to do — after all, he'd done similar good works in his younger days, when he was employed — but he had never realized just how transparently phony such cloying cheerfulness seemed from the other side of the serving table.

The holidays are particularly hard for George because he had so enjoyed the festive season when he was working, married, and respected in his community. In those days, he was a whole man, and not just some fat, unshaven, smelly, nameless bum who couldn't make the grade. The worst part about it is that he still can't say what he did wrong.

For almost 30 years he had devoted himself to his work and his employer. He had been a foreman whose opinions were sought by management and his fellow workers alike. His experience was an asset to the company — and management said so, every year at his annual salary review.

Then the plant closed. "Too inefficient," the hatchet man brought in by head office had said. And while it was true that the tire plant was one of the oldest owned by the company, George suspected the real reason was that the wages the company could pay to Mexican workers at the newly built plant in Manzanillo were about a tenth of what George and his men earned. Even allowing for the Canadian workers' higher productivity, the differential was too great — so George was out of a job.

They'd been fair about it, giving George more than 18 months' salary, and even kicking in extra for vacation time he'd built up but had never taken. But George was almost 50 when they laid him off and making tires was the only thing he knew, the only thing he'd ever known. He tried a variety of jobs, every-thing from bagging groceries to pumping gas, while going to night school to finish his high school diploma, almost 35 years after dropping out of grade 10. None of it worked. The scutwork jobs led nowhere, and there were plenty of younger high school drop-outs who could work just as hard and were willing to put in longer and more irregular hours. After fighting with his latest boss — a punk kid 20 years his junior — George left his last job in a huff. He came home and told his wife he'd had it, that he was going to find something better, and that they were going to sell their home and move to Toronto. Surely somebody there would appreciate his skills.

But this strategy failed. The house hadn't brought much in the depressed local real estate market because there were a lot of other people selling their houses at the same time. And they'd found that living costs in Toronto were much higher than back home. The prospects for work were just as bad in Toronto — maybe worse, because everyone who was out of work went there. Eventually, after something like 150 job interviews, George stopped trying. Then, to top it all off, in a fit of anger and frustration he yelled at his wife to get out — which she had done, going off to live with a sister in Winnipeg. He often regretted shouting at her because he still loved her, but he could never bring himself to ask her to forgive him and come back because he had nothing to offer her now.

He tried part-time jobs that never fit and never lasted; he used up first his unemployment insurance, then his welfare ben-efits. Finally he wound up sponging off his friends and family. He eventually used up every favour, IOU, and resource he had in the world, and came home one day to find that the landlord had changed the lock on his grimy little apartment while he was out, and his belongings were out in the street.

Now life is one long wound, with each day bringing fresh

indignities and insults. He lives on the streets now, begging, stealing and dealing cigarettes and candy, sleeping in hostels and missions in winter and under bridges and in cardboard boxes in better weather.

George never thought he'd wind up like this – and can't for the life of him figure out what he could have done differently, even after all these years of pondering.

I've met men like George, because I've been one of those cheery volunteers at centres for the homeless. I've heard stories from men who were executives at multinational corporations, educated, well respected, and valued, but who were suddenly made redundant by a change in the economic weather. Out of work and feeling worthless, they fell prey to depression and hopelessness. The prospect of suffering such a horrible decline has become the nagging fear we all harbour at the back of our minds these days.

Unemployment has been around forever, its levels rising and falling with the economy. But what's happening now is different from the fluctuations of the past — and the future bodes more of the same. This time it's not just the ups and downs of the normal economic cycle that are throwing people temporarily out of work, but rather a fundamental change in the market and the workplace altering the complexion of work and affecting all of our prospects for the future.

The first cause of this shift is a rise in the level of competition brought about by the emergence of a single, unified global economy that brings with it an emerging global labour force. Individual local economies have been gradually merging and becoming more interdependent for centuries, as improvements in transportation and communications have made it economically possible for people to buy, sell, and trade over greater distances. However, this whole process was given an enormous boost by one of the most significant — and obscure — economic events of the postwar period: the 1971 collapse of the Bretton Woods agreement on fixed exchange rates.

The 1944 Bretton Woods agreement — so called because it was struck in the town of Bretton Woods, New Hampshire — allowed different countries to operate their economies independently of each other. Fixed exchange rates effectively provided insulation between one economy and another, so that the North American economy, for example, might be in recession while the German and Japanese economies were doing well.

The removal of foreign-exchange controls caused the fixed-exchange rate regime to collapse. This removed the insulation that existed between the economies of various countries, so that what affected one reverberated through all of them. Highly successful negotiations on trade, under the auspices of the General Agreement on Tariffs and Trade (GATT), did a lot to foster freer trade and accelerated the integration of national economies. While it has taken a couple of decades for the effects of these changes to become apparent, it is now clear that we are moving into a world where the global economy matters more than individual national economies, and where a labourer's competition for work will come increasingly from distant countries as much as from local competitors.

In the short run this means that countries with low wage rates coupled with decent levels of productivity can produce goods for sale more cheaply than high-wage-rate countries like Canada, the United States, the European nations, and Japan. Companies in rich countries have responded by automating as much as they can to bring the labour content and labour cost of their products down. North American producers have largely been successful in this effort, and the net effect is that they need far fewer workers to produce the same quantity of goods than they did 20 years ago. Indeed, automation is the second great cause of declining employment. Those jobs that involved low to moderate levels of skill are migrating to low-wage countries where industry pays workers a small fraction of what they are paid here, while many highly technical but repetitive jobs are being eliminated by automation.

63

And there is more. Unlike during previous periods of declining employment, today white-collar workers are also being affected. Perhaps as much as or more than anything else, it is the new vulnerability of white-collar, especially managerial, employees that is creating the impression of labour market instability and the tremendous anxiety so evident in the workplace.

But the loss of security has brought an increase in opportunity for those with the flexibility to change direction.

Amanda and Charles were pioneers in using computers in industry in the late 1960s. They were both exposed to computers in college and volunteered to become the guinea pigs in a new computer era in their company. They met each other in the computer systems group, becoming first "an item" and then a married couple. In the course of their work, they looked for applications outside of accounting for their company's mainframe computers and eventually found a great one in financial modelling. Their employer, a pipeline company, was heavily regulated and often needed to demonstrate the effects of rate changes to the regulator. The computer proved a godsend for such detailed calculations, and Mandy and Charles prospered as they became the company's experts at financial modelling.

When timesharing emerged in the early 1970s, they plunged in head first, and were largely responsible for IntraNational Pipelines (INP) embracing the new technology. They set up an internal company mail system using I.P. Sharp Associates' computer timesharing network, foreshadowing the Internet and the use of e-mail by more than 20 years.

But the emergence of microcomputers in the 1980s was a problem for them. Suddenly, the new, cheap, and powerful spreadsheet programs easily allowed almost any trained employee to do what used to take great experience and expertise. Although Mandy and Charles led the move to micros and rewrote most of the models used by INP, they soon found that their services were not as highly prized, or in as much demand. It was a shock when they were given termination notices during the recession in the early 1990s, but not completely unforeseen.

They set up their own consulting firm and survived by selling their modelling expertise, but the market for such specialized services had shrunk as the widespread use of spreadsheets had expanded. The technology that had made them successful had suddenly left them behind. Now in their fifties, and with retirement still a decade away, the future looked bleak. There was widespread demand for computer programmers — but with different skills than they had acquired in the era of mainframes and timesharing.

Then in the mid-1990s the couple became aware of hand-held computers, and they again saw an opportunity created by technology. They created a new application by tying the widely overlooked Apple Newton hand-held computer to the newly emerging Global Positioning System. GPS equipment now cost less than $1,000, was the size of a large cellular phone, and was capable of pinpointing the user's location to within a few feet, anywhere on Earth.

Since there were only two of them, and they had limited funds, Mandy and Charles started marketing their product on the Internet, having mortgaged their house for the capital to get their new venture up and running. It was ironic to find that they had more customers in Australia than Canada in their first year, but then geography had less to do with markets today than in the past.

At first sales were slow because their product was novel. It took time for customers to get used to the idea of a field computer that was easy to adapt to their needs, fit in the pocket of a coat, and produced an accurate geographic location with every observation. Eventually, though, they developed a loyal clientele, hired more people, and worked like the devil to keep up with a blossoming demand and "me too" imitators.

By 2010, Field Work Applications had become the industry standard in a line of new portable — and now wearable — computer systems. Mandy and Charles eventually sold off a third of the company for enough money to ensure their retirement, set up a share ownership plan for their key employees, and continued to market their product with great success through the global communications Net.

Today, at age 70, they have relinquished day-to-day control to two of their key employees and are worth a tidy fortune. They are semi-retired, but continue to consult with — or harass, depending on your viewpoint — their successors from distant locations. They call the office from wherever they are — once from part-way up Mount Everest — with ideas and "suggestions" about new products and marketing thrusts. Most of their ideas are useless — but about one in ten proves to be pure gold. Their hit rate is high enough and lucrative enough that Field Work Applications continues to lead the pack of out-of-office computer applications.

Mandy and Charles, meanwhile, are having more fun than they ever had working for someone else. They travel the world and continue to work as they please.

Life is good, even if it was scary for a few years.

This vignette is loosely based on the lives of two real people. The projection of their eventual great success is speculation, but is reasonable, based on what I've seen to date.

In many ways, the stories of George on the one hand, and Mandy and Charles on the other, are quite similar. In both instances the players were highly competent in their fields, were thrown out of work through no fault of their own, and faced bleak prospects if they could not find alternative careers. But their differences are more significant than their similarities.

The first difference is their respective levels of education. George started work in a world where you could quit high school and walk into almost any factory in the land and find a job. He stayed with that job until it disappeared, then found that the world in which he last sought a job had also disappeared. However, aside from his experience in a job that no longer existed, he had no qualifications that were significantly different from those offered by millions of people in rapidly developing countries around the world who could and would work for a much smaller pay packet.

Mandy and Charles were well educated and had the ability to make the transition from one kind of technology to another. They were used to working with their minds and without much supervision, and they had been innovators throughout their careers. Rather than looking for another employer, they gambled everything they owned and started their own company, inventing their own jobs. That willingness to gamble and the ability to become an entrepreneur is significant, and we'll come back to it later on.

There is one point I want to particularly emphasize. Superior education did not preserve Mandy's and Charles's jobs, but it did give them the mental equipment to find another way to make a living. Education alone will not guarantee anyone a job or a standard of living any more. Mental discipline and agility, plus useful knowledge and a willingness to bet on yourself, will become tools that everyone will need to develop.

While it is true that jobs are disappearing from the economy, jobs are also being created. In fact, more people are working in 1997 than were in 1987, despite ten years of downsizing and the globalization of the work force. However, the *nature* of the jobs on offer has changed. The jobs being created require higher levels of education than the jobs that are disappearing. That is why people like George are going to have a much tougher time finding new jobs than people like Mandy and Charles. Unless the people who filled low-skilled jobs can find a way to invent new ones that suit them,

67

or upgrade their skills to a much higher level, they may never work again. It will be up to the factory worker to turn himself into a computer programmer — and, unfortunately, not many will make the transition successfully.

Please understand that I don't like this trend, nor do I approve of it. I'm merely commenting that this is what *is* happening — and what will continue to happen for the rest of your working life. Having lost my job in a corporate merger early in my career, I can readily empathize with people who have secure and productive employment who suddenly find themselves out of work and on the street. I'll come back to the larger societal issues of labour market changes in a moment. First, though, let's look at younger people just starting out in their careers.

There are two challenges facing young people, both today and in future. First, there are no secure jobs. Today's employment environment is distinctly different from the one in which their parents worked and raised their families, which means that the suggestions and ideas that their parents offer may not be of very much value — unless their parents have had to deal with recent job loss themselves. The second challenge is that the education they have when they leave school may not give them the mental equipment they need for the career challenges ahead of them. I deal with the topic of education in chapter 10. For the moment, let's look at what a student entering the work force today encounters, to see how things are going to change.

Gamal feels cheated, but he is relieved as well. He'd always wanted to be an artist and had really enjoyed the painting and sketching he'd done in high school. His parents, on the other hand, had insisted that there was no future in art, and that he should pursue a career in civil engineering. His grades had been good enough, especially in math, so he had been able to secure a place at a good, but not distinguished, engineering school.

His grades there ranked him comfortably in the top quarter of his class.

But the market for civil engineers wasn't what it used to be because governments weren't undertaking major infrastructure projects the way they had 30 years ago. Top-flight civil engineers were willing to work for entry-level wages just to be employed. While the top students in his class had been able to find employment, most of his peers were knocking on the same doors he was — and with the same results.

Gamal had heard that there were engineering jobs in Asia — and that the competition for them was even fiercer than it was here. Not only were many North American companies competing with Asian engineering firms, but the reputation of the Asian engineers was outstanding. Accordingly, Gamal's career as an engineer looks to be over before it has even begun. Worse, his parents don't understand why he can't find a job with all that expensive education, and they have decided it's because he isn't really trying.

Fortunately for Gamal, he had continued to draw and pursue art as a hobby through college, joining clubs, and taking art electives whenever his engineering schedule permitted. Moreover, he had snuck in some drawing and painting programs for the computer his engineering school had required his parents to buy.

Purely by luck, he is sitting in the waiting room of an engineering firm for a job interview at the same time as the owner of a small marketing firm is waiting for an appointment. Spotting the artist's portfolio case the woman has with her, Gamal strikes up a conversation. The two get on very well, and Gamal finds himself telling her about his love of art. They spend an enjoyable quarter hour talking about the new techniques made possible by the latest computer tools. At the end of the conversation, she remarks that she has just lost one of her graphic artists. She also indicates that if Gamal would like to drop by with some samples of his work, she'd be willing to look at them and suggest where he might look for a job in graphic arts.

He goes in that very afternoon with his portfolio, and she likes his stuff well enough that she offers him some freelance work, with a promise of more if they get on well together. For Gamal, this offer is a dream come true: being paid to produce art, even commercial art. And it seems ironic to him that the expensive engineering degree his parents had insisted he get has done nothing to get him a job while his hobby might turn out to be his salvation.

The point of this story is not that you should let your kids study art, but that there is little value in someone forcing themselves to work in a field in which they are not especially talented. They are going to be competing with people from all over the world, and especially with people who absolutely thrive on what they do and excel at it. If that field happens to be art, then perhaps your kids should study art — with two caveats.

First, it will always be easier to find a job in a rapidly expanding field than in one that is stagnant or mature. One of the biggest challenges of managing a company in a growing field is finding enough bodies to do the work — and that means that sometimes such companies will hire someone with the appropriate qualifications who happens to walk through the door at the right time. However, getting a job does not guarantee a secure employment future.

The second caveat is that it's fine to follow what we used to describe as a "calling," but it's still necessary to make a living. This means that it's not enough merely to do something you love; you also need to find a way to make it pay, and there is no cookbook method for this. You have to invent it for yourself.

There's another aspect of Gamal's story that deserves attention: luck. He happened to be in the right place at the right time — but he also created the opportunity and then seized it. I have seen it over and over in my career; there is no substitute for luck, and every rational person would agree. But there is also the need both to recognize when a door opens and to be willing to walk through it when it does. Moreover, it is possible to create an opening where none existed before. This is a skill that is difficult to teach, because it relies on preparedness, determination, clarity of purpose, and the ability to seize opportunity.

The marketing company owner wasn't sitting in the waiting area to recruit someone to do work for her. Gamal, perhaps unwittingly, created that opportunity by inquiring about her artist's portfolio. He had also prepared himself — again, perhaps unwittingly — by being able to speak knowledgeably about the use of computers in art. But he acted quite deliberately when he followed up immediately by going to visit his new acquaintance to try to clinch the opportunity.

When people ask me what their kids should study to get a good job, I tell them that they are looking through the wrong end of the telescope, that they should first ask what their kids are best at doing. That usually provokes an answer along the lines of "watching television," or "playing computer games," or "talking on the telephone." One parent put it succinctly when he said "eating." The reality is that schools may not offer everything your child needs for her career. Setting aside that issue for the moment, here is a list of the skills that I would suggest children should have beyond their chosen technical specialties, to help them in carving out a career. Those who have read my previous book, *Facing the Future*, will notice several similarities in this list. I'm including it here again because I get so many questions on this point that it is obviously of great interest and concern to people.

1. The ability to communicate clearly, concisely, and persuasively. This encompasses speaking and writing, but it also includes much more:

- The ability to think clearly precedes the ability to express yourself clearly. If you don't know what you want to say, you aren't going to be able to say it well.

- The ability to hold someone's interest depends on being able to express yourself in an engaging way, which usually means being concise, to the point, and witty if possible; using language in novel ways and avoiding overworked clichés; expressing yourself in a manner that is not sexist, racist, or otherwise offensive to your audience; using language in ways that make you appear intelligent rather than ignorant; undergirding your thoughts with appropriate facts and illustrations — in short, all the things your English teachers told you for years.

- Being persuasive means understanding, even empathizing with, your listener's point of view and desires, as well as using the "platinum rule" of human relations: "Do unto others as they like being done unto." It also means having a working knowledge of at least the rudiments of sales technique. Indeed, the ability to sell yourself, your ideas, your services, and your products should be a skill you develop to complement your ability to express yourself.

2. The ability to think and to reason. This means being able to arrive at useful and valuable insights from proper evidence, to separate correctly causes from effects, and to use these insights to project future developments. This ability will allow you to anticipate changes and prepare for them. Reasoning is the substance of science and mathematics. Mere rote memorization of theorems, computational techniques, and historic achievements is no more useful than being taught about someone else's successes without being able to achieve some of your own.

Thinking and reasoning are skills like high diving or performing rap music. They take practice and a grasp of the underlying techniques. You have to work at them, which many

people don't want to do. There's a folk saying that "some people would go to any lengths to avoid having to think."

3. The ability to create, innovate, and synthesize. Creativity is an attribute that everyone has but which few cultivate. The worthwhile expression of creativity demands encouragement, both in schools and in corporations. This usually requires a loosening of hierarchies and procedures, because creativity and innovation, by definition, challenge the status quo. Only an emotionally mature management group will feel comfortable with creativity.

4. The ability to get along with people. In a commercial setting, getting along with people means understanding and being empathetic toward the goals and objectives of your clients, and of their clients, even when you don't entirely agree with them. At the same time, it means balancing your empathy for your clients with your own beliefs. Doing anything for anyone simply for money is neither a healthy nor a successful long-term strategy.

Another necessary skill is the ability to work with and serve the public in a warm and engaging manner. This skill is not only necessary to those who work in service industries; it could be vital to success at a trade show or conference.

The abilities to lead and to follow are increasingly important. More work is being done in *ad hoc* teams, which means that being able to assemble and lead a team, and being an asset to someone else's team, is essential in tomorrow's more informal, more spontaneous working environments.

5. The ability to speak in public. Whether it is to a large audience or to a group assembled around a boardroom table, a facility for public speaking will be an edge for anyone seeking a career. It's a skill that anyone can develop, and one that schools should teach from an early age. Confident public speakers turn into confident people. The ancient Greeks and Romans knew the value of public oration. Benjamin Franklin praised the virtues of public speaking, and advised practising it in weekly meetings with a group of friends to build up confidence. For those who are beyond school age, or whose schools don't offer public speaking, there are organizations like Toastmasters International in most major centres that offer an opportunity to practise and master the art of public speaking.

6. An understanding of how business works. In an age where script writers are short of villains —- Nazis have been overused, and the Soviets are now friendly — business people are frequently being tricked out as the bad guys. Anyone with any experience knows this is largely fantasy (although there are evil doers in business, as there are in every other walk of life), but the negative image of business people, especially white businessmen, persists.

Young people entering the work force should understand at least the basics of economics if they expect to be taken seriously by commercial employers. Also, if everyone had some idea of how the economy worked, there would be more informed public debate on important issues and more thoughtful policy decisions by governments. Too often, lack of understanding leads to emotional responses that have no grounding in reality, and no hope of leading to successful policies or actions. A perfect example is the argument of people who want to put up protectionist barriers to "keep jobs in Canada." Such actions have no hope of accomplishing this admirable goal in the long run but will instead destroy jobs.

7. The ability to use computers and communications technology. Young people should not only be familiar with current technology, such as word processors, spreadsheets, database programs, e-mail, and the Internet, but also have the willingness to dive in and learn about new technologies as they emerge. I must confess that this is one of the hardest aspects of my work. I trained as a computer scientist and emerged from university in 1973 at the cutting edge of my field, but the changes in techniques and technology have been prodigious since then. Accordingly, I have regularly had to give up tools and software that I am comfortable with and master new ones, like the Internet. It's an uncomfortable and time-consuming process, but I know that if I don't keep up, I will be unable to offer my clients the kinds of services I know they will want — at which point I may wind up out of business. The willingness to move beyond your personal comfort zone is now a crucial part of modern business.

Ironically, some of the most important computer-related accessories I buy are games and gaming systems. Games usually push the boundaries of what computers and communications can do, and so are useful precursors to directions that business may move toward. They also give me valuable insights into an emerging mindset that perceives the world as a multimedia data stream.

8. The ability to work for — and sometimes by — yourself. Entrepreneurial skills will be valuable for virtually everyone in the future, whether you are just entering the work force or have only a few years left to retirement. Not only is it much more likely that people will work for themselves in future than in the past, but many corporate employees will have to adopt an entrepreneurial outlook to retain their jobs. Zig Ziglar, one of the best known sales trainers in North America, has said for many years that "everyone really works on commission; it's just that sales people know it."

Corporate Superstars

As anyone who works in a large corporate environment can testify, the differences between employees and entrepreneurs have narrowed significantly over the past several years and will continue to diminish as personal responsibility and accountability continue to grow.

In a significant way, though, entrepreneurship is superior to being employed: unless they are in the very top echelon of a company, employees are unlikely to reap rewards commensurate with their contributions if they engineer a major victory for their employers. They may get a promotion and a fat bonus, but nothing in comparison with the CEOs and a few senior executives. Nor is this inappropriate. It is merely part of the deal; the employee trades the major portion of the upside for the greater security of a steady pay cheque.

However, as the security of pay cheques steadily erodes, more employees are going to start questioning whether they should be getting a bigger share of the rewards of their efforts. For the most part, regardless of how they feel about it, they will not get more. There will, however, be rare occurrences where employees will find themselves able to hold their employers to ransom, if, for example, they develop a very specific, very personal lock on a particular field, expertise, or relationship with clients. The perfect example of this situation is José Ignacio Lopez, whom many credited with reviving General Motors' European business prospects. As a result of his perceived value to the company, Lopez became the focus of a bidding war — and ultimately a series of lawsuits — between General Motors, which wanted to keep and promote him, and Volkswagen, who hired him away from GM.

The Lopezes of the world are rare, and are paid as superstars, much as Michael Jordan in basketball and Ken Griffey Jr. in baseball are paid astronomical sums. Most other corporate employees will receive modest salaries in a two-tier system that differentiates between the best and the merely excellent. The excellent will be paid well; the best will be paid obscenely well. The rest will pick up the crumbs. Whether this is fair or not, this is the direction the corporate world is heading. Young people planning their careers would be well advised to seek a field in which they can be the best, not merely good or excellent.

What, then, might a working day in the life of someone who has just left school today be like in 20 years' time?

"Yes, we can handle that. I'll get on it right away," 45-year-old Judith Maxim agrees, then hangs up. She looks out into space for a moment, whistling tunelessly, then says to her genie, Hobbes, "Commence a new database search on the subject of life insurance sales to individuals over 65 in North America. Search the following databases: Canadian Life and Health Insurance Association, Statistics Canada, U.S. Library of Congress, Toronto Reference Library, National Insurance Association. End list. Discover possible additional databases. Limit fees paid to US$20 per database, $100 total all databases. If there is additional information that might be of use where the cost would exceed these limits, then ask me for permission. Begin search."

Judith then instructs her genie to reach one of her regular subcontractors on the phone. He appears shortly as an image in her Looking Glasses. "Hi, Judith! What's up?"

"What's the name of that graphic artist you used on the cough syrup ads we worked on last August? You know, the one that was so good at creating an old-fashioned, image-of-yesteryear kind of look?"

"Carolyn Kranz — why, do you have something for me?"

"Not this time, Ken. I'm on a tight deadline for a proposal, and my margin's too thin to include you. Next time. Do you have Carolyn's phone number?"

Ken looks uncertain, then says, "You're not going to make a habit of going around me to my people, are you?"

"No, Ken; we work well together, and we will again in future. But this is a rush job on a tight budget to impress a new client. If we land them, there'll be other work for all of us. But first we have to land the account — and I'm out of my depth in terms of what they want."

"Okay — just so long as you still love and appreciate me." He instructs his genie, "James, give Hobbes Carolyn's number." After some more small talk, Ken signs off and disappears from Judith's view.

Next Judith spends an hour surfing the Net, looking for ideas that others have used successfully with mature consumers. Newspaper accounts call what she's doing "just-in-time learning," but she still thinks of it as "research." She can't delegate the task to her genie, because she isn't quite sure what she's looking for until she sees it.

The assignment has come to her from one of the outsourcing specialists of an insurance group. Judith had met the specialist at a conference in Vancouver last year and had added her to the distribution list of newspaper and magazine articles that she writes. Judith had also sent the specialist a copy of her new book, **Yendo: The Way of Marketing** (Toronto: Stoddart Publishing, 2017), which the specialist had liked a lot. This year-long warm-up had resulted in a small, but potentially significant request to propose a marketing strategy for the sale of life insurance to the mature market — a field about which Judith knows almost nothing.

However, Judith is known as a fast learner — and now she's going to have to prove it because all the other bidders had been asked to start their proposals a week ago, and the results are due on Friday. Now she needs a writer, someone with a deft touch and an understanding of finance and marketing, preferably someone in the 65-plus age category. That futurist fellow who had been around since the 1980s and was in his mid-sixties now — Hobbes could dig his name out — he'd fit the bill.

Judith's working world is an unstructured one based on research, a constant, steep learning curve, a network of friends and connections, and a reputation carefully built and nurtured over time. Judith responds with great speed to new challenges, and she is always looking for ways to expand her network of both suppliers and clients.

She follows a marketing path that was uncommon when she started out in business in the late 1990s, which she calls "paid advertising," whereby other people pay her for advertising her abilities through the articles and books she writes, and the speeches she gives. The profile these activities give her cause people to remember her when they have a new and as yet vaguely defined marketing task to address.

Judith went to work for a marketing research firm when she finished her formal education. It was a great place to start, because the people were all upbeat and smart, aggressive but friendly, and happy to take her under their collective wing. Over time, though, she found that a couple of things about working for someone else chafed her. She often wanted to do things her way, but had to defer to someone more senior and, when the firm made a big hit, she didn't share in the financial rewards. She eventually left the firm and started her own marketing research and production organization.

In retrospect, she thought to herself, she had left too early. She could have learned a lot more from the firm if she had been more patient. Indeed, looking back, that had been the single major mistake of her career — and she now had enough experience at having other people work for her (although on a contract basis) to know that a lot of her pay had been in knowledge and experience rather than in straight money.

But the die was cast, and while the lessons she has been forced to learn on her own had been expensive, she has paid her dues, and is developing a prodigious reputation and following. Hers isn't the leading firm of its type — but her inclusion in a group of bidders for contracts is usually enough to make other firms nervous.

Judith is still a one-person show, even though her annual gross billings now exceed $10 million. She has no employees, and only Hobbes, her genie, to assist her. What she does have is a network of people who are very talented, who trust her and her judgment, but who aren't quite as adept at self-promotion and marketing as she is. They are, therefore, quite content to subcontract work for her. For her part, Judith knows the strengths and weaknesses of all her subcontractors, where their individual strengths lie, which ones work best under pressure, and which ones need a slower, more relaxed pace. Even so, she is starting to feel the pressure of doing everything herself. Is she finally going to have to break down and hire an assistant? If so, she'll have to find a way to keep that person happy — not let him become discontented as she had, only to lose him just when he is becoming valuable.

Hmmm. Her old mentor at the firm that originally hired her has just retired. She wonders whether he'd like to work part-time? She tells Hobbes to call him . . .

Individuals working on their own, staying away from hiring employees wherever possible, and spreading their names, reputations, and talents through an admixture of technology, personal contacts, self-promotion, and gumption will become the "virtual corporations" of the future. This is the way many people work already, including me. This doesn't mean that such people will spend their working days alone. Some of my clients include groups of people who work together, share office and equipment expenses, assist and promote each other in business, subcontract work to each other — but who, legally, work for themselves and do not share ownership in their companies.

81

There will still be big businesses because some enterprises require large amounts of capital and large-scale coordination. However, there will be fewer employees than in the past, and more outsourcing for specific purposes. As a result, whether they work for a large organization or for themselves, more and more people are going to be responsible for their own success and failure. This means you will be more exposed to the vicissitudes and opportunities of being in business, and more frequently confronted with the stark reality of success or failure, depending on how well you judge what the market wants.

This prospect is scary. Harry Dent, in his excellent book, *Job Shock* (New York: St. Martin's Press, 1995), makes the point quite succinctly: "The motif of the new workplace is: No more jobs, only businesses. ... If you think big bureaucratic companies or the government will take care of you, you will be crushed when they go down and you find your security has been ripped away."

5
What Happens to the Unemployed?

There have been three great revolutions in human history. The first was the agrarian revolution, which occurred more than 5,000 years ago as humans discovered they could grow their own food by staying in one place and planting crops. This allowed humanity to accumulate more riches than they could transport and to develop a more permanent culture. The agrarian revolution took millennia to work its way around the world. Indeed, there are still nomadic tribes in isolated places today.

The second great change was the Industrial Revolution, which started in England in the 1700s and had spread to Europe and North America by the mid-1800s. The Industrial Revolution transformed a largely rural and agrarian society into one that was primarily urban and industrial. It also allowed the development of a large middle class. More people earned more money from factory work than they ever could have as farm labourers, and mass production meant that there were more goods that were affordable. It also reduced the dependence on brute strength as the primary attribute of a worker, opening the door for women to move toward equal status, which was largely impossible in an agrarian setting. This transformation is continuing today in the developing countries.

The third and latest revolution is the information revolution, brought about by global communications and computer technology. The primary transformation here is the change from working with our hands and muscles to working with our minds. This revolution is happening in a matter of years or decades, rather than centuries or millennia, which means that it is hitting people in the middle of their working lives and interrupting their career paths and plans. In the digital age, physical size and strength are irrelevant; it's mental ability that's important.

Let's look at a typical worker caught in this manner today. A baby boomer born in the 1950s who started work in the 1970s emerged into a working world where the idea of a "steady job" still meant a great deal and was the accepted norm. In the 1950s someone with only a high school diploma, or even someone without a diploma, could walk into a factory and find a steady job (except during recessions) and stay there for as long as he wanted. By the 1970s, recruiters were lining up for college graduates, who had their pick of jobs and careers, and few earnest workers, regardless of qualifications, went without a job for long.

Today this same boomer is about 20 years into his career, when he suddenly finds that there are no steady jobs, and that he may have to start from scratch in a world that no longer values his knowledge and experience. The *Toronto Star* gives an account of one such boomer:

> Linda Fry had never thought of herself as old until she began looking for work last fall. After 24 years in the transportation and courier business, she began to sense what an employer was thinking as soon as she walked into a job interview. "I've been in interviews where I just know that because of my age, I'm not going to get the job," says Fry. "It's just a young person's world."
>
> Whether that's an accurate observation is the subject of ongoing debate. As the Canadian population ages and baby

boomers are "downsized," a ballooning number of older, or "mature" workers, have found themselves on the unemployment lines. (July 8, 1996, page C3)

Linda Fry is in her mid-forties. Although the newspaper does not give much of her story, it's likely that Linda was one of those who lost their jobs due to downsizing. But downsizing is really a symptom of a number of different trends coming together in the corporate world.

The first is the steady rise of foreign competition, especially from the Rapidly Developing Countries (RDCs) with low wage rates and rapid rates of growth. Domestic companies have responded by using automation to decrease the labour content of their products to combat the rising competition from countries where labour is cheap. In the process of saving their businesses, domestic producers wind up eliminating a lot of jobs.

The advances in automation and the capabilities of more sophisticated equipment would have made inroads in jobs, even without a rising level of foreign competition; foreign competition has just accelerated the process. As Jeremy Rifkin describes in his 1995 book, *The End of Work* (New York: G.P. Putnam's Sons):

In the United States, labor costs in the past eight years have more than tripled relative to the cost of capital equipment. (Although real wages have failed to keep up with inflation and in fact have been dropping, employment benefits, especially health care costs, have been rising sharply.) Anxious to cut costs and improve profit margins, companies have been substituting machines for human labor at an accelerating rate. (page 6)

Domestic companies also need to cope with a marketplace that moves faster and requires successful companies to respond to changes more rapidly. Shuffling paper is a horribly inefficient way to disseminate information through a company. Accordingly, those companies that intend to survive in the future are replacing paper memos with electronic networks and integrated working teams that cycle market impulses more rapidly from the consumer to design to production and back. Shuffling paper between isolated groups of specialists takes more people on the payroll than e-mail and computers, so as companies switch to more responsive corporate structures, they can do more with fewer bodies.

Rifkin offers a classic example of this in describing the computerization of credit approvals by IBM Credit, which finances the purchase of computer equipment for IBM clients. Sales people were complaining that they were losing orders because it was taking more than seven days after they had closed a sale to get a credit approval. IBM executives, concerned about such reports, took a single order and walked it through the credit approval process, asking each person involved to process that order right away while they waited. By doing this, the executives found that it actually took only about 90 minutes to process a credit approval. Paperwork and passing memos from one place to another ate up the rest of the time.

They solved the problem by setting up a computer system to handle the flow of information and assigning each credit approval to a "deal structurer" who rode herd on it until it was complete. In the process, they cut the approval time from seven days to four hours — and eliminated five separate offices and the people who worked in them (Rifkin, page 103).

As discussed in the last chapter, companies will rely more and more on the creative and innovative abilities of their employees, so they will favour people who are self-starters who can work within a more decentralized, less hierarchical corporate structure. This is already happening with information technologies (IT). The new IT systems — fax, modems, e-mail, the Internet, corporate Intranets, telecommuting, telework, videophones and video-conferencing —

will increasingly allow companies to place their operations in low-rent locations, including the homes of their employees and the offices of their clients, rather than concentrating them in one expensive, central location. And a more autonomous, decentralized work force doesn't need as many managers and supervisors. Accordingly, many of the middle management jobs that the baby boomers strove for are disappearing — just when they were reaching the age when they expected to get them.

The sheer size of the baby boomer generation is creating the next trend. The boomers, born roughly between 1946 and 1967, constitute about 35 percent of the Canadian population. When they started into the labour force, they entered a corporate world structured roughly like a pyramid, with many jobs at the bottom and one job at the top. As the boomers aged, they moved up in seniority. However, although now there are virtually the same number of boomers as before, there are far fewer jobs in the upper levels of the corporate pyramid. As a result, baby boomers are being let go in record numbers and falling into a market that requires them to be very different kinds of workers from what was wanted when they last went job hunting. But while they may be classic examples of what's happening in the workplace today, the boomers are not by any means the only ones affected by these changes. Workers of all ages, from those just starting out to those trying to hold on until retirement, are finding life far more precarious than before.

So what happens to those people who can't adjust to the changes, who can't adapt to new ways of working, or can't find a new niche into which they can fit?

What Happens to Those Who Can't Adapt?

Not everyone will want to establish his or her own business and make a success of it, or become a freelancer with a network of contacts and clients. Not everyone is comfortable with computer systems or can profitably surf the Internet. It's unlikely that a 50-year-old factory worker who has spent his life making vacuum cleaners, or a corporate administrator used to supervising groups of people who aren't needed anymore, is going to transform himself into a cutting-edge graphic designer or an HTML (HyperText Mark-up Language, the principal language of the Internet) programmer. So what will happen to such people?

This is a tough question, which, unfortunately, has a tough answer: they're going to stay unemployed and may well fall straight through the cracks in society, as illustrated in George's story in the last chapter. The world in which they started work has vanished, and the world today is much less accommodating. Secure jobs no longer exist, and whole categories of occupations will disappear with shifts in business and trade.

Again, please understand that I don't like this trend, nor do I approve of it; I'm merely commenting on what is likely to occur over the next 20 years. But better to be forewarned and prepared for trouble than to be ambushed by it. Accordingly, if your job has disappeared, and you aren't able to find another one like it, then you may have no choice but to find some other line of work, or another way of making a living. The world is the way it is, not the way we want it to be. Don't waste time deluding yourself that the world will change back to something you like better.

Many people resist this answer, like children throwing a tantrum when they can't hold the moon in their hands. They come up with a variety of arguments, all of which add up to a denial of reality. Let's go over some of the major themes of these denials.

Can't the Government Do Something?

On the whole, governments can't do much about this situation, and for a variety of reasons, the most important of which is that the forces at work are bigger and more powerful than our governments, singly or in combination. In fact, what governments *can* do, for the most part, is get out of the way and not make matters worse.

People expect governments to support those who have lost their jobs, whether through extended unemployment insurance, welfare, or some other financial means. However, just as individuals who have lost their jobs face financial trouble, today's governments, too, have financial problems. First, government revenues are not rising as quickly as they did in the past. As the incomes of the work force go, so go the revenues of the various levels of government. When many people are out of work, tax revenues decline. Add the costs of welfare payments and unemployment insurance, and governments face a real cash crunch.

Next, the demands on government funds are changing. As the average age of the population increases, and as average life expectancy rises, the costs of health care are skyrocketing, eating into government budgets. This problem is going to get steadily worse as time goes on, and I'll come back to discuss it in chapter 9. Finally, debts accumulated by governments since the mid-1970s have left them crippled with huge interest payments. This makes it much more difficult to finance programs that might alleviate the pain of structural unemployment.

Some people seem to think either that we can just ignore the debts our governments accumulated on our behalf, or that human issues are more important than mere money, so we should spend the money we don't have regardless of the financial consequences. This isn't possible, no matter how hard we might wish things to be different. Spending money we don't have will only make things worse later on, in a world that is going to get progressively meaner.

Accordingly, we now face a situation where governments just do not have the financial capacity to support people who cannot find work for an extended period of time, regardless of why they are unemployed or of their personal situations. Like it or not, we are returning to a world where people will succeed or fail, even live or die, on the basis of what they can contribute to the economy. If they cannot contribute, they will not have a claim on the income or profits of those who are working. If this statement seems hard-hearted, it's because it runs counter to the policies that the developed countries have been pursuing since the late 1800s, and especially since Franklin Delano Roosevelt's New Deal policies of the Great Depression. We can no longer afford such policies. Though we may not like it, the world of today and tomorrow is and will be hard-nosed and hard-hearted.

For those who are not convinced that we need to be this way, or that the world will force us to be this way, I suggest that they look at the RDCs that are working hard to compete with us. In the Asian Tiger countries of Singapore, Hong Kong, Taiwan, and South Korea, spending on social welfare is a small fraction of what it is in the developed world. There, generally speaking, people who do not work do not eat, period. To the governments of these countries, it makes no sense to support people who do not contribute, and a great deal of sense to pour money into activities that will make people more productive, such as education and appropriate tax and export policies. Such countries are increasingly setting the agenda for Western nations by forcing us to respond to their competition in the global marketplace. If they can be highly competitive and lure business away from us, then we must become equally competitive or slip into Third World status ourselves.

Can't We Protect Jobs from Foreign Competition?

In a word, no. It doesn't matter what we try, the result will be that domestic companies cannot avoid competing with foreign companies, which will put domestic jobs at risk.

A simple solution might be for us to erect trade and tariff barriers to prevent cheap goods from entering our markets in competition with goods made here, thus apparently protecting our producers and their employees. But passing legislation does not change the economic laws by which the global economy works. Legal actions on matters of our economy have, in the long run, about as much effect on the workings of the global economy as legislation repealing the law of gravity. What's more, foreign trade is too important to Canada — indeed, to any developed country — for protectionist policies to work. Let's look at a simple example to see why.

Suppose we decided to protect all Canadian-made goods from external competition in order to preserve Canadian jobs. This would mean we would have to erect some form of trade barriers against goods from abroad. There are many barriers to choose from, but let's pick the easiest: tariffs. The first impact of tariff imposition would be the increased price of imported goods. Everything from Korean VCRs, Japanese cars, and French wines to American medical equipment would cost more, producing a dramatic and unpopular increase in the cost of living. It would also mean a dramatic decline in our ability to export our products for two reasons. First, our trading partners, noting our desire to keep their products out of the Canadian market, would retaliate with trade barriers of their own, which would do significant damage to our economy as exports account for about one-third of Canadian GNP (depending on how you account for them). Secondly, it would cost more to produce products, because the imported materials and equipment used to produce them would cost more, and because labour costs would be higher as people strove to achieve higher wages to offset higher prices. Eventually we would all have lower incomes, sell fewer products abroad, have less money to buy the products made here at home — and wind up with fewer jobs and a lower standard of living, the exact opposite of what we set out to do.

Protecting some industries and not others would mean that those people who were not protected were being taxed to line the pockets of those who were. This is what is happening with dairy and poultry products, for example. Canadians have to pay substantially more to support the 0.1 percent of the population who are engaged in raising these products.

This inability to protect jobs affects every country in the world, but the bigger ones can disguise the effects for longer. The biggest nations, like the United States, can pretend that they are doing something effective by protecting jobs, and if they can cheat and bend world trading rules to give them an unequal advantage, they may be able to get away with it for a while. But their consumers will eventually pay for this protection through higher prices, and their industries through poorer and more expensive materials and equipment. Ultimately their exports and economy will suffer.

The government of the former Soviet Union "protected" their industries and jobs from competition outside the Iron Curtain for more than 70 years. But over time, their industries fell further and further behind their free market competitors. When the Soviet government ran out of money to prop up the illusion of a strong economy, the protectionist barriers fell, and the world discovered that the Soviet economy was largely trash, worthless and incapable of supporting its workers. This is why economic activity in the former Soviet Republics fell so precipitously after the Soviet Union came apart, and why it would be a mistake for Russian voters to assume that they can regain their former standard of living by returning to communism.

Over the long run, protectionist measures do not preserve jobs; they destroy them. This is an uncomfortable truth, and one that people who have jobs that are being protected work hard to deny.

Training Is Not the Answer

There are few issues on which those who debate government policy agree, but training seems to be one. Everyone wants to help people move from older, dying industries to new jobs in rapidly growing industries, and training is viewed as the way to make this happen.

This strategy has some validity, but nowhere near as much as every-one supposes; as a result, there is an awful lot of money spent on training schemes and very little to show as results. The *Economist* magazine commented on this in an April 6, 1996, article on training:

> Unions like training programmes because they can use them to push up wages. Academics like them because they increase the demand for education. Parents like them because they give out-of-work, out-of-school youths something to do. Prophets of a post-modern society praise them as part of an ethic of life-long learning. ... All in all, then, the case for publicly supported schemes seems solid. There is just one problem. In practice, they rarely work.
>
> In a growing body of research, economists have compared groups of unemployed people who enter government training schemes with similar groups that do not. In almost every case, these studies have found that the schemes have failed to improve either the earnings or the employment prospects of their clients. (page 19)

The *Economist* goes on to describe a variety of research studies on the effects of training produced by the United States, Great Britain, Australia, and the Organization for Economic Cooperation and Development (OECD). All of these studies indicate that government-run training programs do virtually nothing to improve the prospects for employment for those involved. Indeed, some of the studies seem to indicate that such programs can actually slightly decrease the earnings of young people. Moreover, simple training in how to conduct yourself during an interview seems to have more effect than elaborate — and expensive — training schemes.

Recently I was a guest on an open-line radio show in Winnipeg. A very scared and angry woman called to criticize me for talking about the kinds of changes that I've described in this chapter. She told me that her husband, who had been a factory worker for many years, was thrown out of a job when the factory closed. He then retrained as a welder and now couldn't find work in that profession either. She seemed to believe that I bore some blame for this situation because I talked about what was happening in the labour market.

Regardless of her high opinion of my ability to influence the economy, she had a valid point. "Training" is not an undifferentiated commodity. Training people in useless skills is a waste of time and money, as well as of the emotional capital that gets used up when their hopes are raised and then dashed. Yet there is little debate about what training is offered, how it is provided, or to whom. Instead, training has become a motherhood issue that no one dares attack.

Does this mean all training and, by inference, all education are a waste of time and money? Of course not. If you have decided on a career area that involves technical knowledge and training you don't have, then training from a community college or university, or from a reputable commercial training group that specializes in that field, can be invaluable. In addition, learning how to conduct yourself in an interview, assistance in preparing an effective résumé, and lessons about job hunting can be beneficial. But entering a training program — any training program — without a clear idea about how it will lead you to a new career is like hoping your fairy godmother will make your problems go away.

Meanwhile, governments should pay attention to the studies and scrap most, if not all, public-sector training. I'll have more to say about training and education in chapter 10.

Why Job Sharing, Shorter Work Weeks, and Higher Minimum Wages Won't Work

I was initially profoundly impressed, and then profoundly disappointed, by Jeremy Rifkin's *The End of Work*. His analysis of what was happening in the global labour force was so clear, so insightful, and so soundly argued that I couldn't wait to get to the end to read his recommendations for job creation and employment. When I got to the section, I found it horribly weak. He made, in essence, two suggestions: institutionalized job sharing and legislated shorter work weeks. Neither of these will work, despite his historical analysis to show that shorter work weeks did help employment markets earlier this century. The reason they won't work is that he assumes that the global labour market is homogeneous around the world, and that we can select labour policies in North America and Europe and ignore what is happening elsewhere. This is no longer the case, even if it was so earlier in the century.

Job sharing is popular with those who are out of work and unpopular with those who have full-time jobs, because job sharing usually means pay sharing as well. Those who are receiving a full pay cheque for a full-time job are likely to resist being asked to saw off a significant chunk of it to give to someone else. If job sharing did not mean pay sharing, then it would substantially raise the cost of employing people — which would reduce the demand. The same is true of a legislated shorter work week. If companies are required to pay the same amount of money for less work, then the cost of workers goes up.

If our labour markets operated in isolation, the way they did earlier this century, then these proposals *might* work. If more people were working, then more people would be buying things and spending money. This would increase corporate profits, compensating companies for higher pay costs. Today, however, this model no longer works because of foreign competition and automation. If the cost of labour rises, then the cost of products and services must rise as well. This would make our products and services less competitive with those produced by the RDCs, and would cause us to lose market share, profits, jobs, and income. To compensate for higher labour costs that threatened their ability to compete, companies would either move their operations to some country that had less expensive labour or increase their use of automation. Either way, job sharing and a shorter work week would result in less employment, not more.

In essence, jobs and profits are like elusive fish that need to be coaxed into coming to you, not forced. Job sharing, shorter work weeks, higher minimum wages, pay equity laws, and similar forms of labour legislation are all attempts to bend employment to a social agenda. I oppose them out of pure pragmatism, not out of any knee-jerk, right-wing, "let-'em-eat-cake" philosophy. I have no ax to grind here as I neither employ people, nor am I an employee of others. These measures just won't work.

What Can Governments Do?

So far, all I've done is criticize the things that governments have done wrong and demonstrate how powerless they are. But is there anything that governments can do to help, other than sit by and watch their citizens be hurt by these changes? Is there a role for governments? Yes, but it is a very different one than they are used to filling.

First, governments can give people information about what is happening in the economy and the job market. Statistics Canada has been praised internationally for its data collection, accuracy, and integrity, a sentiment I echo. Although not perfect, it is a wonderful government operation, and one that has been valuable in my own studies.

The government should commission Statistics Canada to watch the trends in business and the labour markets, and publish observations about what occupations are in the highest demand, and which ones offer the greatest stability, the highest pay, and so on. In the business field, StatsCan could produce reports about which industries are growing most rapidly in sales, profits, and employment; which small industries are emerging; and so forth. The net result would be information that people could use to select career paths, seek new employment, or choose an industry in which to become entrepreneurs. This task would be relatively simple and inexpensive, as StatsCan already collects and prepares most of this information. It is really more a matter of collecting it in one place, writing clear, jargon-free text to go with it, packaging it, publicizing it, and making it available at the lowest possible cost to the widest range of people.

Next, all levels of government should work in collaboration with businesses, educators, and community groups to define a desirable future for Canada as a whole, and for each community as a microcosm. These collaborations should identify obstacles to the desired future for the members of a community, then seek ways in which the group can work together for the common good.

If this sounds like pie-in-the-sky, it shouldn't, for such steps are already being taken in a variety of places. The techniques being used are similar to those described in a 1995 book by Marvin Weisbord and Sandra Janoff, *Future Search: An Action Guide to Finding Common Ground in Organizations & Communities* (San Francisco: Berrett-Koehler). These same techniques also formed the basis of a conference on the future of communities in Silicon Valley that was jointly organized by Stanford University's North American Forum and the North American Institute.*

In a world where competition for markets and jobs can come from a company on the other side of the globe that no one has ever heard of, and where profits, jobs, incomes, tax revenues, and government

---

* David Crane, "Silicon Valley's strategy for the future," *Toronto Star*, March 31, 1996, p.D2.

services are so closely linked and interdependent, it makes no sense for differing groups to fight with each other. When business and labour argue over how they're going to divide the pie, or when governments and community groups fight over ideology, everyone suffers because the real competition is no longer your neighbours or your counterparts across the table. Instead, you should be worrying about hungry, ambitious workers and companies in RDCs that make a fraction of what you make, and would be happy to serve your customers with better service and lower prices if you give them the chance. Accordingly, people have to understand that the health of their community affects them both personally and professionally. Governments can serve a pivotal role by taking the lead in collaboration. The Japanese have a folk saying: "You can fix the problem or you can fix the blame, but you can't fix both." We have spent far too many years fixing the blame for our problems rather than fixing the problems themselves.

We need to change and rebalance legislation governing the relationship between employee and employer. Let me revisit a quote from Jeremy Rifkin's 1995 book *The End of Work*: "In the United States, labor costs in the past eight years have more than tripled relative to the cost of capital equipment. (Although real wages have failed to keep up with inflation and in fact have been dropping, *employment benefits, especially health care costs, have been rising sharply*)" (page 6). I've emphasized that last phrase because it demonstrates quite clearly one of the biggest obstacles to increased employment — and it is one that we've created ourselves.

Payroll taxes — unemployment insurance premiums, health insurance taxes, Canada or Quebec Pension Plan payments, and the like — and similar employee benefits increase the cost of having employees. Legislation on issues like employment equity, wrongful dismissal, and workplace discrimination make it less desirable to have employees or to hire more.

Most of the current legislative acts were passed during a period when they seemed appropriate and enforceable. Indeed, no one can fault the intention or the spirit of these taxes and pieces of legislation. From now on, though, they will have the unintended effect of dissuading companies from hiring employees. As one entrepreneur described the situation in the *Globe and Mail*:

> [So] decidedly one-sided is current labour law in favour of employees that owners of small businesses are virtually defenseless, another disincentive to job creation. In my experience, employment law does not exist to protect employees from their employers but from themselves. They can walk out on a moment's notice and retain their rights while an employer has to give notice or pay in lieu. (January 27, 1993, page A20)

It's time to rethink labour protection laws and payroll taxes, to come to a balance between the legitimate need to protect individuals and the legitimate needs of companies for flexibility and accountability. This realignment will be highly unpopular with many — especially those in labour unions — but we have to choose whether we want to offer protections for jobs that don't exist or whether we want jobs. The reality is that the market is creating the flexibility employers need, without legislative changes, by turning so many people into contract workers and freelancers instead of employees. Indeed, the so-called "contingent work force" — which includes part-time workers and self-employed people working on contracts — is now the fastest-growing sector of the labour market. Accordingly, governments should acknowledge the reality of the marketplace, and look for a new legislative balance that will encourage employment rather than destroy jobs.

One area where governments could accelerate job growth is business franchises. People often ask me what I think about franchising as a business opportunity. My reply sounds flippant but isn't. I tell them that buying a good franchise can be a good way to buy a job. For people who decide that they need to create their own jobs by going into business for themselves, but lack the confidence or experience to do it safely and properly, buying a sound franchise can be a good alternative to starting a business from scratch. A properly run franchise already has market studies, a business plan, employment policies, legal documentation — in short most of the things necessary for the creation of a successful business. The reasons why a franchiser sells the concept to a franchisee as opposed to doing it themselves should properly be: (1) the franchisee brings his own capital to the franchise, allowing the franchiser to expand more rapidly than he would otherwise be able to do; and (2) the franchisee brings the management and hours of work that the franchiser would otherwise have to hire. In effect, the franchisee brings two of the four things necessary to a successful business: money and manpower. The others — know-how and a feasible market niche — should be supplied by the franchiser.

But there are franchises and franchises. Unfortunately, Canada has very little legislation protecting people who buy franchises through one-sided or even near-fraudulent franchise agreements. Accordingly, someone buying a franchise needs to be very careful and do his homework before committing himself to a legal agreement that is almost certain to favour the franchiser. Indeed, I suspect that someone could create a healthy business in assessing the potential of a given market area, suggesting the best franchises for the market, and giving information on the reputation of various franchise opportunities — sort of like the books produced on used cars.

The franchising business is going to continue to expand rapidly as people look for ways of "buying a job." Governments need to encourage this trend not only by regulating the industry — lightly — to avoid fraud, but also by requiring sufficient disclosure so that potential franchisees can see clearly what competition and problems they are likely to face, and what kinds of returns they can reasonably expect in a given franchise.

What Can You Do for Yourself?

If you accept that you are going to carry the primary responsibility for managing your career, and that there is no job security any more, what can you do for yourself? This is a broad topic, and is discussed in a variety of other books, including the previously mentioned *Job Shock* by Harry Dent, and a variety of books on finding employment, such as the perennial job-hunting book, *What Color Is Your Parachute?* by Richard Nelson Bolles (Berkeley: Ten Speed Press, 1996).

But I have a more basic answer, which I described in the previous chapter: do something you love and at which you excel, and then find a way to get people to pay you to do it. This is easy to say but difficult to do, and there are no pat answers as to how you can accomplish this. One suggestion I can make is that you take a hard look at the list of skills new job entrants should have, as I outlined them in the previous chapter.

The odds are that doing something you love, and finding a way to get paid for it, will mean working for yourself, either in your own company, or as a freelancer or consultant. There are books on entrepreneurship that can make the transition easier — including one I wrote myself, if you can find it. It's now out of print, but you might be able to track it down in your local library. It's called *From Employee to Entrepreneur: How to Turn Your Experience Into a Fortune* (Toronto: Key Porter Books, 1989).

I started this chapter by asking: what happens if you're unemployed, if you don't fit into the working world as it has evolved? The final answer is that you'd better start changing until you do fit in, because the world has become a very unforgiving place. I don't like this uncomfortable answer any better than you do, but it's the truth, and it will govern your future.

Managing for the Future

If you do have a job and work for an employer, what kind of a company will it be? How will it be different from today's companies? If you are an owner or a manager, how will the employer–employee relationship change over the next 20 years?

To begin, there are a couple of themes I've already introduced that are going to affect companies and their managers. There will be more opportunity coupled with less security. Among the forces that make this true are the faster pace of business, the growth of international markets linked with increases in global competition, the new fields and industries opening up because of new technologies, and the potential to serve clients at long distance (or lose them to a long-distance competitor) because of the communications revolution.

As routine work disappears, whether eliminated by automation or lost to workers in developing countries, routine workers will also vanish. The crucial work — and the crucial workers — that remain will be more entrepreneurial, more creative, more thoughtful than the average worker of the past. They will also be more challenging to manage because they will think for and of themselves; they will decide whether they are receiving as much as they are giving and whether they can demand more and get it. Indeed, many will not be employees at all, but outside contractors, in which case they will routinely demand what the market will bear. However, if you are a

manager, regardless of whether the people doing the work are internal or external, and regardless of how you organize them, you are going to have to be a leader, not a boss. To be sustained, creativity cannot be commanded, it can only be encouraged. This point is being lost in some of the uncertainty surrounding management today, and the practice that typifies the current fuzziness of thought is downsizing.

The Downsizing Fad

Downsizing represents a strange paradox. Today's companies increasingly compete on brains more than products or market position, which means that the greatest asset a company has is the collection of brains represented by its employees. When, then, does it make sense to downsize?

There is no simple answer because several trends are coming together at the same time, which creates great confusion. One part of the answer is that many companies that are downsizing are making a major mistake. A company should never keep employees that are not productive. A mass firing, then, is normally an admission by a management team that it has not been doing its job of making sure that all employees are sufficiently productive. If employees are productive, they should not be fired. If they are not productive, they should be fired individually as their lack of productivity becomes apparent rather than *en masse*.

The only exceptions are companies that have had a major change in management and ascribe previous bad results to incompetency; companies in markets driven by technology, where a major advance makes it possible to automate the functions of employees doing routine work; and companies that get out of a market segment, either because they have been beaten or because the market is no longer attractive. Accordingly, much of the downsizing going on today is really a tacit admission by management that they don't know what they are doing.

Downsizing also carries several hidden costs that show up only over time. First, it makes companies too lean to meet market demand during periods of strong growth. This forces them to pass up sales they would otherwise have gotten and damages relationships with customers. Secondly, over time it makes employees less productive because downsizing tends to destroy company morale. Moreover, the remaining employees tend to burn out from overwork as they struggle to stay ahead of the ax. Thirdly, and most importantly, downsizing tends to destroy the corporate creativity that companies need to survive. Employees know that the people most likely to keep their jobs in a major downsizing are those that keep on their boss's good side. They also know that creativity is dangerous: if you put forward an idea that doesn't work out, then you tend to get the next chop. As a result, companies that indulge in downsizing will find that their remaining employees spend much more time playing politics and much less time thinking about ways to invent the company's future.

Downsizing, then, is a fad that will die out as a general practice except in those situations described earlier. Even so, leaner companies are the way of the future. The average number of employees per company has been declining in the developed world since the 1960s, and that trend is going to continue well into the future.

The Company of the Future

Before I get into the details, let me summarize the major differences between the companies of the future and those of today. You might want to consider how your company measures up to tomorrow's standards:

- The concepts of "core competency" and "outsourcing" will produce virtual corporations that may have brief existences. Even longlived companies will change shape and function rapidly.

- Corporate hierarchies are going to give way to corporate marketplaces.
- The people who work for a corporation will make an enormous difference to its success or failure, which means hiring the best people for the job is of crucial importance. Companies will be looking not just for a "good fit" between employer and employee, but for the best possible fit. The differences between one individual and another will be thrown into sharp relief.
- Because people will be so important, making the best use of their time will become a major strategic initiative.
- Communications and shared resources, easily and immediately available throughout the company, will become key. Corporate secrecy will decline.
- Competition will occur inside as well as outside a company, yet individuals and corporations will cooperate with competitors to an extent that we would now consider unthinkable.
- The need for capital and access to financing will become the prime determinant of whether a company needs to be big or small. Even so, small companies will begin to manage projects that require huge amounts of capital.
- A company's flexibility will determine whether it survives. Rigidity and bureaucracy will be dangerous to corporate health.
- Quality will become so widespread that it will be irrelevant. The defining moment of your relationship with your clients will come from their worst experience with any employee (or any aspect) of your company.

- A company's ability to assist its employees to upgrade their skills and learn new ones will be the key to responding to new changes in the marketplace. Accordingly, those companies that are serious about survival will become serious about helping their employees learn.

Now let's look at these points in some detail.

The Virtual Corporation

For some time now we have heard rumblings about the emergence of virtual corporations, but few are in evidence. There's a good reason for this scarcity: a virtual corporation, almost by definition, vanishes when it completes its task. As a result, it's not going to produce many headlines or leave a lasting impression, although some of the individuals involved will.

But the virtual corporation is going to be more common. Indeed, in many ways, business is going to look more like a film production company than a traditional business. Someone will decide that there is a particular need or opportunity, assemble a team, arrange financing, and exploit the situation. When the game is over, there will be a wrap party, everybody will laugh, drink, and cry on each other's shoulders, then scatter until some of them meet again in another project.

Moreover, even traditional companies are going to start taking on the elusive trappings of a virtual corporation. Interdisciplinary teams are going to replace isolated groups of specialists. Oftentimes these teams will be created on an *ad hoc* basis, then disbanded. They will certainly be more flexible, and have a much broader mandate, than traditional workers. The companies themselves will become much less substantive than a traditional company, outsourcing many or all of their functions, but labelling the overall result as being theirs. For instance, there is an American firm, TopsyTail, that has sold more than $100 million of a hair-styling product, yet has no permanent employees other than management. Instead, it outsources almost everything, from design, manufacturing, and marketing, to packaging and distribution.

Hierarchies Versus Markets

Businesses organize their activities in two major ways, hierarchies and markets. Hierarchies tend to move slowly, but according to a central plan. Markets move quickly, but often in messy, erratic, unpredictable ways. But since the pace of development and competition, and the rate at which new technologies and products evolve, are all speeding up, market-oriented activity is increasingly taking over from hierarchical activity. Accordingly, 20 years from now, a successful business will be more market driven, and less hierarchical, and may look something like this:

> Kamil Venmura's creation of the first true twenty-first-century company is a case study in sizing up an opportunity and making the most of it. His creation of The Partnership Network (TPN) is a stroke of genius, brilliantly executed. This 69-year-old, silver-haired consultant came out of one of the major accounting and management firms. He saw the difficulty that his senior partners had in making the transition from a world where seniority meant respect, money, and position to one that seemed to say, "What have you done for me lately?"
>
> But Kamil also saw the potential for a loose amalgamation of high-powered people tied together in such a way as to make it easy for them to draw on each other's talents, while always working for their own personal interests. TPN is structured much like some of the major accounting and management consulting firms — but without the hierarchy that causes these firms to be so top-heavy.

Kathy Higginson, a 47-year-old mother and computer leader from Swift Current, Saskatchewan, knows all about TPN, and so is nervous when she receives their slim envelope in reply to her application. Taking a deep breath, she slits it open, then lets out a sigh of relief as she reads that her application for partnership has been accepted. A letter signed by Venmura himself says that he hopes theirs will be a long and mutually profitable relationship.

Kathy's acceptance has come at the end of a long interview process. TPN had asked her to fill out an eight-page application form, which requested, among other things, a list of every award, prize, and accomplishment she had attained since birth. She had gone through three separate interviews with a professional recruiter, which included both a timed intelligence and aptitude test and a vocational inclination test. She had to supply a raft of references, both personal and professional, vouching for her integrity, her ability to get along with other people, her determination to get things done, and her success in business. She has travelled to the company's headquarters in Vancouver for what TPN described as a "mutual interview" with three partners, all of whom went through the same recruiting process one year before. The purpose of the last interview was not only to size her up, but to let her ask her own questions about the partnership. At the end of the mutual interview, the three partners each had to answer three questions: 1) Would you be willing to pay this person out of your own pocket to work for you? 2) Would you be willing to work for this person? 3) Is this person truly outstanding? Kathy had to answer one question: did she still want to join TPN?

All three interviewers had given her thumbs-up on all three questions, as had the professional recruiter. Now that TPN has accepted her application, she will invest $30,000 in TPN and agree to pay a $2,000 annual communications and referral fee. Half of her investment will go to cover the cost of the interview process, including the fee for the professional interviewer, the tests, and the travel costs to Vancouver. The other half will go into TPN's Partnership Capital Pool, which will earn her a share of the profits based on her investment.

TPN goes to extraordinary lengths to recruit partners, adopting the slogan: "Competent people are common; great people are hard to find." Many outside people think this is boasting. In reality, it is nothing more than a statement of fact — and of TPN policy. Kathy has been invited to become a full partner in one of the greatest organizations of her time.

TPN has no employees, only partners. TPN operates no companies and owns no facilities or equipment. Properly speaking, TPN is not a business at all. It has no CEO, only a managing director engaged under contract. The managing director's function is to coordinate the day-to-day relationships between partners.

This story highlights the reinvention of our concept of what a business is. A business — any business, big or small — is really the cooperative efforts of the individuals who work within it. Its success is the result of the talents and skills of individuals. TPN organizes all its efforts around that principle by doing everything possible to maximize the abilities of individuals to get things done.

Let's go through some of the things that could make TPN-type organizations one of the paths to success in the next century. The first thing to note is the focus on individual strengths. In an increasingly competitive world, business will eventually come down to who does things best, not merely who does things. The traditional corporation has a much harder time maximizing the talents of its people because their motivation is limited to what rewards they can expect as employees, and their ability to initiate and experiment is limited to what their employer will allow. If you've ever worked for a small company, you know that the owner always works later than

anyone else and is constantly unhappy with how lightly her employees treat business matters.

Some organizations work hard to overcome this. The classic
example is 3M, which allows technical staff to engage in "bootleg-
ging," working on pet projects for up to 15 percent of their working
hours. Moreover, they have a corporate policy that pushes them to
innovate: they seek to generate 25 percent of each year's sales from
products that are less than five years old.

Yet, even in 3M, employees still spend 85 percent of their time
on what the company wants done. This is completely understand-
able where an employer is paying a salary to its employee — but it
does not maximize a worker's motivation or ability to innovate. A
TPN-type organization contains nothing but entrepreneurs. Their
dedication to their own businesses is absolute. The only constraints
on their freedom to innovate are the realities of the marketplace
and their ability to make an idea work. In the terms of currently
popular management buzz words, TPN not only has a "flat" organization chart, but one in which there is no hierarchy at all.
Everybody working within the TPN umbrella is a partner, and all
partners are equals. By emphasizing the quality of each individual
they recruit, TPN vastly increases its odds of success.

We are seeing a two-tiered system develop in which good people
are paid good money, but the best people are paid extraordinary
amounts of money. This superstar system is moving into business
because in a sharply competitive world, having the best dealmaker,
the best turnaround artist, the best cost-cutter, or the best litigation
lawyer can make the difference between success and failure.
Consider what happens when two companies are bidding for the
takeover of a third, strategically important company. There is no
prize for second best in such a competition, so the difference
between hiring the best and the second best dealmaker is crucial.
Accordingly, the increase in levels of competition is throwing the
differences between one individual and another into sharp focus.

This is another reason why companies need to start focusing on the talents and abilities of individuals rather than on viewing them as boxes in an organization chart.

Another key feature of TPN is that all its partners have unfettered access to the best-quality information.

> Like Kathy, every TPN partner is a principal of his or her own business. TPN provides the support mechanisms and network connections that each partner needs to be as successful as possible. The $2,000 annual communications and referral fee gives Kathy unlimited access to the Partnership's Intranet communication system, as well as to Central Reference, an all-purpose group of "can do" problem-solvers whose task is to field requests for help and information, and to find the best possible solution for a partner's needs for a particular task.
>
> Central Reference — usually called CR by the partners — will advise on the latest and best office, computer, and production equipment a partner may need. If the partner wishes, it will source that equipment, either in a direct purchase, or on lease. If the partner has unusual requirements, CR will find someone with the expertise to give the best possible advice, researching and hiring from outside if necessary, or more usually finding and hiring the talent from its database of TPN's worldwide partners.
>
> If a partner needs office space or airline tickets or secretarial help or banking relationships or almost anything else, she can usually get it better and cheaper through CR than on the open market. She doesn't have to waste time searching, as she knows she's unlikely to find a better deal than the one offered by CR. She always has complete freedom to buy things from outside the organization, but will find that it's hardly ever worth doing so. TPN not only has the bulk buying power of a major organization, it also has some of the best purchasing and negotiating talent in the world. These people find the best deals going on

virtually everything that their partners commonly use in their professional and personal lives. The purpose is not so much to save money — although that happens, too — but to save the partners' time by saving them the need to shop around.

As a result, Kathy can concentrate on what she does best. She can subcontract all the administrivia, tax filing, form-filling, marketing campaign snags, sales follow-up calls, manufacturing hassles, shipping problems, distribution foul-ups, or anything else that is not central to her main strengths. Moreover, since she is buying such products and services through CR, she knows that they will be absolutely top quality, and at a price that is likely to be better than she could find for herself. TPN service providers who don't provide great results quickly find their services are not in demand and their businesses languish. Accordingly, they bust their butts all the time, for every customer — and especially for every partner, big or small.

Central Reference is legendary in the business world. Whenever partners run into a problem or a need, whether personal or professional, the first thing they normally do is call CR. The abilities of Central Reference, coupled with the worldwide reputation of the partnership, have allowed individual partners to bid for and win multi-billion-dollar projects, handling the parts they do best, and subcontracting out everything else. Each partner knows that he can rely on CR because it is run by other partners who are just as eager to win the business as he is.

Information is the lifeblood of business organizations today — and not just random information either. For TPN, I included two communications services: a partnership Intranet and Central Reference.

An Intranet is like a privately run Internet; a computer-based communications network, where the users probably employ something like Netscape Navigator or other graphic Web browsers, but which is accessible only to people within a given business group. It serves as a communications funnel for people working together, even if they are spread over a wide geographic area. Being able to make information available instantly, either to carefully selected groups within a company or to everyone all at once, is going to be crucial to companies that are competing on their ability to respond to the market.

The Central Reference communications service in this vignette so far exists only in my imagination. It is a central problem-solving group whose sole purpose is to find information and make connections within an organization. To corporate bean counters, this system looks like that most feared of all corporate luxuries: overhead. However, if management can assemble an effective group that makes the knowledge workers of an organization more efficient, such a group can pay for itself many times over. In TPN, they do pay for themselves, partly with an annual flat fee and partly with fees-for-service based on special assignments.

One of the biggest problems facing working people today is the sheer quantity of information. This information avalanche has many ramifications, but the one relevant to a Central Reference-type operation is that, especially in large organizations, the left hand often doesn't know what the right hand is doing. Moreover, everyone is having difficulty keeping up with developments in their field these days. If there were a group that could monitor developments in a given field and alert you of new developments, it could prove to be the crucial difference between success and failure in a competitive business venture. But the Central Reference group of TPN is more than just an information conduit.

Although there are significant motivational differences between employees and entrepreneurs, one of the biggest problems with being an entrepreneur is dealing with a lack of resources. The TPN structure overcomes the difficulties of getting a large organization to change direction and of providing the necessary back-up and support. Central Reference is not the only such structure that could offer support; it is merely one possibility.

The most noteworthy aspect of TPN is its support for individual talents. TPN's aim is to allow individuals to run as fast as their talents will let them. Accordingly, it provides them with the support they need to complement their talents. Ask any professional whether he enjoys his job and you will likely get an answer like, "Sure, when I get a chance to do it." Much of any professional's time is taken up with a flurry of administrivia that interferes with the ability to get a job done. Accordingly, the best thing any company can do to improve the productivity of its people — and, incidentally, to improve their overall job satisfaction and personal motivation — is to get everything not directly relevant to their work off their desks and out of their minds.

My own experience mirrors this, even though — or perhaps especially because — I work for myself. During the period when I was trying to work most intensively on this book, I made a conscious effort to push everything else aside but still found myself devoting almost half of my working days to doing things that were necessary, but not directly related, to my writing. I would have loved to have been part of a partnership like TPN, where I could hire someone to come in and do the research; client contact; government filings for tax, registration, and information; expense claims; travel planning; and everything else that goes on in my professional life, and be confident of getting a first-class result at a good price.

Computers will, over time, start to do many of these things, and companies should work hard at finding systems that liberate their people from administrivia, like the reorganization of IBM Credit described in the last chapter. They should seek ways of maximizing the creative, thinking, and productive time of their knowledge workers.

Another challenge for most entrepreneurs is marketing themselves.

TPN also markets the services of its partners, who are all experts in their fields, and among the best, or else TPN wouldn't have invited them to join the partnership. Those partners who specialize in marketing, advertising, sales, and related disciplines read the published descriptions of every new partner carefully to see if there is a fit, to determine if a "newbie" can provide something more that they can sell to their already established markets. If they see a fit, they contact the new partner directly and offer a marketing relationship, which the newbie can accept or decline as he or she sees fit.

Partners also compete with each other, both inside and outside TPN. They bid for business from other partners, and they compete in the open market. Despite this, partners are amazingly open with each other about what they are doing, because they know that in the long run they will make more money by working with each other than by cutting each other's throats. They rely on their ability to think clearly and act decisively for their success rather than on keeping secrets. Indeed, their openness about what they are doing, and their willingness seemingly to give away information in an age where information is the highest currency, is one of their greatest sales tools. Clients know that the information they receive is merely the tip of the iceberg — and that makes them eager to have more permanent access. This openness also makes it easier for competing partners to work in cooperation for mutual benefit.

The next important aspect of TPN is cooperation even in competition. TPN partners will frequently compete with each other, yet often work in cooperation as well. This reflects the trend in corporate strategy of including outsiders in the planning stages of development, most notably suppliers. The Japanese car companies pioneered this concept when they started including their parts suppliers in the early, secret design stages of developing new cars.

If, as discussed earlier, companies are going to move (selectively) away from vertical integration to concentrate on core competencies, then they are going to have to include outside suppliers in their planning processes so that suppliers can keep up with the development process.

The computer industry and especially the Internet have brought this trend to its next stage: tell the world what you are doing, when it will be ready, and even give away copies of your products. Netscape, the wildly successful marketers of the Internet graphic browsing software that has become the industry standard, embodies this trend. Anyone with the necessary equipment can download Netscape software free of charge and use it for up to 90 days to evaluate it. If he decides to keep it and continue to use it, he pays a relatively nominal fee (around $40) to become a registered user. Meanwhile, early adopters — people who can't wait for the latest and greatest stuff — can download early copies of software that has not yet been fully debugged, free of charge. This arrangement gives Netscape a ready-made focus group of users whose feedback is incorporated into new designs.

How does Netscape make money doing this? It's a bit like the old retailing joke: "We lose money on every sale — but we make it up in volume!" Companies like Netscape make money because their distribution costs are almost nothing (people download most of their stuff on the Internet, which means users pay the costs of distribution), they sell in volume, and they make lots of money on developer software and corporate packages for things like Intranet installations. By making their graphic browser the Internet standard and forcing the pace of development, they can generate a regular flow of repeat sales to customers (which they call "software subscriptions"), and make those with commercial designs on the Internet happy about paying stiff fees for their developer products.

It's important to understand the strategy here. Just setting the standard for everyone else isn't enough, although that is certainly important. If you rely on speed and fast reactions to your customers' likes and dislikes, you can afford to tell the world what you are doing. It doesn't matter if your competitors steal your ideas — as long as you stay ahead of them. As Rudyard Kipling put it in his poem *The Mary Gloster*:

> *They copied all they could follow,*
> *but they couldn't copy my mind.*
> *So I left 'em sweatin' and schemin',*
> *a year and a half behind . . .*

First and foremost, TPN sells intellect. Major companies are increasingly trying to sell more thought and less product. The thought component of products and services represents a steadily increasing proportion of their cost. Most of the major costs in producing semiconductors comes from the research and development necessary to their design, with only one to three percent coming from the cost of the raw materials used. In comparison, 40 percent of the cost of an automobile and 60 percent of the cost of pots and pans comes from the materials used to make them.*

Accordingly, a twenty-first-century company in a developed country will focus on maximizing its sales of intellect, knowledge, ideas, and creativity rather than on selling mere products and services. This is the logical response to competition from mass producers in the RDCs, who will reduce the price of non-specialized products to the lowest possible level through the use of low-wage labour and automation.

TPN's structure also solves one of the thorniest problems of small business: venture financing.

---

* Peter F. Drucker, *The Frontiers of Management* (New York: Harper & Row, 1986), p.27.

Many times TPN partners will need outside financing to allow their personal businesses to grow. They take their needs to TPN, paying a TPN management specialist to help them prepare a business plan and proposal. A TPN venture capital investor then helps them assess their investment potential and arrange financing. If it gets to that stage, the TPN Partnership Capital Pool almost always makes the all-important first commitment. Outside venture capital investors, knowing TPN's incredibly successful track record on such investments, will usually follow. Accordingly, access to capital is rarely a problem.

One of the biggest problems facing Canadian small business is access to capital. Most Canadian small business people start out by thinking that they'll be able to borrow the money from a bank. However, any bank's first obligation is to ensure the safety of the money loaned to it by its depositors. Accordingly, they can lend money on secure terms, but they cannot really invest it. This means that banks are largely incapable of becoming partners in a new venture.

But true venture capital is in short supply in Canada. When I'm not writing, researching, speaking, or consulting on the future, I work with long-time friend and business associate Bob Shoniker. He has a long and successful record in raising investment capital for young companies that have solid track records and need between $1 million and $50 million to expand their operations. This relationship allows me to work with the small companies that are at the cutting edge of the economy, which is very useful to me as a futurist. I can tell you from direct experience that while there are four stages of investment capital — idea money for testing a concept, seed money for starting a company, roll-out capital for moving a proven idea into a wider marketplace, and expansion capital for helping an already successful company get bigger — there is only serious investment money in Canada for the last and least risky of these four stages. Indeed, this is one of the major structural disadvantages Canada has relative to the United States, where all four stages of venture investing can find funding.

Having a source of true venture capital, such as I've proposed for TPN, coupled with expert advice and support, would make a big difference to Canadian small business. The Business Development Bank of Canada, an arm of the federal government, attempts to provide both support and capital to small business and is pretty good at it. However, there are limits on what the BDC can do, and there is need for much more.

TPN measures carefully whether it wants to recruit partners who specialize in a new field before taking them on. The partnership committee makes the final decisions about whether to enter new fields, looking for synergies with the existing core competencies of its partners, plus exciting opportunity and potential in the field itself. Meanwhile, though, individual partners are free to move into new areas. Indeed, by the time the committee finally assesses a new field, it has probably already been penetrated by TPN partners, which makes the decision process easier. If there are too few partners in a new field, it may be too early to enter it, or it may lack the potential TPN wants.

The result is an amorphous, poorly defined organization that outside competitors hate with a passion, but would join in a heartbeat if they could. It is an organization that moves into new territories by many different means: by creating a new market through innovation; by muscling in through sheer, raw talent and power; by establishing beachheads and then expanding; by oozing into markets through stealth and cunning and artifice; and by doing whatever else talented individuals can think up to increase market share and profits.

Partners who are the CEOs of substantial corporations often wait for much smaller partners to move into an area, then subcontract for them as a means of identifying successful new market niches. As one partner puts it, "It's rather like pouring a bucket of water over a flat surface: most of it will just run off, but some of it will find the cracks. We follow the flow into the cracks by first helping our smaller partners find the opportunities, then by helping them make a bundle by exploiting them. That's what's helped us be the first major player into so many new markets."

Kathy's successful application and her $30,000 investment do not guarantee success, but they do guarantee that all she needs to do to succeed is to excel at what she likes most and does best. That is TPN's greatest strength.

TPN is market driven, flexible, and highly responsive to changes in the marketplace. It automatically expands by success and cuts off failure without the need for a high-level decision-maker. Because its people all work for themselves, or own their own companies, they are constantly on the lookout for new opportunities. And because there is no central management committee to consult, partners can move into a new area as soon as they decide it will be profitable, bringing all the resources of the organization — hired on a contract basis — with them. They can also subcontract parts of a project, often to corporations of significant size in which partners are principals. Accordingly, each partner doesn't need to own or be owned by a large organization to have the facilities of a big organization available to him.

This autonomy coupled with support and resources makes it possible for individuals with a great deal of initiative to move rapidly into a market as new opportunities open up, without the impediments of office politics or bureaucracy. At the same time, having top management consultants available to help in the planning process, as well as research people to dig out the best available information, makes it possible to move into new markets in a big way. And because all the partners are entrepreneurs themselves, it is possible for someone who doesn't have much money to offer profit points rather than up-front cash in exchange for service and support.

For those not able to see the value of joining an organization like TPN, consider what would be available to you if you could become a partner. Someone else would market your services for you. You would be nearly guaranteed of finding competent, well-priced help for almost any task, on either a short- or long-term basis. You could outsource all the difficult or time-wasting tasks that you need done and that distract you from your real job. You'd have access to the most up-to-date information in virtually any field. And you could find patient investors, eager to help your company grow.

Is there a nascent TPN out there that you can join? Not to my knowledge. Many organizations have some pieces of the puzzle, but none that I know of embody the complete package, especially the right mindset. Several of the major management consulting and accounting firms have the research and consulting talents, plus the back-office support in things like accounting, collections, and payroll services, that could be marketed to entrepreneurs. Temporary employment agencies market the services of a range of people and have some of the characteristics of TPN, without the entrepreneurial elements. But, in the main, the mindset of such organizations, and many others that have some similarities to TPN, is: "How can we make this business captive, make it all ours?" This runs completely contrary to the central concept of TPN, which is: go with whatever works best, regardless of who owns it. The corporate mindset of "we need to own it" must give way to "whatever works best," or corporations are likely to disappear.

Another aspect of TPN's unique organizational structure is that, unlike hired managers who worry about employees wasting the company's resources, which is why they need to supervise their workers, each TPN partner has complete control of and responsibility for all the resources he or she uses. It is this combination of authority and responsibility that would make an organization like TPN work.

TPN is merely a hypothetical illustration of the trends I see evident in management today, but what can a real management group do, starting right now, to move into the next century, and what business and management trends are likely to grow in importance and influence? Here are some guidelines to keep in mind with regard to your own business.

- **Consider the structure and function of your organization**. You should consider outsourcing — and even downsizing — if there are parts of your organization that do not operate as efficiently as they would if they were in direct competition with outside suppliers. But before you downsize and outsource, consider time, cost, and reliability. Would an outside supplier be able to do things as promptly and be as responsive to the needs of your company? Would the loss of integration with other parts of your company carry hidden costs that you might not initially be aware of? What priority would an outside supplier give to your business as only one of their clients?

  Outsourcing is a trend that is likely to continue, but it is important to treat it with caution. Indeed, you might consider allowing your organization to source products and services from outside suppliers in competition with comparable offerings provided by internal groups. This would help you determine how good your internal people are and prompt them to improve their operations.

- **Shift your organization's focus beyond quality**. Quality is crucial, but quality is no longer enough. A high-quality product or service — for its market segment — is now necessary if you want to compete. As global competition rises, however, so does the level of product and service quality. And as consumers become used to higher-quality offerings in one area of their lives, they begin to wonder why they can't have them in others. J. M. Juran, one of the grandfathers of the quality movement, was quoted in *Business Week* as saying, "When 30 percent of U.S. products were failures, vs. 3 percent for Japan, that was an enormous difference. But at failures of 0.3 percent and 0.03 percent, it'll be difficult for anyone to tell" (January 15, 1991, page 8).

When quality is widespread, it becomes less important as a means of differentiating your offerings from your competition's. Accordingly, your clients will increasingly judge your company by other criteria. My belief is that they will judge on the basis of their worst experience with your firm. This means that everyone who either relates directly to the customer, or who supports people who relate to customers — and that means all employees — can be responsible for the defining moment of the customer's relationship with your firm.

Let me give you a personal example. The last car I bought is a wonderful car in just about every way. I had researched both the car and the dealership carefully until I was ready to buy. Because time was at a premium, I asked about trading in my old car at the dealership, even though I have always sold my old cars privately in the past. The quote I got from the behind-the-scenes employee who prices used cars was less than 40 percent of the street value of the car. Worse, the salesman with whom I was negotiating presented the offer in "take-it-or-leave-it" terms with no explanation. Had he merely said something like, "We couldn't give you enough to make it worth your while. We recommend a private sale," I would have been satisfied. As it was, I felt offended and came within a heartbeat of walking out of the dealership and buying my second-choice car instead. The car manufacturer, who had nothing to do with this part of the transaction, came close to losing a sale because of the actions of an employee who never saw or met the customer. This is what I mean by looking beyond quality. The car I bought is consistently rated at or very near the top in its class for quality, but there were three other comparable cars I would have been pleased to own. The defining (negative) moment in my purchase of a new car came close to changing my mind. In the end, I sold my old car myself and got full market value for it, which confirmed my annoyance with the dealership, to which I am unlikely to return.

- **Play to your company's strengths**. Karl von Clausewitz, the nineteenth-century military strategist, once remarked that the only purpose of strategy is to make tactics work. This is the complete opposite of what most corporate planners believe. They think that corporate strategy consists of sitting in a corner office pondering on a grand design for the company, and then telling the troops that it's up to them to deliver such pipe dreams. In fact, top management should develop corporate objectives with the company's strengths in mind, and then look at how they can use those strengths to create a corporate strategy, not the other way around.

- **Treat your employees as your most important asset**. Hire the absolute best people for the job and reward results. Think about how to design the operation of your organization around your employees. Think about their individual strengths and how you can make best use of them. Find out what interferes with people's ability to do their jobs and eliminate these problems. Talk to your employees and make sure they want to talk to you.

- **Recruiting is one of your most important strategic skills**. When recruiting, you should look not only for people who have the technical skills but for those who also hold values and ideals similar to yours and your company's. A group that has a common outlook on the world, holds the same principles, and agrees on social goals and objectives is more likely to make a unified team than people whose skills fit but whose personalities don't mesh.

- **Communicate the objectives, hopes, and goals behind your management decisions**. This may sound simple, but one of the major reasons why corporate restructurings and downsizings don't produce the results that managers want is that, in the large majority of cases, management doesn't tell its employees what it is hoping to achieve by the change, and how it intends to accomplish its results. Not only does this create anxiety among your employees, but if they have no clear idea of what they should try to accomplish, it is much more difficult to get people to work together.

- **Give people authority as well as responsibility**. The only way an employee can respond effectively to a situation is to have the authority to make a decision and implement it. A friend of mine who works for a brand-name, multinational company once said that with all the chatter about "re-engineering the organization," "flattening the organization chart," and "empowering the employee," it was difficult to determine whether an individual had more ability to act or less. He said that in his mind there were two tests of the sincerity of an organization. Are whistle blowers who spot and report problems and screw-ups rewarded or punished, and does the individual employee have authority to spend money without getting approval? Obviously, there has to be a budget to determine how much an individual can spend — but does your organization have such budgets to begin with, or is every expenditure a unique case requiring specific approval?

125

- **Let leaders, not just managers, lead**. Frequently the person with the title is not the right person to lead a project, especially when specialized knowledge is important. In such situations, it makes tactical sense to let the logical leader lead, which will help your people grow into more valuable employees.

- **Enable individuals to learn new skills that will help the organization**. Whether your people take courses on their own, attend professional development seminars through an industry association, or hold corporate planning and strategy sessions, you should find ways of encouraging people to become more valuable, both to you and to themselves. Some of the most useful workshops I've conducted have been for corporations or industry associations that have focused on creating future scenarios. The purpose of creating these scenarios is to develop a common understanding of the challenges they are likely to face, and to come up with possible solutions they need to consider. The collaboration they share during these exercises creates a sense of cohesion and purpose. This can be especially useful if you are in an industry or an environment that is changing rapidly, or where new developments are coming at a furious pace.

- **Never give your clients a reason to consider changing suppliers**. I described the fundamentals of this idea — called "clientship" — in *Facing the Future*, and still feel it is crucial. The basic idea is that today we all feel that we don't have enough time to do everything we want. Since this applies to your clients as well as yourself, if you never give your clients a reason to look elsewhere, they probably won't bother. Making sure they never have a reason to look elsewhere means making sure your prices are always competitive, your offerings are up to date, and your quality and service always meet or surpass expectations.

- **Cultivate "informed intuition."** This concept comes from Gerry Hirshberg, president of Nissan Design International. It can take six years or more from design to delivery to produce a new car. Accordingly, while it may be useful for a car manufacturer to know what its customers want today, what it really needs to know is what they are going to want six years from now. Most other businesses are in similar situations. It's not possible to make such a projection without first gathering all the information you can, so that you are informed about your clients, your competitors, and the market. Add to this information your intuition, to help you decide where the market will be in the future. That should be part of your purpose in reading this book.

7
The Rise of "Assassin Marketing"

Over the course of the next 20 years, what you buy, and how and where you buy it, will change, often dramatically. But the biggest changes will come from the integration of technology, advertising, marketing, and retailing, which will bring about a new kind of marketing: "assassin marketing." Until recently, retailers have relied on print and broadcast advertising, which marketers describe as "hunting with a shotgun." A retailer throws his message out into the wild blue yonder by advertising in a major newspaper, or on television or radio in hopes that somebody somewhere reads, sees, or hears his ad and likes it enough to buy his product. Marketers measure such advertising in terms of "cost per thousand," i.e., dollars spent to reach a thousand people through a chosen medium.

But even the best advertising people can't really tell to what extent such ads encourage or develop sales, which gives rise to the long-standing advertising quip, "We know that half of our advertising is wasted; we just don't know which half." Accordingly, marketers have developed new techniques in the last two or three decades that allow companies to reach much more tightly focused groups of potential clients. Marketers call these techniques "narrowcasting" and describe them as "hunting with a rifle." The retailer identifies potential customers who present the desired socio-economic or psychographic profile, then fires a message aimed directly at them. Narrowcast techniques include direct mail, telemarketing, and advertising in special-interest magazines or on specialty television programs. Marketers measure the value of such techniques by "cost per sale," i.e., how many dollars does it take to produce each sale?

The next logical step is to be able to aim a message at a specific individual, about whom the advertiser knows such things as how often he buys the product, how frequently, and at what price. Assassin marketers will hunt for specific individuals, one at a time, and aim a message at them with a sniper scope so they don't miss. While narrowcasting techniques allow marketers to assess the cost per sale, and even track profits per sale, assassin marketing will allow marketers to start choosing among a variety of sharply honed strategies to optimize profits.

Let me give you an example of what might happen when an assassin marketer gets you in his sights. This example is not from the distant future, but probably from the next five years.

Tim has done the shopping for his household ever since he retired two years ago. Not only does he enjoy it, but he gets a chance to pick up some goodies that his wife doesn't approve of. As he puts it, patting his paunch, "Martha is watching my weight for me."

Once Tim finishes unloading this week's groceries on the counter at his local Bag-It supermarket, he pulls out his direct debit card, plus the "frequent buyer" discount card issued by the store. When the cashier finishes running all his purchases over the optical scanner, she rings up the total and debits Tim's chequing account to cover it. He loads his groceries back into the cart, including a large box of Oreo cookies, and trundles his purchases out to his car, whistling.

Tim might not be quite as serene if he knew everything that had taken place during his transaction. The supermarket chain recently introduced an assassin marketing campaign aimed at boosting the sales of its own private label brands at the expense of national brand products, thus increasing the chain's profit margins. The store is starting its campaign by targeting the sale of its private label cookies. Having spent the last five months sifting and collating a mountain of data about what products every customer with a frequent buyer card purchases, how frequently they buy them, and at what prices, the chain takes its first step.

First it looks for all customers who buy Oreos, Dad's, Peek Freans, or some other national brand of cookie. Then it screens the purchases of these customers to see who buys them regularly. Next it determines whether such customers are sensitive to price — whether they buy them when the prices are slightly lower, and pass them by when the prices are slightly higher. In preparation for this campaign, the chain has deliberately been manipulating the prices at which it sells cookies to see how different customers react.

As a result, the chain has determined that Tim likes to buy a large box of Oreos about every two weeks, and that he prefers Oreos but will switch to another kind of cookie if there's more than about a 27-cent difference per box. He's never bought the private label Oreo-type cookies over the five months the chain has been accumulating data, even though they are usually more than 27 cents cheaper than Oreos.

Tim is surprised when ten days later he receives a letter from the manager of the store where he normally shops. "Dear Mr. Altair," it reads, "as the new manager of your local Bag-It supermarket, I really appreciate your shopping at our store. It's my job to do everything I can to ensure that our customers enjoy their shopping experience. As my way of showing my appreciation, and to introduce you to our new line of Resident's

Choice cookies, I'm enclosing a coupon for 75¢ off your next purchase of Resident's Choice Eat-the-Creme cookies. I hope you like them — and thanks for shopping with us. Please stop by and say hi any time you're in the store, or call me if you have any questions."

The chain sent out a total of 853 such letters for the stores in this region, each one "signed" by the actual manager of the store in question. Each letter includes a coupon for Eat-the-Creme cookies with a different discount, set according to the estimated price sensitivity of the customer. The letters also include a taste-test review of the national brand cookies and Resident's Choice equivalents, published by a major national newspaper.

Tim's a bit puzzled by the letter. He shrugs, briefly scans the newspaper article — which finds only minor differences in taste between one brand of cookie and another — and sticks the coupon in his wallet to use when he next goes shopping. On his next trip to the supermarket, Tim remembers to pick up the box of Resident's Choice cookies, but forgets about the coupon. He's at the check-out counter, and has already presented his debit and frequent buyer cards for the groceries, when the check-out clerk sees a message on his cash register screen and turns to Tim. "Our new manager has been sending out coupons to a few selected customers. Do you have any coupons today?"

Tim remembers the coupon stuck in the back of his wallet and quickly pulls it out. The cashier smiles and, since Tim has already paid for his groceries, gives him 75¢ in cash from the till. Tim pockets it with a smile and walks off, smug that he's paid less than he would normally pay.

Two weeks later he buys Resident's Choice cookies without a coupon because they're 31 cents cheaper than Oreos — as they have been, on average, for the last couple of months. The chain selected a 31-cent discount for Resident's Choice because that price gave them the highest total profit — the optimum number of sales at the optimum price, especially among new purchasers. A higher price gave them more profit per sale, but fewer sales. A lower price gave them more sales, but with less profit. Because first-time purchasers like Tim were slightly more price-conscious than previous customers for Resident's Choice, it was vital to draft a coupon campaign that gave their cookies both the exposure to attract new customers and generated the data necessary to produce the highest possible profit.

Sixteenth-century English philosopher Francis Bacon said that "knowledge is power," and this example shows how technology can make it so. Today's technology is well on its way to making this scenario a reality; only a few impediments stand in the way. The first is data collection. If a grocery chain collects information on all the purchases of all the customers it can identify, it will quickly be overwhelmed with data. This problem can be solved in several different ways. The chain can start by collecting data selectively. If it wants to target sales of, say, private label cookies, then all it needs to do is to collect information about cookie sales from people who buy cookies, ignoring everyone else for the time being. As computers become faster and data storage becomes cheaper, a retailer can start with small trial projects, and work up to more ambitious ones, building both an organized body of data and expertise in using it.

Over the next 20 years, the application and uses of assassin marketing will be perfected, to the point where marketers' computers will analyze each transaction you make, so that it seems as if you are being watched under a microscope. In *Facing the Future*, I predicted that the threat of Big Brother would give way to the threat of many Little Brothers watching you. I've seen nothing to change my view and much to confirm it since then. Indeed, protecting our personal privacy will become a key political and ethical issue.

Given the developments in technology, it will become possible for marketers to develop psychological profiles of such enormous accuracy that they will come to know you and your behaviour better than you do. With this knowledge, hard-driving merchandisers will appeal to your impulses and desires, both conscious and unconscious, in ways that will be close to irresistible.

The tools I've listed are the thin edge of the wedge. Added to the mountain of data and the software to analyze it are new kinds of computer programs that can "reverse engineer" solutions. These tools don't yet have a widely accepted name. I've seen them called "adaptive programming," "solution-seeking software," or "data-driven programming," and they are just starting to emerge. Neural network software, an established category of software that mimics the way neurons work in the brain, is included in this category, but the category goes far beyond mere neural net techniques.

I have a mere glimmering of what this type of computer software might be able to do, but I know it is astonishing. Because the technology is new, and we have no other tools quite like it (at least outside of our own brains), it is difficult to describe. In a general sense, though, these programs take a mass of data, get you to describe the results that you want repeated, and then look for the patterns that would precede these results. When the computer finds them, it gives you a cookbook formula for achieving what you want — "First you do this, then this, then this . . ." — until the desired result pops out. And the programs are relentless; every success or failure gives them more information to make better judgments on how to obtain the desired result. Whether or not you buy something, the software helps the programs decide how to approach you next time.

For example, a retailer making use of adaptive software tools could supply the program with all available data on cookie sales to perform what is called "data mining" as the first step. The software might identify people who shopped on Tuesday afternoons between

2:47 and 4:48, and Thursday evenings immediately after the 15th and 30th of the month, as being those most likely to buy cookies. The store might then start changing the locations of the displays, and the prices of cookies during those hours, and publicizing these changes with point-of-sale advertising. With the results shown, the adaptive software might suggest a particular combination of location and price to see how customers respond, eventually producing a plan that would increase sales and decrease costs. The software would then monitor sales on an ongoing basis to identify and exploit new trends or changes in behaviour as they occurred. One of the drawbacks of these software tools is that there is no explanation of *why* certain things are done, and management will have to work out the answer to this question for itself.

Most retailers and marketers will use the new technological tools responsibly because they know that abuses will lead to a consumer backlash and to restrictive legislation. But the desperate, unscrupulous, and downright fraudulent will abuse these tools. Accordingly, if I were a retailer with a modicum of foresight, I would start to establish rules of conduct to head off abuses right now. The Canadian Direct Marketing Association has such a code for current direct marketing practices, and I would encourage companies to work in cooperation with them to benefit from their expertise in this area. New techniques will need new rules, and I strongly urge retailers to get started before the problems start cropping up.

Properly handled, assassin marketing will have significant advantages for the consumer as well. It will mean that the companies and people who try to sell things to you will, by and large, be those that have something you are likely to want. Retailers will start anticipating your needs and offering what you want, when you want it, where you want it, how you want it, and at a price you are willing to pay.

Delivering the Marketing Message

In chapter 3, I talked about a new information delivery technique that I called "multi-dimensional media." These new media will allow

you to ask for more detail, or individually branch off into related areas while you are watching a particular program. The same flexibility will work in reverse. Suppose that Procter & Gamble is about to launch a new product and, through assassin marketing techniques, decides that you are a perfect candidate for the new product.

At present, if a company wants to reach a consumer like you, it could buy ad time in a program you are likely to watch. However, in the coming era of video-on-demand and multi-dimensional media, it will be able to target you much more precisely. The company could contract with an ad agency to buy advertising time on your television, no matter what program you choose to watch, or where the program originates. The advertiser would pay each program originator the appropriate toll for access to your household through their programming, just as advertisers pay television and radio stations today for including commercials in their broadcasts.

As a result, you won't be able to change channels to get away from a particular ad — it will turn up on any and every channel you select (except pay or public channels that don't carry ads). And it won't matter what time of day you choose to watch; the ads directed at you will appear whenever you turn on the set.

Moreover, suppose you have more than one television in your house, and you watch certain programs on certain sets at various times of day while other members of your household watch other programs on other sets. The signal delivery system (cable, satellite, telephone, or whatever) may well be able, over time, to predict which set you are watching and pipe your commercials to you, with a completely different set of commercials for your children, even if you are all watching the same program on different sets.

Let's take it a step further. Soon it will be possible to create video programming, including ads, without camera operators or actors, merely by using computers. Accordingly, it's conceivable that computers could create a unique ad specifically for you, using story lines that had been predefined by an ad agency.

How about print media? A newspaper such as the *Globe and Mail* or a magazine like *Maclean's* could produce a specifically tailored edition for each subscriber, as well as more general editions for street distribution. Moreover, they could do so at approximately the same price as a mass-produced single edition. My copy might have stories that the publisher's computer selected for my individual tastes, and would certainly have ads aimed directly at me, such as a full-page ad on page 3 saying "Richard Worzel, you may already have won $15 million!" or some such. This would, after all, merely be an extension of what print publications do now in different regions, whereby an advertiser can buy exposure in one specific area of the country. This extension would merely define a "region" as comprising one consumer. As computers become more powerful, and customer profiles become more detailed, the technology will be able to deliver on such promise.

Publishing such earmarked individual editions of a magazine or newspaper would require more organization and more pre-planning than current operations, but those are the kinds of tasks at which computers excel. But why print an individual publication when you can deliver the same individual-specific message electronically without killing all those trees? Why drive to the grocery store when you can have your computer genie reorder your supplies as you use them up? Are newspapers and trips to the store going to disappear?

My expectation is: probably not, at least not within the next 20 years.

Which Retailers and Media Will Survive?

Any message that a newspaper (or a magazine) can deliver can also be delivered at a fraction of the cost by the Internet. That does not

mean that all of the experiences delivered by a newspaper can be delivered electronically. The rustling sound of the pages of a newspaper, the big visual spread of an open page, and the smell of the paper and ink are subtle but enormously important aspects of "reading" a paper. That's why publishers place so much emphasis on the typeface used, or the weight and finish of a grade of paper, and why they agonize over even minor changes.

Moreover, it's easy for a customer to "operate" a newspaper, and just about anyone who can read can do it. The Internet, on the other hand, is much more difficult to use, it's not transportable (you need to be sitting at your desk), and it demands a mode of thinking that relates more to work than to relaxation. It is possible to speedread a newspaper, but most people read a paper precisely because they don't know ahead of time what they might consider important. The ability to browse through news is possible electronically, but it is far less enjoyable.

This doesn't mean that the messages you now receive through print publications (or broadcast media, for that matter) won't be delivered by other means in future. They clearly will, and these traditional media will be under increasing pressure as more people become accustomed to getting their messages that way. But there will be a place for print publications that work hard at delivering an experience, not just a message.

The same concept applies to retailers. Yes, it will be possible to order your groceries, your clothes, your roof shingles, and just about everything else that you might want electronically, but that doesn't mean you will do it.

Miranda tells Chlöe, her genie, that she's finished work for the day. She is about to push back from her desk when Chlöe reminds Miranda that she needs to do some shopping. "Show me the list," Miranda orders, and Chlöe complies. Miranda scans down it. "Order the routine stuff from Mark's, and remind me Saturday morning about the other things."

Chlöe confirms the reply, but for greater certainty she asks, "You want me to order everything but the skirt, earrings, and car stereo from Mark's, is that right?" Miranda thinks for a moment, then says, "Almost right. I don't want to shop for a stereo. I hate going to Consumer's Universe. That store reminds me of an airplane hangar, and there's no one to help you. Get the **Consumer's Reports** review of car stereos under $200, then shop for the best deal on the top two picks. Confirm the choice with me before you buy, and tell me where and when it will be installed." She then has Chlöe show her any new e-mail messages while she waits the 30 seconds for Chlöe to finish shopping for the stereo.

When Chlöe finds the best deal, she displays a picture of the two best stereo systems in Miranda's Looking Glasses along with a list of their features, and offers a choice of two installation locations: one superstore way out of town and one local store around the corner that will match the price but that wants an extra $20 to install it. Miranda picks the system that looks most retro, opts for the closer location, confirms the proposed time, and goes off to dinner.

Meanwhile, Chlöe has contacted Mark's Shoppers' Service, to which Miranda pays an annual membership fee of $75, and given them the list of groceries and supplies. Mark's is a shopping and delivery service that serves the area where Miranda resides. For each item on Chlöe's list, Mark's matches the items against the current prices of all the stores within a 20-mile radius, selects the best prices, then uses an optimization program to trade off delivery costs against low price. Because Miranda has Chlöe keep household food and supplies at reasonable levels, Miranda never pays a surcharge for same-day or next-day delivery. Instead, she gets all of her goods at a low service charge because they always go on Mark's regularly scheduled delivery rounds. She saves money, as compared with doing her shopping for herself, and she never spends her precious hours of leisure doing routine shopping. Mark's guarantees each participating retailer a certain minimum annual profit. This combined purchasing power makes Mark's annual membership fee a bargain.

On Saturday morning, after Miranda has finished reading the paper in bed, Chlöe reminds her that she wants to shop for a new skirt and earrings. "Add that new Alfred Sung perfume to the list," Miranda commands as she stretches, "and find me a couple of places where it would be fun to shop." Chlöe considers for a couple of seconds, then offers three shopping areas, including one mall. The first two areas are old favourites of Miranda's that have the appropriate stores and merchandise, but she's feeling a bit bored with them. The third is a relatively new shopping mall that Chlöe has suggested two or three times in the last month. It uses a Casablanca-inspired theme, and this week Cirque du Soleil is performing in the Casbah Court at the centre. "What fun," says Miranda, and decides to go. She bounces out of bed, changes into comfy but elegant clothes, and heads off for a day of shoppertainment at the mall. She may pay a bit more for the things she buys — but, then, she's getting much more than just a skirt, earrings, and perfume. Indeed, the purchases are really more of an excuse for the trip.

Over the course of the next two decades, retailers will divide into three major categories already in evidence today: utilitarian, convenience, and shopping experience. The utilitarian category will include the super stores and category-killers like Price Club, Office Depot, Toys-R-Us, or Wal-Mart, which emphasize price and breadth of selection as their main draws. They may have some service, or they may emphasize no service to underline their low-price, no-frills image.

The convenience category will include small stores that may not offer great selection, but are right around the corner and stay open around the clock. Service is minimal, and you can beat their prices almost anywhere, but when you want it now, they're the place to go.

Shopping experience stores will be just that. Their prices will not be the best in town, but they will offer exquisite service and be fun to visit for more than just their merchandise. This is already happening with isolated stores today, but will become widespread over the next two decades. There are grocery stores in California where singles dress up to shop primarily because they can meet other singles. There are grocery stores in New England where the service is so extraordinary that some people drive more than 100 miles one way just to be pampered and treated like royalty.

In addition to these retailers, catalogue merchandising is here to stay. A catalogue is not just a means of delivering a message, but also a publication that consumers read for entertainment. This means that the best catalogue merchants, such as the venerable L.L. Bean or the upbeat Lands' End, which provide top-notch quality, no-hassle guarantees, and fast delivery at reasonable prices will thrive, as the mediocre ones come and go.

Electronic shopping is just beginning to come into its own. The Home Shopping Network is a harbinger of this way of selling; multi-dimensional media will make electronic retailing much more powerful. You may well do much of your routine shopping electronically, even automatically, and people who enjoy shopping as a form of home entertainment will be able to buy from the comfort of their couch or bed.

Which retailers will fall by the wayside? Department stores. Unappealing mom-and-pop shops. Catalogue shopping stores. Plain

Jane shopping malls. Stores with rude service staffs or so-so prices. And good riddance to them all.

The Decline of Demographics

Retailers have traditionally spent a lot of time, effort, and money scrutinizing demographics in a bid to focus their marketing efforts as efficiently as possible. This practice is starting to change for two reasons. First, society is becoming more idiosyncratic and less homogeneous. People are marrying later, divorcing, having kids in and out of wedlock, becoming single again at ages that would have been unusual in an earlier day, and generally breaking with past patterns of behaviour. The clearly defined ages and stages when people buy particular goods or services are crumbling as the shape and structure of our society shifts. The second reason is that the future of marketing and retailing belongs to the assassin. With its ability to find and focus on specific individuals, assassin marketing will gradually replace less effective marketing methods, and those who can't keep up will fall by the wayside.

8
Age and Money:
Opportunity and Strife

Let me start at the conclusion, then back up to explain how I arrived at it: *How you manage your money over the next ten years will determine how much money you will have for your retirement and how affluent you will be for the rest of your life.*

Because the baby boomers are entering their major saving years, the current stock market boom is being talked about by a wide range of commentators, to the point where sophisticated market investors are getting tired of hearing about it. I've been talking about this market boom — and the corresponding major decline in interest rates — since I was an investment market analyst in the late 1970s, and I've been writing about it for public consumption since the mid-1980s. Accordingly, what is happening on the Toronto Stock Exchange and elsewhere comes as no surprise to me.

However, like all market moves, this one will have surprises and textures that are not widely known. First let's trace the underlying causes.

Your Financial Life Cycle
Everyone goes through changes in financial position as he or she

progresses through the different stages of life. Let me characterize those changes through the example of one individual.

Kurt was born in 1952 and is a classic baby boomer. When he first emerged from university, there was a line-up of corporate recruiters waiting to interview and sign him — just as there was for all of his peers. He took a promising job with a major corporation at a starting salary of $13,000 a year — pretty good pay in 1974.

He rented an apartment and was careful with his money, paying for purchases mostly out of his monthly pay cheque. The dishes, curtains, cutlery, and working clothes he acquired gradually, but for a few items — living room furniture and his bed, for instance — he took out a small bank loan, which he paid off without much difficulty. After a couple of years, he bought a car on credit, which bumped up his monthly bank payments. He was making more now and was quite comfortable with carrying his loan and car payments.

He had paid off about half of his car loan and had finished paying off his other bank loan when he met Tonia. After dating, then living together for three years, they finally married when he was 28 and she was 26. Between them, they were making decent money, each had bought a few Canada Savings Bonds and put some money in an RRSP. They lived in his apartment until the lease ran out in 1982, then went house hunting when Tonia became pregnant.

They bought a small bungalow — a starter home, really — which was big enough for the three of them, knowing that they would need to buy a larger home later. It cost $78,000, which they financed by taking out a $58,000 first mortgage and a $6,000 second mortgage, and cashing in their CSBs and a Registered Home Ownership Savings Plan for the balance. After Mitch was born, and Tonia's pregnancy leave was up, she went back to work, paying off the second mortgage, and saving as much as they could for their next house.

By 1985, Tonia was pregnant again, and the real estate market was heating up because of all the baby boomers buying homes. Kurt and Tonia decided they'd better buy their family house while they could afford it. They found a smallish but attractive three-bedroom house in a downtown area for $159,000. It had a good-sized lot, so they figured that if they needed more space, they could build an extension. With the sale of their bungalow, they were able to finance the house with a first mortgage of $120,000 and second mortgage of $5,000.

Although they had little in the way of liquid savings, they didn't try to build up their savings account much. Instead, they put about $1,000 each into RRSPs each year, mostly for the tax savings. The rest of their financial planning consisted of bumping up their mortgage payments as much as possible to pay them off early.

Kurt was laid off from his job in 1992, which caused the couple a great deal of anxiety. However, he was fortunate in being able to get a slightly lower-paying job relatively quickly. It was with a much smaller company that had good prospects, and where Kurt could play a more important role. Kurt and Tonia did, however, have to remortgage their home to lower the monthly payments, much as this ran against their philosophy.

By year 2000, they thought they were going to have to remortgage again to help finance their son's entry to college, especially as their daughter was likely to follow three years later. However, by cutting corners, they were able to get by, although they had to skip some RRSP contributions for a couple of years. This worried them. By this time it was obvious that they weren't going to be getting anything like the Canada Pension Plan benefits that they had expected earlier in their careers. Moreover, governments seemed poised to tax heavily many of the benefits that they did receive. But the couple really had very little choice, especially when Tonia lost her job during the 1999 recession.

She looked for another job for a while, then finally decided that she could do better on her own. She bought a financial planning franchise and, after a rough couple of years, started making real money at something she was good at and enjoyed.

By the time the kids had finished college and had more or less left home it was 2008, and they finally paid off their mortgage the next year. By now, both Kurt and Tonia were making excellent incomes, and they really started socking it away for retirement — after all, he was 56 and she was 54, and they both hoped to retire early. But higher taxes and CPP contributions meant that it was harder to save money. To ensure having enough for retirement, they realized that they were going to have to work longer than they wanted to. Neither minded this much, they told themselves, because they enjoyed their work, especially once they built themselves an office at home and started working there two or three days a week.

They had to change their plans again in 2013 when Kurt developed high blood pressure and started showing signs of heart trouble. His doctor told him to start easing off on the stress, which meant working fewer hours. He did so, reluctantly, taking early retirement from his company at a reduced pension, and helping Tonia with her business three days a week. They sold the franchise to Tonia's junior partners in 2019, when Tonia reached 65, and finally retired.

This is a typical life cycle pattern. It consists of the six major stages of adult life, which are described below:

1. Entry into the labour force. This period runs roughly from the time someone enters the labour force until about 25 years of age. People in this group don't make much money and have to buy most of the basic necessities for establishing a household. As a result, they tend to borrow small amounts of money to finance major purchases like furniture and automobiles.

145

2. Home buying. Typically more people buy homes in their late-twenties to mid-thirties than at any other time of life, so this stage runs from approximately age 25 to 35. Some generations will buy homes later than this, as described later in the chapter. People in the 25-to-35 age group have enough income to be able to support a mortgage. As a result, this group goes more heavily into debt than any other.

3. Consolidation. People in the 35-to-45 age bracket typically finish making major purchases and stop borrowing money. In fact, as their incomes go up, they start paying down their debts and start saving money through a variety of means: making mortgage payments and payroll contributions to a company pension plan, paying premiums on whole life insurance policies, making investments in an RRSP, and so on.

4. Heavy saving. Between ages 45 to 55 people save, on average, more money than at any other time of their lives. This group, as a whole, reaches their highest income levels, although this is not necessarily true for every individual within the group. The reason for this difference is that some members of this age bracket, especially men, start experiencing health problems that force them to start cutting back on their working time, which shaves their incomes. The other major change in this age group is that they realize that they need to start planning for retirement, and so they start saving as much money as they can, given their lifestyles. Some will have children in college, which will make it more difficult to save.

On the other end of the spectrum, this is the time when

significant numbers of people in this age group start inheriting money from their parents, some of which goes to make luxury purchases or to help pay for the kids' college education, but most of which winds up going toward debt retirement and savings.

5. Pre-retirement. The 55-to-65 age group are dedicated to saving for retirement. However, because of individual health problems, the average income of this group is starting to decline, even though some members are still seeing their incomes rise. Moreover, people traditionally start retiring, on average, shortly after age 60, which also drags down the average income and savings rate.

As a result, this group shows a slight decline in income, and typically they start to withdraw small but steady amounts from their savings.

6. Retirement. From age 65 on, most people are retired. Their incomes show a distinct drop from when they were working, and they continue to draw on their savings to supplement their incomes.

You may not follow this pattern precisely, but it does portray the average tendencies of the population as a whole. The chart on the next page shows which stages the Canadian population is at today.

Now mentally move Canadians forward two stages to allow for changes that will occur in the next 20 years and you can see why the stock market is likely to experience another tremendous boom. Because of the bulge of baby boomers currently in the 30- to 50-year age brackets, there are going to be a lot of people saving and investing money, and not as many people borrowing money. This is one of the primary causes of the low interest rates and the stock market boom we are currently experiencing.

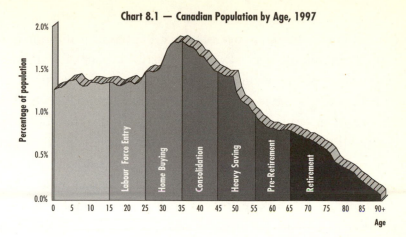

Chart 8.1 — Canadian Population by Age, 1997

Note that demographics is not the only thing that will affect the investment markets. Other traditional factors, like technology, foreign competition and investment, weather, changes in the patterns of commodity usage, and all the legendary emotions of the marketplace will also have sway over investment prices and trends.

Moreover, the effects of demographics will not be uniform over the next 20 years, as different groups move through different stages. And, while I can't anticipate the effects of all the factors that affect the markets, I can estimate what effects demographics will have in isolation. My best guess for the course of the stock market over the next 20 years (using the Toronto Stock Exchange 300 Composite Index) is shown in chart 8.2 below:

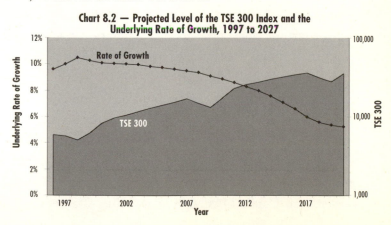

Chart 8.2 — Projected Level of the TSE 300 Index and the Underlying Rate of Growth, 1997 to 2027

This is a very dangerous graph because it can be so easily misunderstood. Let me hasten to describe what I'm trying to illustrate.

The financial life cycle I've just described, coupled with the demographics of the population, produces the long-term trend of chart 8.2. I've also projected the major market ups and downs due to the economic cycle. Please note that this chart does not take into account all the other events that will undoubtedly happen in the world and should, therefore, be treated with great caution.

You should use this chart not to predict stock market indices, but to plan intelligently for one of the major factors — demographics — that will move the market over the next 20 years. Toward this end, let me make the following observations:

- Because more people will be saving than borrowing, there will be a greater supply of money than demand for money, and interest rates, on average, will be substantially lower over the next 20 years than they have over the last 30. Accordingly, if you are retired, you will not be able to live off fixed income securities as you have in the past. You will have to diversify into investments that will, individually, offer more risk because they also offer higher rates of return.
- The stock market will almost certainly experience a major boom over the next 20 years. At time of writing the TSE 300 Index is hovering at around 6,000. By the year 2017, when the leading edge of the boomer generation reaches age 70 and the trailing edge reaches age 50, the TSE 300 will likely have punched through the 30,000 mark — an increase of almost five times its current level. Indices in the United States, such as the Dow Jones Industrials and the S&P 500, will experience similar explosions owing to the similar demographic trends. Accordingly, you should have a significant portion of your assets invested in stocks. Which stocks you own should jibe with your ability to accept risk,

your tax status, your age, your need for income, and your ability to make additional investments. You should assess these factors and arrive at a suitable asset mix with a qualified investment advisor.

- The rise in the stock markets will not be evenly distributed. More money will pour into the market between now and 2007 than between 2007 and 2017. As a result, I would expect that more than half of the stock market boom (in percentage terms) will occur within the next ten years. This means that the investments you make in the next ten years will be the most important ones you make in your lifetime.

- Labour force growth is a major contributor to economic growth. The labour force will grow as the echo generation, born between 1980 and 1994, moves into the workplace early in the next century. However, such growth will start to stagnate by about 2010. At the same time, the aging of the remaining adult population will mean that growth in personal income for the nation as a whole will slow by 2005, further restraining economic growth.

- The long-term growth rate in consumer debt, already low today, will continue to slow as baby boomers move out of their prime borrowing years. The next 20 years will, therefore, see further increases by banks and other lenders in fee-based and non-loan-related revenues as interest income from lending continues to lag. Please note that I am talking about the *rate of growth* of personal debt, not the *level* of personal debt, which is at a historic high.

- Several commentators have wondered whether the stock market will collapse around 2017, when the boomers retire in significant numbers and start to cash out on their investments. I was concerned about that myself. However, my recent studies indicate that although the rate of stock market increase due to demographic influences will slow significantly after 2007, there will still be more money flowing into the stock market than out of it because of demographics.

150

To be honest, I was surprised by this result. Accordingly, I ran a number of sensitivity analyses on the projections, and discovered that it almost doesn't matter what demographic assumptions you make — within reason. The projections under almost any assumption indicate that the savings of an aging population will continue to flow into the stock market well into the middle of the next century.

In short, there is no reason to anticipate a massive stock market crash between 2010 and 2020. The indices just won't move up as quickly as they will over the next ten years.

- The length of economic cycles has more than doubled from four years to eight years. This is being caused by the integration of individual national economies into a global economic whole that has both more momentum and longer leads and lags built into it. As a result, I've estimated that over this period there will be long-term bull markets averaging approximately 90 months in duration, and bear markets averaging approximately 18 to 24 months in duration. However, it is my expectation that the periodicity of the economic cycle will continue to change, even though it is not clear just *how* it will change. Stay alert; you can't just invest mechanically and expect to win.

Planning Your Investments for Tomorrow

All of these points lead to the conclusion stated at the beginning of this chapter: from an investment planning point of view, the next ten years will be the most important ones of your life in determining how affluent you will be during your retirement. Right now you should be straining to save and invest, even if you are not at that stage of life where it is convenient to do so.

But the stock market's upward march will not be smooth and steady. Quite the contrary. With so many newcomers to the markets, when the market does dip, as it must from time to time, many investors will panic and flee to investments like GICs that offer low but guaranteed returns. This will produce dramatic ups and downs in stock prices, and you will need to work out a coherent investment strategy ahead of time to avoid being whipsawed by the volatile emotions of the investment markets.

At the same time, investment profits will not be evenly distributed. There will be significant winners and losers because of the steadily rising level of global competition and the dramatic changes brought about by new technologies. As a result, investors are going to have to spend more time than ever before weighing which investments to choose. Indeed, the task of picking the next round of winners is going to mean knowing which individuals are managing which companies, rather than just being knowledgeable about the companies themselves. The pace of change is going to make the investment process significantly more complex than ever before. Hiring a professional investment advisor is going to be invaluable. You may do this by having your portfolio privately managed if you have upwards of $250,000 to invest. Most people, though, will pool their money with other investors in mutual funds. Then the trick becomes finding a mutual fund that is suitable to your needs and situation in life, because there are thousands of mutual funds available these days. In the United States, for instance, there are more mutual funds than there are stocks listed on the New York Stock Exchange.

Achieving solid investment performance is going to be crucial, especially if you haven't retired yet. Steadily rising taxes and user fees for many public services and medical treatments, coupled with continuing cuts and clawbacks to public pensions and old-age payments, will mean that if you do not adequately provide for your old age, you will wind up living in cold poverty.

It is also important to recognize that conservative investments are not necessarily *safe* investments. As I mentioned earlier, I expect interest rates and the demand for loans to remain low over the next 20 years. Accordingly, investing in fixed income securities, while it can be wise and profitable from time to time, and for portions of your portfolio, is not your best long-term strategy. Indeed, relying exclusively on GICs, Canada Savings Bonds, and similar, supposedly "safe" investments may turn out to be one of the riskiest things you can do, because you could end up with significantly less money than you will need.

Please note, though, that stock market investing does have risks, and not all of them are evident, even to sophisticated investors. One of the things that is most important in determining your medium-term success is whether you buy stocks for the first time when they are expensive, or when they are relatively cheap. If you buy at the top of a bull market, and have to wait out a bear market crash and subsequent recovery, you can fall several years behind in your investment program. If, on the other hand, you buy close to the bottom of a bear market, you will look like a pundit in short order, and your long-term performance will get a real boost. This is one reason why mutual fund companies may quote their performance records from the bottom of the last bear market and try to downplay what came before.

The problem with market timing is that few can do it well. One of the members of the Rothschild family of Europe is supposed to have remarked, "The only people who buy at the bottom and sell at the top are liars." Accordingly, it is important that you develop a solid, sensible strategy for stock market investing that will help you ignore the emotions of fear and greed that gallop through the market. If you need professional help, get it. A good advisor will recoup his or her fees many times over.

The same flood of money that is pouring into the investment markets is also attracting a flood of johnny-come-latelies eager to profit from it. The next 20 years will probably witness a historic number of market scandals brought about by fraud, deception, incompetence, laziness, and knavery. It's important to pick an investment advisor who has an established track record; has had sound, professional training; and has the back-up, research, facilities, and support to provide the services and information you need. Just because someone calls themselves an investment advisor or financial planner, and has a fancy office and business cards, does not mean that he or she is competent or has your interests at heart. There are many so-called advisors who recently sold used cars or shoes, and have put on a three-piece suit to sell mutual funds and tax advice, purely because the commissions are higher. Just as you need to find the right investments for your portfolio, you also need to find the right advisor. The time and effort spent in doing this will make a big difference to your financial future.

Foreign Money, Foreign Investments

The foregoing analysis ignores the rest of the world and treats Canada in isolation. However, as discussed earlier, the global economy is of steadily rising importance to the Canadian economy, and to Canadians as individuals. This is equally true in investments.

Indeed, one of the principal ingredients of the formula that allows an underdeveloped country to follow in the footsteps of the Asian Tigers is to attract significant outside investment capital. Since that capital has to come from somewhere, and since most investment capital is held by affluent investors in wealthy countries, almost all of it comes at the expense of domestic investments in those same wealthy, developed countries. Accordingly, the stock market boom in North America could be curtailed by a boom in investments in faster-growing, rapidly developing countries.

Note, however, that this won't prevent the stock market boom in North America — only that it may reduce its rate of growth. Most Canadian investors, even those who have a completely free choice, unfettered by government restrictions on pension funds and RRSPs, still invest the majority of their money in Canada. Moreover, it will take years before investors become comfortable investing abroad and are willing to accept the higher levels of risk involved. North America has the highest requirements for financial reporting and the highest levels of investor protection against things like stock market fraud and market manipulation in the world. Accordingly, North America is still the most secure place to invest, even if its rate of growth will be distinctly lower than that of developing countries.

As a result, Canadian investors should be aware of investments in fast-growing countries, and should think about putting a portion of their portfolio in an appropriately structured mutual fund that specializes in that kind of investing. Most of your portfolio, though, should probably remain in the North American markets.

What a Difference 20 Years Makes!

In 20 years' time, you and your family will be very different. For one thing, you will all be 20 years older. If you are of the baby boom generation, there's a strong possibility that one or both of your parents will have died, and you will have inherited their estate. If you have children now, they will likely have finished their schooling, and either be in the work force or worrying you because they aren't. Depending on your age and stage in life, you will be somewhere in the process of thinking about, saving for, planning, or experiencing your retirement. Your health and that of your spouse may not be as good as it was, and you will be concerned about the future of the Canadian health-care system.

All of these changes have financial repercussions that will affect your personal finances, as well as the finances of your city, province, and the nation as a whole. Although population patterns do not dictate everything, they have a powerful influence on the ebb and flow of money.

Accordingly, let's start our examination by considering where we,   155
as a people and as individuals, will be in 2017. First, let's look at how many of us there will be in each age group, and talk about what each group will be experiencing. Remember, though, that these generational characterizations are based on my own speculations. They won't apply to everyone in any age group and should be used with care for planning purposes, not as a specific forecast of events.

Table 8.1
Projected population by age, 2017

Birth Years	Group	Age range	% of pop. in 2017
1937 and before	Pre-Second World War	80+	4 percent
1938-1946	War babies	71 to 79	6 percent
1947 to 1957	1st half boomers	60 to 70	13 percent
1958 to 1967	2nd half boomers	50 to 59	15 percent
1968 to 1979	Baby bust	38 to 49	16 percent
1980 to 1994	Baby boom echo	23 to 37	20 percent
1995 to 2006	2nd baby bust	11 to 22	14 percent
2007 & beyond	2nd echo	0 to 10	12 percent

- **Pre-Second World War.** If you are in this group, you are already elderly in 2017. There will probably be a significantly higher proportion of elderly people in Canada in 2017 than at any other time in history, largely because we are living longer. These people will place the highest *per capita* demands on our health-care system, which will have experienced another two decades of ever higher demands, and ever rising budgets. I'll be talking more about health care in the next chapter.

If you are in this group, you have had great financial opportunities with the boom in real estate and stock market prices. Now, though, you may be wondering whether you put aside enough money for your retirement. To paraphrase the words of Cary Grant, "If I had known I was going to live this long, I would have taken better care of my finances." Moreover, government financial support for the elderly is undergoing tremendous strain in 2017. Accordingly, governments have either flatly reduced the benefits they pay, or given with one hand then taken back with the other.

This group is either thinking about or already living in some alternative kind of residence, like a lifestyle community or seniors' residence, that supports the elderly by taking over some of the day-to-day chores of living.

- **War babies**. If you're a war baby, you are probably comfortably retired in 2017. You had some anxious moments toward the end of your career in the late 1990s and the early years of the twenty-first century when jobs were disappearing and job security vanished, but you and most of your peers made it through with enough money to retire in your early sixties. You have invested in stocks, both directly and indirectly, for many years, and are more comfortable with the idea than the Pre-Second World War crowd, who prefer investments like Canada Savings Bonds and GICs that don't fluctuate in value. Your financial worries for the future relate primarily to your children and grandchildren, because you see taxes eating up their incomes and gnawing away at the estate that you had hoped to bequeath them.

  You have either moved from the family home or have had it renovated to make a more suitable residence for your old age. There are fewer snowbirds travelling south for the winter than there were 20 years ago because provincial health plans no longer cover stays of more than three weeks outside the country, and the cost of private health care for someone in their seventies is tremendously expensive. This has produced a new winter migration pattern to those parts of Canada, notably the West Coast, that have more moderate winters.

157

Generally speaking, you and the other members of your generation are comfortable and enjoying your retirement. Most of your concerns centre on shrinking government benefits, the health-care system, and your children and grandchildren.

- **First-half boomers**. If you are in the first half of the baby boom, you are now reaching the stage of life that has long been considered "retirement age." Despite this, many of your peers are still working, although mostly part-time and from their own homes. Your generation has done well financially, but is concerned about the high level of taxes, the steadily rising costs of health care stemming from the continuing cuts in government funding, and the reductions in public pensions.

  Many of your peers are still working because they are not sure they have saved enough money to last them through retirement. They spent the early part of their adult lives in relative insouciance, secure in the belief that the future was theirs, and that everything would work out just fine. They spent the second half of their careers concerned about whether they'd be able to hang on, stay employed, and save enough for retirement. Now that they are at retirement age, they feel uneasy about whether they've provided enough for themselves, and so feel compelled to continue bringing in some money, knowing that if they quit working, it's going to be nearly impossible to start again.

You and your generation are savvy investors, having invested in mutual funds, stocks, and overseas investments for 25 years and more. You can be both tremendously fickle, jumping from financial fad to fad, and tremendously loyal, sticking with specific financial planning and management groups that you feel pay close attention to your needs. If there is a pattern to your fidelity, it is that you need to know that the people helping you with your affairs care about you as an individual. If you believe your advisors have violated your trust, you leave without a backward glance.

You have sold your family home — or had it renovated — before real estate really started to slide. You didn't get quite as much as you had hoped from the sale, but it was still, generally speaking, significantly more than you paid for it. Now you're living in a smaller house or a luxurious condominium, and feeling relieved that you've done as well as you have. Still, you can't shake that gnawing feeling that you'd better continue to sock money away "for your old age."

- **Second-half boomers**. If you're a second-half boomer, then you've spent your life following along behind your older brothers and sisters and picking up their leavings. The jobs you got were not as good as those of the first-half boomers. There was tremendous competition for every job available, and you were paid less. You had to live with your parents for the early part of your adult years while continuing your education in hopes of finding a better job, and it has only been in the last 15 to 20 years that you've been able to form your own household.

You're now approaching the age when you would traditionally be thinking about putting the kids through college and starting to really sock away money for retirement. Situated as you are, though, you're finding it difficult to do either, and are worried about how you're going to manage to scrape together enough for your retirement. You have almost no confidence in the ability of the Canada Pension Plan to help you out, you're becoming cynical about the health-care system, and you're taking your lack of faith and trust out on any politician who dares to utter the word "tax" except in the phrase "tax cut." As a result, tax cheating for you and your peers is rampant and socially acceptable. You feel cheated and have no compulsion to "pull your weight," choosing instead to fight against what you see as an inequitable system.

Nevertheless, you continue to struggle to find an annual contribution for an RRSP, largely because it's about the only tax shelter left. If the government ever does finally increase its tax on RRSPs to the point where they are no longer appealing as tax shelters, second-half boomers may just give up on saving for retirement altogether.

Most second-half boomers have a modest home by now, but with a largeish mortgage. You'll probably keep your house well into your old age, renovating it as a retirement home, first, because real estate prices will be under significant pressure by the time you think about selling, and because it will do just fine as an "empty nest."

- **Baby bust**. The generation following the boomers is significantly smaller than the baby boom. If you belong to this group, then you, too, have had to live in the shadow of the first-half boomers. However, because there are fewer of you, you haven't had to experience the excruciating competition for jobs that the second-half boomers did. Although the recession of the early 1990s made finding your initial jobs difficult, since then it has been slightly easier for you to find jobs than for second-half boomers. However, advancement up the corporate ladder has been as slow, in part because boomers are still hogging most of the jobs.

More of your peers have created their own businesses than earlier generations. This has been a mixed blessing. There are many success stories to inspire your generation, but there are also large numbers of people who tried and failed in their own businesses. Even where such people have succeeded later on, their earlier failures wiped out their savings, forcing them to start from scratch.

Your generation also feels cheated on taxes and government services and seeks opportunities to cheat. Indeed, tax cheating is more than just socially acceptable; you and your contemporaries view it as justifiable guerrilla warfare against the selfish baby boomers and the generations before them, who neglected to pay anything like the full cost of the government benefits and services they have received and are still receiving.

Even so, you are starting to accumulate some net worth, and are looking seriously at the stock market, envious of the small fortunes that the boomers have made in stocks. Your generation has been buying houses as the boomers have been selling theirs, and so have benefited from the decline in general real estate values. You, too, make full use of RRSPs, and are strongly against the creeping tendency to tax RRSP assets. Indeed, your generation is allying with the echo generation that follows to fight against what they see as further unfair government favouritism toward the boomers. You are fighting for limits on health-care payouts for the elderly — although with reservations because this is affecting your parents. You are looking for greater clawbacks on old-age benefits as well as further reductions. The tensions caused by such actions are threatening to burst into full-scale political polarization between generations, which may yet happen. "You want your old-age benefits," snarl members of the baby-bust generation, "then *you* pay for them. Stop stealing from us!"

- **Baby boom echo**. The echo generation is by 2017 firmly entrenched in the workplace — or at least in the cycle of looking for work. If you are an echo kid, then your experiences range all over the map, and depend tremendously on how good your schooling has been. Those of you who went to schools that adjusted to the changes in the world, and who learned how to be independent researchers, creative thinkers, and team builders and players are doing very well. You have moved into entrepreneurial situations, both in your own businesses, and as entrepreneurial employees working for others. The older members of your generation are also buying the houses being dumped by the boomers, and they are starting to save money. Your generation, too, is aware that you are being unfairly taxed for too-generous benefits for the boomers and the generations before them, and you are starting to catch the militancy of the baby busters.

  Other members of your generation who went to schools that resisted change, or were stuck in schools that proclaimed that they were going "back to basics," are struggling now. They enjoyed school far less than their more fortunate peers, they came out of it with lower skills for independent work and research, and they are now trying to find traditional, secure jobs in a world that no longer offers them. Many in this group had great potential, but drifted through school, making poor use of the resources offered to them. Instead, they spent their time watching the tube, playing video games, and deliberately avoiding thinking about the future.

Such people are now chronically unemployable, a burden to themselves, their families, and their society. A dismayingly large number of them live on the street with lifestyles equivalent to those found in a Third World nation. They are bitter, estranged from their peers and their society, and have few scruples about ripping off other people. Partly as a result of those attitudes, the nationwide rate of crime, including violent crime, has been climbing again for the last ten years or so, after 15 years of more or less steady decline.

Many people worry about this generation and the large numbers who are disconnected from the economic system. They also worry about the growing animosity between generations over government-sponsored benefits. Owing to their numbers, the baby boomers, war babies, and pre-war generations make a potent political force that is almost impossible for later generations to defeat. Contempt for the rule of law, cynicism about the political system, and strife between younger and older generations are becoming pervasive. The growing number of politicians who are younger than the baby boomers, and who share in the outrage, compounds the intergenerational conflict.

There are those on both sides who try to find common ground. But the voice of calm reason stands little chance against the ability of older generations to vote for their own greedy, selfish interests, and the anger of the rabble-rousers from the younger generation who want to proclaim an intergenerational war. Evidence of this conflict began to emerge in the 1996 Canada-wide consultations on the Canada Pension Plan. The depth of animosity has been reconfirmed repeatedly in political campaigns since then.

- **The second baby bust**. Although this generation is still in school in 2017, they are already smarting from the injustices perpetuated by earlier generations. Their schools are being closed because of dwindling enrolment, so class sizes are going up. Education budgets are being systematically looted to pay for government benefits for the mature and elderly. Day care is almost all privately funded as governments long ago gave up even the pretense of helping working families. This generation, too, will live in the shadow of a disproportionately larger generation, but it won't make much difference, as age and seniority now count for little in the workplace. Instead, advancement will depend on ability from now on, and the disparities in educational opportunities will become key factors in the success or failures of the members of this generation.

One key development of the next 20 years is a virtual certainty: the conflict between generations. I made a presentation and submission to the 1996 federal-provincial hearings on the Canada Pension Plan, and received the interim report from these hearings, along with the panelists' recommendations. As one might expect in any issue relating to money, no one wants their ox gored, which means that those who have the greatest political clout wind up with most of the goodies. Consequently, it is a certainty that today's young people and the succeeding generations will pay more toward the pensions of older generations than those generations will contribute for themselves. At the same time, the younger generations will experience higher levels of taxation, lower levels of government services, especially in such areas as day care and education, and will get lower pensions at the end of their careers as a legacy of our greed.

I am ashamed of my generation and the generations before mine for stealing from our children in such a blatant and unrepentant manner. When I said so at the CPP hearings, one man spoke to me on the way out, justifying this theft by pointing out that he was paying property taxes to finance my children's schooling. It never occurred to him that the generations before him paid for *his* education, and that he was merely repaying a debt, not advancing money out of generosity. In contrast, people who retired before the 1960s did not finance their retirement by stealing from their descendants. Those of my generation and older have established a new precedent in our society: robbing from the young to pay for the old. It is a shameful act, but one that we seem intent on perpetuating. We will all pay a price for it in growing strife and division in our society.

There will be many, particularly among those currently retired, who will be unhappy with my comments. They will point to the sacrifices they made for our country and for present-day generations. They endured the deprivations of the Depression, fought in the Second World War, and financed our educations, social benefits, and health care through their hard work in the postwar years. All of that is true, but it does not change the fact that they and the baby boomers will take out of the retirement system far more than they ever contributed to it. Moreover, it does not justify our actions in leaving an unpaid bill of enormous proportions for the children of today and tomorrow.

How Long Will You Live?

One question about the future is of interest to virtually everybody, even if they don't really want to know the answer: How long will I live? Fortunately (or unfortunately), we can't know that, but we do know a number of the factors that will affect our longevity. Let's start with the most obvious factors: how old are you now, and are you male or female?

The longer you live, the longer you will live. One reason that this strange statement is true is that by living through various stages of your life, you avoid the stumbling blocks that might have tripped you up earlier. For example, a 50-year-old won't die of Sudden Infant Death Syndrome. A 20-year-old male today can expect statistically to live to about 73 years old. A 60-year-old male can expect statistically to live to 78 years old, largely because he has already lived through many of the perils and risks that strike down younger men.

Your gender also has a lot to do with what age you'll live to. Being a woman is a definite advantage, because women tend to live several years longer than men. That's changing somewhat as women are becoming more susceptible to diseases, like heart trouble, that can be exacerbated by stress and the lifestyles associated with high-powered business lives. The table below shows current life expectancies for men and women of different ages.

Table 9.1
Average Canadian Life Expectancy

Current Age	Men			Women		
	Average Life Expectancy	1 of 10 Dies by	1 of 10 Lives to	Average Life Expectancy	1 of 10 Dies by	1 of 10 Lives to
20	73.4	55	89	80.1	62	95
25	73.8	56	89	80.2	62	95
30	74.1	56	89	80.4	63	95
35	74.4	57	90	80.5	63	95
40	74.7	58	90	80.7	64	95
45	75.2	59	90	81.0	64	95
50	75.8	60	90	81.5	65	95
55	76.7	62	90	82.1	67	95
60	78.0	65	90	82.9	69	95
65	79.6	69	91	83.9	71	95
70	81.6	72	91	85.1	74	96
75	84.0	77	92	86.8	78	96
80	86.9	81	94	88.8	82	97
85	90.1	86	96	91.5	86	98
90	93.8	90	98	94.6	91	99
95	97.7	95	100	98.0	95	100
100	100.8	100	102	100.8	100	102

Source: Statistics Canada, IF Research

This table indicates what your average life expectancy is, and roughly what your chances of dying sooner or living longer are. Hence, if you are a 40-year-old woman, this table says that you will, on average, live to age 80.7 years. Of this group, 10 percent will die by age 64, and 10 percent will live to age 95.

But this table uses historical data, and this century has clearly demonstrated that we can expect to live longer than those who lived before us. Since 1900, life expectancy has increased from around 45 to around 76 years, which averages out to an increase of three months per calendar year this century. Improvements that have steadily increased life expectancy have come from better nutrition, housing, and sanitation, and from the widespread refrigeration of food. The introduction of antibiotics in the early 1940s gave an upward jolt to health and life expectancy. But what major factors will affect your longevity in the future? The three principal ones will be technology, disease, and money.

New Tools for Health

We are on the verge of leaving the age of trial-and-error medicine and entering the age of scientific health care. What I mean by trial-and-error medicine are the techniques and treatments that we have derived from watching the healers of earlier days and of different cultures, and identifying what helps the sufferer. This is how curare, used as a muscle relaxant in surgery and as a treatment for certain medical conditions, and digitalis, used to treat heart conditions, were developed. Researchers tried strategies based on a hunch as to what would work, and retained and refined those that were effective. Occasionally, researchers would discover cures or treatments by accident. The discovery of penicillin and X-rays both came about this way. Although the executives at pharmaceutical companies don't like to think of the billions they spend on R&D in this light, they develop many contemporary pharmaceuticals through trial and error.

In future, we will seek specific new treatments using a variety of techniques. Extending and refining techniques already in development, we will discover the etiology, or cause, of a disease by systematic study; we will analyze the effects of the disease on the molecular structure of the body; and we will invent specifically targeted cures based on this understanding. In particular, computer simulations of molecular biology and chemistry, coupled with computer manipulation and analysis of cells and DNA fragments, will lead to new knowledge and new treatments. We do, of course, have a long way to go before we understand the many complex functions of the human body and all its parts. But the more we understand and know, the more scientific will be the tools we use to invent treatments.

The Human Genome Project (HGP) is an international effort to map all 100,000 human genes and all three billion DNA sequences that make up the human genetic pattern. The Project started in 1990 and should be finished before 2005 and, unlike most projects of this size, promises to come in early, under budget, and to produce more results than originally expected. It will take decades before we can explore all the results that emerge, and develop new treatments based on this knowledge. But there have been a few immediate discoveries, and there will certainly be more within the next 20 years. Researchers have already identified the locations of genes that cause or are related to a number of diseases and conditions, including certain kinds of breast and colon cancer, cystic fibrosis, Duchenne muscular dystrophy, Huntington's disease, Alzheimer's disease, Type I diabetes, and a variety of other ailments.

The kinds of treatments that this research might lead to include rewriting a defective gene in the human body to correct a condition, as has been done on an experimental basis with cystic fibrosis and the so-called "bubble baby" syndrome of children born without an immune system. It might also lead to various kinds of "silver bullets," which is what physicians call treatments that target diseased cells or disease-carrying organisms, but which leave normal cells and structures alone. For instance, experiments are now going on to treat glioma, a cancer of the brain, with gene therapy that effectively instructs the cancer cells causing the tumour to switch off and die while leaving normal cells unaffected.

This research might lead to treatments like the ones described below. Please note that these treatments are not available today. I've made them up as illustrations only, and they are not based in medical fact.

Kendra, a 34-year-old mother of two, is concerned, but not distraught, when her doctor diagnoses her as having multiple sclerosis. MS is a chronic disease in which the central nervous system gradually breaks down, resulting in progressive loss of sight, speech, balance, and coordination. Twenty years ago, back in the "Grey 90s," this diagnosis would have condemned Kendra to a slow and distressing decline and an early death, because the causes of MS were then unknown, and there was no cure. Doctors could treat the symptoms, and ameliorate the course of the disease somewhat, but they were merely postponing the inevitable.

Now the cause of MS has been traced to the interaction of three separate and apparently unrelated gene sites, with the onset triggered by exposure to a particular kind of protein after a certain age. In Kendra's case, the trigger was a protein contained in corn. The trigger changed a subtle code in the chemistry of the white blood cells that are part of the body's defence mechanism. As a result, the white cells identified the fatty sheaths that surround Kendra's nerve cells as a threat and started to attack them. If left untreated, this process would progressively destroy the nerves that control Kendra's body, causing all of her major body functions to deteriorate.

By the year 2017, however, MS can be treated, although not cured. After performing an analysis of Kendra's genetic code and her now defective white-blood-cell chemistry, Kendra's doctors will supply her with a personally tailored supply of a chemical transmitter that compensates for the improper chemistry of her white cells. Every five years Kendra will need to have a new capsule of the chemical implanted under her skin, where it will slowly release the necessary chemicals into her bloodstream, allowing her body to repair the damage done to date, and preventing the degeneration that would otherwise occur. As long as she follows this treatment, she can continue to live a healthy, normal life.

Her family's main concern is financial. The diagnosis and genetic analysis cost almost $250,000. Her provincial health insurance will pay for 85 percent of the cost as part of Kendra's lifetime Medical Savings Account (MSA), with Kendra's family paying the rest. The five-year implants cost $67,000 each, because they are specifically tailored and produced to fit her genetic pattern. Her provincial health insurance does not cover these continuing expenses.

Although it means taking out a second mortgage, Kendra's family would rather endure the financial strain than let her suffer the ravages of multiple sclerosis.*

A similar story might apply to many other conditions that we now are helpless to cure in normal circumstances, such as diabetes, cystic fibrosis, organ transplant rejection, or degenerative bone diseases like osteoporosis. Regardless of the condition, this story illustrates several themes I expect to see appear over the next 20 years. First, the decoding of the human genome will lead us to understand what causes a variety of genetically linked diseases and conditions that have previously baffled us, and allow us to start treating them successfully. Secondly, I believe we will find that some of the diseases that bedevil us are triggered by environmental conditions, such as exposure to certain kinds of food, resins used in

---

* For those who suffer from MS, and for their families, please forgive me for inventing a fictitious knowledge and cure. As far as my sources tell me, MS is, at this time, still beyond our ability to cure or treat successfully. As I have friends and acquaintances who have MS, I find this difficult — but believe that we will see successful treatment within the next decade or so.

certain kinds of woods or plastics, pollen, or other things with which we come into routine contact. We might even find that coming into physical contact with certain individuals, because of where they have been or the kind of work they do, might be dangerous. I suggested this earlier in chapter 2 when Marc and one of his interviewers declined to shake hands after their genies alerted them to a possible medical incompatibility.

We are just beginning to understand how such triggers work. In this example, I chose corn merely because I know that some individuals develop strong allergic reactions to it as they age while others can eat corn happily all their lives. My example could just as easily have been almost any food, or any airborne substance, or materials with which we come in contact on a daily basis. The knowledge of such triggers is probably going to revolutionize all kinds of normal activities. Construction companies will list the components in the building materials they use, just as prepared foods now must list all their ingredients. Toy manufacturers will have to be aware of new developments in this field and will also be forced to label their toys with the materials used in their manufacture. Towns and cities will have to take such reactions into account when they plant gardens, trees, and shrubs. Health practitioners will have to start performing individual sensitivity assessments to advise people what substances to avoid.

Unique treatments keyed to the specific genetic pattern of an individual are another likely development. This does not mean that every treatment of every disease will have to be unique. But if your genetic pattern is specifically related to a certain disease, you may require an unusual or custom remedy. Overall, though, most genetically linked cures and treatments will be usable by a wide range of people. Not everyone with a particular genetic quirk will be subject to every kind of disease. As a result, even though you may share a widespread weakness that could lead to illness, it may be that only a small fraction of people will come down with it. It may be cheaper to develop a unique medication than to develop and store a wide variety of different medicines for thousands of small groups of people.

Whatever such research as the Human Genome Project might bring, one message is clear: the way we finance health care will have to change in future. In Kendra's case, a large part of her concern was financial because she had to dip into both her own family's savings and into her Medical Savings Account to finance the best available treatment. The idea of an MSA, which some American health organizations are starting to use, is that each person will, on average, use a certain dollar amount of health care during a lifetime. If you are unlucky, and need more, or need it early in life, you would have to pay for anything beyond that average amount. Our present Canadian system, where everyone theoretically has unlimited access to as much health-care service as they need — or want — is destined for extinction.

The aging of the baby boom, coupled with those who are at or past retirement age already, will place severe pressure on health-care costs, which will continue mushrooming until the baby boomers die off in significant numbers. I'll talk about this later in the chapter, but keep in mind the kinds of structural changes I suggested in Kendra's treatment.

In chapter 1, I noted that computer genies may well monitor our health from second to second, and identify conditions or diseases early on. Early detection has always been important in treatment. If we can identify diseases before they can become fully established, we may be able to stop them much faster and more effectively. This principle applies to almost everything, from cancer to the common cold.

Marcia is in the midst of making a business presentation when Machiavelli, her computer genie, signals that he needs her attention as soon as possible. Since his request did not indicate that his need was urgent, she carries on, finishing up as quickly as she can without missing any of the major points that might persuade her client. When her team leaves the client's offices, she excuses herself, ducks into the ladies' room, and tells Mac she's free to listen.

He informs her that some symptoms of breast cancer have shown up in her bloodstream. Since Marcia is in a high-risk category for breast cancer, her mother made sure when Marcia was in her teens that her genie regularly downloaded information from the relevant databases. Every morning, Machiavelli has tapped into all the current data from a public database on symptoms to watch for, but they've never been of any use — until now.

Marcia is shocked. She's 48, leads a hectic life, but watches her weight, exercises regularly, and makes sure she gets enough rest. She long ago decided that she wasn't going to get breast cancer. She never thought it would happen to her, and certainly not without some warning.

Mac tells her that she should go immediately to the Women's Centre, an outpatient clinic belonging to her private insurance group, where she can have an appointment for complete diagnosis and treatment either within the next 23 minutes, or at 4:45 that afternoon, whichever time she can make. She decides she can grab a cab and make the earlier appointment, so she instructs Mac to set it up. She also tells him to inform her team what's happened, and to keep her team leader apprised of her progress. She steps out onto the sidewalk, where Mac has arranged for a cab to be waiting, using a medical priority code to jump the queue. En route, Marcia instructs Mac to tell her mother (Marcia's not feeling strong enough), then Marcia calls her life partner, Janet, so they can talk about what they're going to tell the kids. When she signs off, she refuses all incoming calls below priority one, and jitters in the back seat until she arrives, 14 minutes later, at the Women's Centre.

As she walks through the entry hall, Mac checks her in and authorizes release of her medical database to the care centre, while directing Marcia to the proper section of the clinic. She walks through the clinic's door, which unlocks when Mac gives the proper authorization. Because Mac has warned her what to expect, she immediately starts stripping off her clothes, depositing them in the locker designated, and affixing her thumbprint on the lock. She dons a hospital gown, which is just as useless and embarrassing as such garments were 50 years ago. The hardest things to leave behind are her Looking Glasses and her Listening Post. She is now electronically out of touch with the world — a concept that makes her nervous.

A nurse walks through the door — the first employee of the Centre she's seen — and asks her to lie down on a gurney, which then rolls itself into a procedure room where two technicians are waiting. The nurse accompanies Marcia and stands by her in the procedure room.

The technicians start the diagnostic series for breast cancer. One sticks tubes in her arm that will allow the computer to perform a detailed analysis of her bloodstream. Meanwhile, Machiavelli relays Marcia's normal baseline metabolism to the procedure room computer so that it can gauge how she will respond to the various aspects of her subsequent treatment. It takes note that she is allergic to penicillin and various related antibiotics, and adjusts the prospective treatment accordingly.

Meanwhile, the nurse stands next to Marcia, describing in detail what's about to happen, answering her questions honestly, knowledgeably, and as fully as she can, and holding Marcia's hand to reassure her. This particular procedure room nurse was hired to work here not only for her knowledge and experience, but also because she exhibits high levels of empathy, and patients are comforted by her presence. Long experience has demonstrated — with statistical and scientific rigour — that the patient's state of mind affects how well her body responds to treatment. As a result, practitioners now know that the presence of the right kind of medical caregiver significantly improves the prognosis and decreases the time and cost of treatment.

Once the technicians have taped the bloodstream tubes to Marcia's arm, they roll her into a CompScan, which is like a tunnel that encircles her entire chest cavity. The machine creates a detailed, three-dimensional, real-time image of what's happening inside her breasts and chest cavity by using a variety of scanning technologies, then integrates them into a single, complex image. Concentrations of white blood cells and T-cells, the higher temperatures associated with cancerous areas, and other indications become immediately evident to the computer, which highlights those areas affected on the physician's screen. When the CompScan is approaching completion of its work, it signals the attending physician, who walks in seconds before the CompScan finishes.

After chatting briefly with Marcia, the physician looks over the screen, which is not visible to Marcia, and starts reading through the information displayed. She notes the computer's selected diagnoses, as well as the probabilities given for a variety of alternative possible diagnoses (which are all negligible in this case), the range of alternative treatments available, plus one-line abstracts of relevant research documents available for her perusal if she wants more detail. She agrees with almost everything the computer suggests, silently checking points off with a light pen, but stops when she comes to the final follow-up treatment. She hesitates, then asks for a test not suggested by the computer, and indicates a site on the left breast where she wants the test performed.

Seconds later the procedure room computer releases a cloud of nanobots — microscopic robots — into Marcia's bloodstream. Under the computer's direction, they navigate to an apparently healthy region in the left breast, sampling the surrounding cells at random. What they discover is that the cancer has, surprisingly, already started to metastasize, or spread, beyond its original site. This indicates that follow-up must last longer and be more intense than the computer originally allowed. Once again human judgment has proven to be not fully replaceable by computers and statistics. If asked, the physician would not be able to articulate clearly why she felt the need for the additional test, but the truth is that her subconscious recognized incomplete pattern fragments that led it to what people call a hunch — and the hunch proved correct.

The procedure room computer initiates treatment immediately, with a second group of nanobots delivering specifically tailored chemical "keys" to the region around the cancer cells. These keys connect with chemical receptor "locks" on the exterior of the cancerous cells that instruct the cells to stop functioning. This means that most of the cancer cells will die off, and they won't reproduce or cause healthy cells to turn cancerous. The body's own natural defences will deal with those few cells missed by the nanobots, now that the treatment has eliminated the majority of the cancerous cells. The tailored chemical keys do not fit on the receptors of healthy cells, and so have no effect on them. Within two days, all the cancerous cells at the identified sites will have died off, and Marcia will be healthy again.

Which leaves the metastasis. For now, the doctor injects her with a specially tailored virus that reproduces in the bloodstream, hunts and destroys the cancerous cells of the type that are loose in Marcia's body, then dies off when it fails to find enough such cells on which to feed. This will slow the development of any new cancers and may allow Marcia's body to fight off the disease entirely.

The physician also deposits a third series of nanobots into her bloodstream. These nanobots, unlike the two earlier series that will shut down and be flushed out of her system in a matter of hours, are relatively longlived, reproducing in limited numbers before shutting down about six months later. On Marcia's follow-up visits to the centre, her doctors will scan her for concentrations of these nanobots in any one site, which would indicate the development of a second cancer. The manufacturer tags the nanobots with low-level radiation so they are much easier to spot than the body's own cells. Accordingly, the Women's Centre medical team can use a much faster, and less expensive, system to scan her body, with the entire procedure taking no more than five minutes and requiring only a technician in attendance.

The nanobots are programmed to stop working one by one. The body then flushes the inactive nanobots from its system. Depending on the results of these subsequent tests, Marcia's health team will inject a new group of nanobots if there are signs that cancer cells are still floating around in her bloodstream, or stop all treatment if it seems likely the danger is past.

For now, though, Marcia's getting ready to go home. As she dresses, she puts her hands on her breasts and breathes a sigh of relief. In an earlier day, she would have had to have all or part of her breasts surgically removed. Early discovery, coupled with new technologies that allow the precise delivery of "silver bullet" treatments, have cured her within three hours of the first signs of cancer, weeks or months before earlier measures would have discovered it.

There's a lot of material for discussion in this story, so let me cover it in point form:

- First, as discussed earlier, a personal genie will be able to monitor your health on a second-by-second basis. For individuals who have a high risk of disease for genetic or other reasons, a genie will be able to download detailed data on specific signs and symptoms to watch for, allowing for early diagnosis and treatment, thereby improving the odds of success.

- An integrated health-care system, in which patients and the system share data, will build up a base of early warning symptoms with astonishing rapidity. When you add the likelihood that solution-seeking or adaptive computing software will analyze these data to come up with ever-better diagnoses and treatment, you get a powerful, nationwide health management tool that is unparalleled in history. Moreover, different societies or nations will pool data to increase the odds of catching diseases that may be unusual in one climate or locale, but not another.

  As a result of this information sharing, diagnosing, say, a tropical disease for a traveller returning to northern Manitoba, where health-care practitioners may not be familiar with the symptoms or the treatment, would become much simpler. A physician in northern Manitoba will be able to confer and share data with a physician in Malaysia, for instance to get assistance in diagnosis and treatment. Doctors around the world will have the ability to access the entire global knowledge base about a particular condition or disease, and to confer directly with other physicians familiar with it. They will also be able to identify epidemics and their vectors (carriers) much earlier than we can now.

- The CompScan is a device that I made up, but it's a logical extension of today's Computerized Tomography, Magnetic Resonance Imaging, Emission Tomography, and related imaging devices, which are themselves lineal descendants of the X-ray machine. Under the guidance of computers, it is already possible to integrate a variety of imaging techniques to come up with detailed, real-time images. In future, these images will become ever better, and practitioners will be able to switch from one examining technique to another to reach as definitive a diagnosis as possible.

- The use of computers for diagnostic purposes is not new. Experiments with such systems in the past have occasionally been done poorly, leaving many physicians with the impression that computer diagnostics are unreliable. But properly designed and written computer systems will, over time, produce superior diagnoses for the vast majority of illnesses and conditions to those produced by humans. Computers can keep millions of facts "in mind," can collate these facts, can seek patterns in apparently unrelated data, and can "learn" how to improve results.

Such systems should always be subject to human judgment, though, for two reasons. First, computers have no sense of what is reasonable, so that if their diagnosis is wrong, it can be wildly wrong. It will still be essential to have highly trained human beings assessing computer diagnoses, and people must never assume the computer is always right. Second, solution-seeking, statistically based software is only as good as its historical data; it will be of little value in assessing new diseases or conditions. More so than computers, humans are adaptable in their thinking, and able to recognize novelty when they see it, so there is and will be no substitute for human medical judgment.

I propose that the health-care management establishments of the world, particularly government ministries of health, should start immediately to establish such diagnostic databases. They could then begin to pool data, although they should always tag the origins of that data in order to gauge its reliability. They should also share with other countries techniques and software for diagnosing disease, to help each other up the steep learning curve these tools will require. The impetus for following this course of action in the developed countries that have rapidly aging populations is money. Such systems may become the single greatest tool humanity has for prevention and early diagnosis and cure, and their early implementation could save billions of health-care dollars.

- In my vignette, the CompScan screen also offered the physician a range of abstracts that apprised her of relevant new research developments in an up-to-the-minute fashion. Physicians, of all professionals, probably have the hardest task in trying to keep up and would welcome any system that could help them do so. Human librarians managing a computer-based, point-of-use system could make it much easier for physicians to manage their information overload and keep costs down. Such systems already exist; my minor refinement is to have this online information available in the operating theatre.

- The presence of an empathetic nurse in the procedure room in Marcia's story was deliberate. We already know that helping the patient to understand her condition and providing information and support to deal with it makes a positive difference in treatment and results. It makes financial sense to invest in whatever improves patient outcomes. At present, though, we are moving in the opposite direction. In our concern to keep down our expenditures on health services, we are making it difficult for physicians, nurses, and other health practitioners to offer empathy and support. Instead, they have to rush from place to place, performing tasks and procedures rather than treating people. I hope we will finally come to see that cutbacks in the human side of health-service delivery can be costly; let's start managing our system wisely rather than cheaply.

- The use of tailored viruses and specifically designed chemicals to act as "silver bullets" is already happening experimentally. As we learn more about molecular and cellular chemistry, these techniques will become more widespread, and we will be able to start treating disease with precisely designed missiles rather than with crude and clumsy tools like broad-spectrum antibiotics. We're not there yet, and 20 years certainly won't complete the process, but by 2017 we will think of precision medication and treatment as the norm rather than as an experimental exception.

- I may have been overly optimistic about the use of nanobots in Marcia's story, for they may not be as highly developed as I have portrayed them. They will exist in our future, but they may take longer to develop than 20 years.

The field of molecular nanotechnology is young and highly controversial. We know we can manipulate individual atoms and molecules, place them where we want, and get them to stay there. It is a long leap to being able to create complex structures of precisely planned and placed molecules to produce microscopic robots. However, that is precisely what is being discussed in the field.* For those interested in reading further in this field, there are few resources because it is so new. Perhaps the two best non-technical books are *The Engines of Creation: The Coming Era of Nanotechnology* (New York: Doubleday, 1986), by K. Eric Drexler, who is widely considered to be the leading pioneer in this field, and *Nano — The Emerging Science of Nanotechnology: Remaking the World — Molecule by Molecule* (New York: Little, Brown, 1995) by Ed Regis. As in any brand-new field, the literature is not keeping pace with the developments. Therefore, you might want to visit the Internet website http://www.foresight.org/index.html as a starting point, or use a good

---

* Note that there is much more to nanotechnology than applications in health management. See *Facing the Future*, chapter 9.

search engine on the subject of nanotechnology. It is my view that nanotechnology will become widely used in health management, largely to augment the body's own disease-fighting mechanisms.

The Ethical Problems Ahead

Although many exciting improvements to health-care delivery and to personal health will arise from this new technology, they will bring with them new and ever more complex ethical dilemmas as well. We are wandering into fields where there are few clear markers to tell us what is right and what is wrong, and we will find ourselves hard pressed to come up with answers to equal the life-and-death decisions that will confront us. Let me give you some possible examples:*

- Your health service has just told you that your pregnancy test is positive, and you're going to have a baby. However, based on genetic screening of the fetus, they also tell you that the child will be born with severe physical handicaps. The provincial health service tells you that the child will consume more than its lifetime Medical Savings Account within the first year. This means that you will have to pay, out of your own pocket, a sizable amount of money to keep the child alive in the first year, and much more every year thereafter. Do you abort the fetus, as the provincial government recommends, or bring it to term?
- You are a practitioner at a genetic testing facility. A husband and his pregnant wife both carry the gene that causes

---

* Some of these examples come from an excellent and thought-provoking discussion of this question found in "Beyond the Genome: The ethics of DNA testing," *Science News*, November 5, 1994.

achondroplasia; that is, they are both dwarfs. Dwarfism can be a serious disorder in some cases, producing abnormal bone structure that will sometimes confine the individual to a wheelchair for life. But many dwarfs live long, healthy lives and do not think of themselves as disabled. This couple want you to test their fetus for dwarfism. They tell you that they intend to abort the fetus if it will *not* be a dwarf, because they are worried about the problems facing two dwarfs raising a normal-sized child. Do you perform the test?

- There is a bill in federal parliament to require practitioners to screen all fetuses for the gene that causes polycystic kidney disease, which is one of the most common inherited, life-threatening diseases. If a fetus has the gene, it will have to undergo a genetic transplant in the womb to guarantee the child is not born with the defective gene. The intent is to eradicate polycystic kidney disease within a generation. While there is an 85 percent chance that such a transplant will succeed, there is a 15 percent chance that it will cause a miscarriage. Are you for or against the legislation?

- Your 18-year-old son has been accepted by Harvard University, which will cost you close to US$200,000 over the next four years. Through genetic testing performed before he was born, you know that he has a degenerative nerve disease that will almost certainly kill him within the next five years. You've never told him about his condition to avoid burdening him with it through his childhood. What do you do?

- You are an obstetrician. A husband and wife have a child who suffers from cystic fibrosis, an incurable disease that is almost inevitably fatal in early adulthood. CF is caused by a recessive gene, and occurs only when both parents are CF carriers. A child who receives only one recessive gene is a carrier, but does not get the disease. The couple have come to you together. They yearn for another child, but want to know the likelihood of that child being born with CF. During testing, you discover that while the woman has the CF recessive gene, the man does not, which means that he is not the genetic father of the first child. If you tell them there is no risk of a second child having CF they will want to know why. Remembering that they came to you together, and are both equally entitled to the information you now have. What should you do? Moreover, the genetic father of the first child does carry the recessive gene and could conceive another child with CF. Should he be tracked down and told?

While knowledge is power, power is sometimes a mixed blessing. New medical technologies will convey to the medical establishment — bureaucrats and legislators as well as practitioners — enormous power over people's lives. The challenge for the rest of us will be to decide how this power should be used.

The Skirmishes Are Over; the Battle's Just Beginning

Life is persistent, and that's a problem. Bacteria, viruses, and parasites are especially tenacious, and are constantly inventing new ways around all the wonderful cures that we've invented to kill them or stave them off. Over the next 20 years, you, a member of your family, or someone you know may become seriously ill or even die, because of a disease you thought medical science had beaten. Something as simple as a sore throat could wind up killing you, if it is caused by a *Staphylococcus* bacterium of an antibiotic-resistant strain. Or someone you know could die of "consumption," as they called tuberculosis 100 years ago. TB is making a comeback as new, drug-resistant strains are emerging that are untreatable, leaving little for doctors to do except isolate the sufferers and helplessly watch them die.

You may be out doing something healthy, like backpacking, and drink some water from a stream without purifying it properly, and die from *Escherichia coli*, or *E. coli*, a bacillus that is commonly found in your own digestive system. Or there could be another great influenza epidemic, like the one in 1918 that killed over 20 million people worldwide, including more soldiers than all the bullets and artillery of the First World War. You could be vacationing in Florida, get bitten by a mosquito, and die of malaria. Or you could be sitting in a theatre with 300 other people, including someone who has just come back from Africa, and catch a brand-new airborne disease that no one has ever heard of, and for which there is no known cure. Worse, it could be the beginning of a major global epidemic, like the Black Death, which killed something like one-third of the population of Europe in the mid-1300s.

All of these scenarios may sound like a bad science fiction movie or a cheap medical thriller, but I warn you that there is a high probability that events like this will happen in your community, and perhaps to you or a member of your family, within the next 20 years. But why?

Penicillin was first discovered by Scottish bacteriologist Alexander Fleming in 1928, and first used to treat infection in 1941. Since then scientists have developed scores of synthetically derived antibiotics, which for decades have been robustly effective against a wide range of bacterial infections. Today, however, new strains of these bacteria have evolved into drug-resistant forms for which there are few, if any, effective drugs.

Over-prescription and improper use of antibiotics, primarily in developed countries, and particularly in the United States, are the chief causes of their declining efficacy. We have become so comfortable with the notion of doctors being able to dispense instant cures that we've forgotten what humanity knew before the discovery of penicillin: that the battle against disease is a constant life-and-death struggle. Our success in fighting disease due to the widespread use of antibiotics has made us overconfident, so that we believe that we've won the war when we've merely won a few of the opening skirmishes.

Nor are old diseases the whole story, as we may we be faced with new ones that are even worse. An airborne hemorrhagic fever, like the Ebola virus if it were transmitted the ways cold viruses are, would make almost all other diseases seem pleasant in comparison. A minimum of 50 percent, and perhaps more than 90 percent, of all the people who contract Ebola die within a period of days, and it's not a pleasant or pretty death. At present, it is transmitted only by direct physical contact with a carrier, but if it, or a similar disease, were carried by air currents, we could well see a repeat of something like the Black Death in our time.

Most people are serenely ignorant that these life-threatening bacteria and viruses even exist, especially in the developed world where we have become complacent. On a personal level, we should all follow the basic rules of hygiene — careful hand washing and food preparation, and so on. On a societal level, the following recommendations make both public health and financial sense:

- Subsidize those for whom prescription medications are a major expense. It's cheaper to subsidize those that can't afford medicine than to have them become breeding grounds for diseases we can't cure. Penny pinching here is foolishness.
- Make it illegal to use antibiotics in livestock feed. Farmers routinely put one of humanity's greatest weapons against disease into animal feed, even when there is no evident threat of disease. This is a dangerous misuse of an important health tool.
- Undertake a major education campaign, in the schools and to the general public, about proper sanitation, disease prevention, and nutrition.
- Develop new guidelines for restraining the use of antibiotics

and other medicines. Antibiotics may need to become our last-ditch defence against disease rather than the first thing we try. We should also start thinking about cycling less effective antibiotics out of use for a period of years. If we're lucky, bacteria will start mutating out of their resistance to such antibiotics, and we can start using them again.

- Undertake a public information campaign about the cautious and proper use of antibiotics to wean people off the overuse or improper use of these potent medications.

Beyond these steps, we should increase subsidies for research and development to find new antibiotics, plus new ways of countering both bacteria and viruses. At present, while research goes on, it does not receive the funding or the priority it should. I understand, for instance, that the money spent making the film *Outbreak*, which is about a highly contagious new disease, exceeds the annual research budget for finding cures or vaccines against such diseases. Surely this is a misuse of our resources. Technology has a great deal to offer, and, particularly with the results of the Human Genome Project now starting to emerge, we should be able to find effective new treatments for disease, even as our old standbys lose their efficacy. This research is expensive — but so is dying.

Without these, or similar, measures, we could be faced with a major epidemic against which antibiotics are of no use. In the wake of such an epidemic, we could well see a move to punish the abuse of antibiotics.

Connor is a busy man, always flying from place to place for important meetings. He's the mainstay of his media empire, wears elegant, expensive suits, and has developed a tendency to talk down to people because he's obviously richer, and therefore smarter, than they are.

One day he comes down with a "bug" in the midst of buying

a new publication. He doesn't have time to waste in bed, so he goes to his doctor and tells him to prescribe something to get him well. The doctor looks at Connor long and hard, and reminds him that the authorities have issued a final warning against the abuse of antibiotics. If the doctor is going to prescribe "something to get him well," then Connor is going to have to promise to go home to bed, take his medicine as prescribed, and keep doing so until he gets a doctor's certificate of wellness. Connor nods, accepts the reluctantly given prescription, and proceeds to ignore everything his doctor told him. He has his secretary fill the prescription, then he hops a plane to Dallas that very evening.

He forgets his bottle of medicine in his hotel when he leaves Dallas. In irritation, he arranges for the bottle to be couriered to him at home. He arrives to find that the doctor has phoned him at home (not through his genie), and hurriedly changes into his pyjamas before phoning back from his bed.

The doctor is not convinced that Connor has been following his instructions and, as required by law, he reports his patient to the province's Health Authority. The Authority calls Connor in for an examination and investigates his activities. They quickly discover that he has been travelling, that he has not taken the medicine as prescribed, and that he is dismissive of his failure to do so, even now. They confiscate the prescribed antibiotic, and place a lifetime ban on any physician, anywhere in the developed world, prescribing antibiotics for him. This ban is transmitted through the global medical database.

Connor responds by first suing the doctor and the Health Authority, and then buying antibiotics on the black market. Unfortunately, the drugs he procures are useless against the disease he has. He finally dies – alone at home – on the day the courts summarily dismiss all of his claims out of hand.

The abuse of antibiotics may become a crime in our lifetimes, punishable by banning you from ever having access to them again. Or perhaps I'm overreacting, and this is merely a paranoid fantasy. But before you decide, I urge you to read *The Coming Plague* by Laurie Garrett (New York: Farrar, Straus and Giroux, 1994).

The Currency of Life Is Money

When I speak to American audiences, they learn that I live in Canada. As a result, I'm often asked questions about the Canadian medical system, and how it compares with its American counterpart. This is what I tell them:

Both the United States and Canada ration health care, even though both countries pretend that it is freely available. In Canada, we stand in line, waiting our turn for medical attention. If we die before we get to the head of the queue, too bad. In the American system, they ration health care based on the size of your credit card. If your credit card is too small and you die, too bad. Both are means of rationing health care — and not necessarily the most intelligent ways. I discussed some other possibilities in *Facing the Future*, and refer you to that discussion rather than repeating myself here.

But the truth is that no matter how we do it, we are going to have to ration health care for the same reason that the stock market is going to boom over the next 20 years: the baby boomers are aging, both in the U.S. and Canada, and older people are heavier users of health-care services.

According to *National Health Expenditures in Canada, 1975-1994*, published by Health Canada, Canadians currently spend just under 10 percent of Gross Domestic Product on health care. Only Americans spend more. Moreover, this 10 percent is up from 7 percent in 1976. If we continue to run our health management system the way we do at present, then I estimate that by 2017 we will be devoting about 14 percent of GDP to health care, which is about one dollar out of every seven we spend. In Canada, we pay for most of our health care through our governments. This means that expenditures on health care are going to steadily eat up a larger and larger share of government budgets — unless we start changing what we do and how we do it.

In order to get a handle on what might happen to health-care costs over the next 20 years, I developed an econometric model based on Canadian demographics. For this analysis, I assumed that all other economic variables remained the same, and the only thing that changed was that we would get older. The result was that rising health-care costs, which already constitute the single largest government program expenditure, will gobble up about 45 percent more of our governmental budgets in 2017 than they do now. This will mean that we will have to cut something like $25 billion per year (plus inflation) from other government programs to finance the increases in health-care costs.

This one fact — that the baby boomers are going to consume more health services as they age — will overwhelm all other factors relating to health care. We cannot afford to spend $25 billion a year more on health care even if we wish to. Even with all the cost efficiencies of new technology and a better understanding of disease and human physiology, we will still be forced to radically alter how we manage our health-care system and how we spend our dollars. This is going to lead to a number of changes we don't want and don't like, but the alternatives are worse, not better.

Some of the changes are obvious. For instance, governments are going to restrict access to health services, and we're going to start paying directly for a steadily rising percentage of the services that we use. In Ontario, for instance, the provincial health service no longer pays for certain kinds of physicians' services, as well as for some tests and procedures. The list of such exclusions is going to get progressively longer as time goes on.

Seniors, who have in the past enjoyed significant subsidies for prescriptions, are going to pay more for them and for other medical services. Seniors will fight this move, and, because their political power is rising steadily, they are going to be successful some of the time, to the detriment of younger people. This will especially be true once the baby boomers start retiring in significant numbers.

Governments will place more restrictions on health service professionals relating to where and when the licensee can practice, and how much money he or she can make. This is not to say that I believe these restrictions are fair. Quite the contrary. Governments are choosing to make practitioners the scapegoats for the mushrooming costs of health care, and the general public is acquiescing to their actions because people believe that doctors make lots of money. This perception may have been true in earlier decades; it is not nearly as true now, and it almost certainly won't be in future. By 2017, a young person will become a nurse or a physician to fulfil a personal calling or out of dedication to others rather than for the money, which will be much less enticing than in the past. Nor will it help to move south to the United States. Studies done by a variety of think tanks in the U.S. indicate that both physicians' incomes and the number of physicians will drop steadily in future. Some estimates indicate that there will be a need for somewhere between 100,000 and 150,000 fewer specialists within the next ten years than there are now, for instance.

But how can it be true that there is going to be an ever-rising demand for health services, and a declining number of health professionals? The simple answer is: more services are going to be delivered by people other than physicians, people who have less training and are paid less. We will use a steadily rising amount of automation in health care, as illustrated in Marcia's story. We are going to rely more on computers, software, and "smart" equipment, and less and less on highly trained human judgment and skills for routine diagnoses and procedures. Already, for instance, there are robots in a few specialties, such as prostatic cancer and neurosurgery, that perform surgery (under a physician's direction) faster and more accurately than human surgeons.

Already a number of Canadian jurisdictions are talking about licensing nurse-practitioners to diagnose the more routine illnesses and to prescribe certain medicines and tests without referral to a doctor. Although it is likely that most nurse-practitioners will work in health management teams that include doctors, it's possible that a few will set up practices on their own.

This is one picture of the health management system you may face in the next 20 years: fewer services, longer queues, greater numbers of people dying before being treated, dramatically lower incomes for physicians, continuing pressure on nurses' incomes, more stressful work environments for all health-care workers, and higher out-of-pocket costs for patients.

It's not a pretty picture. But while we can't stop the underlying force — the aging of the population — we can manage our resources better than we are now. Below is a list of the steps that we might take to improve the overall situation, for I believe we need to approach the management of individual health in a radically different way, or we will all pay a heavy price in human suffering.

Our Health-care System Is Aimless

At present, health care is largely financed by governments in Canada. Government budgets list health care as a cost centre, but make no provision for the real economic benefit of making a sick person well again. Furthermore, there is currently no measuring system to tell us — or government policy makers — whether we are getting good value for our (tax) money or not. There are few yardsticks to indicate whether a given practitioner, hospital, or region is performing effectively and efficiently, or whether a given procedure is the best one to use.

As a result, we have a health-care system that has no defined purpose because the only thing that is measured is money. Individual practitioners may have a purpose, as defined by their ethics or oaths of practice, but our system as a whole is undefined and unmeasured, and counts failure as being equal to success if they cost the same. In Marcia's story, the purpose of having an empathetic, knowledgeable human nurse involved was primarily to improve the effectiveness of treatment by improving the morale of the patient. There is no room for these kinds of initiatives in our system because the system — not the individuals in the system, but the system itself — does not gauge their effect, only their cost.

We need to change this mindset, perhaps by developing a national mission statement and then assessing the system's effectiveness by measuring results. There are some attempts to move in this direction by monitoring the kinds of procedures used by practitioners, and measuring them against a statistical norm, but this is a process still in its infancy.

Let's Stop Practicing "Medicine"

Think about it: isn't "medicine" a pill or potion? Granted, when we use the term "medicine," we really mean more than just pills and potions. But words have a way of shaping our perceptions and expectations, and using the term "medicine" has made us come to view our strategies for creating and preserving health through too narrow a lens. Too few physicians know much about diet and nutrition, sports therapy, human genetics, psychology, eastern health practices, and a wide range of other useful arts and sciences. If we start talking about "health management" rather than "medicine," we open our minds to examining a wide range of possible approaches to health, wellness, and disease, approaches such as aromatherapy, homeopathy, herbalism, yoga, Tai Chi, and eastern health practices, to name only a few. We don't now accept any of these practices under the title of "medicine," but all of them might be welcome in the practice of "health management."

Of course, we should also apply the same standards of scientific rigour to these practices as we demand of traditional western medicine. Otherwise we risk blundering into practices of questionable value.

Centralize and Automate Health Records

Centralized and automated health records make the diagnosis of a condition easier, more certain, and faster by eliminating unnecessary duplication of tests and procedures. If you were travelling in rural Saskatchewan on business, and became violently ill, having all of your health records available to a local hospital would allow the attending health-care professionals to know about any allergies, pre-existing health conditions, or previous surgeries that might complicate treatment. Your life could ride on this information being available in an accurate and timely fashion.

Such a system could also handle physician and hospital billing and records, and pay practitioners promptly by electronic funds transfer. Doctors could do with fewer support people, thereby reducing their overheads and increasing their net incomes. These systems could also help physicians stay abreast of current information relating to the illnesses they treat. Physicians could file prescriptions electronically, with appropriate records going to their own files, the pharmacy, and the provincial ministry. Moreover, they could write such prescriptions with a complete knowledge of the negative interactions between medications. And patients who are taking a variety of medications prescribed by different physicians could be confident that they aren't taking them in dangerous combinations.

The biggest danger with centralized, computerized health records is the potential for the abuse of privacy. Accordingly, there must be ironclad safeguards against the invasion of our personal records, and these safeguards must be more than mere legislation. There have been cases of politicians and civil servants making improper use of health records to further their own ends. We should make this impossible, not merely illegal. One way of ensuring the confidentiality of health records is through data encryption. If, for instance, my health records are encrypted, and I have one of two keys required to access the records, the other being held by the Ministry of Health, then my records could only be used with my consent and assistance.

195

This will create complications in situations where I may not be conscious or able to provide the key, but there are fall-back procedures that have been developed in the computer industry that can be adapted for such situations.

Develop an Integrated Health Management System

Before the widespread use of personal genies monitoring health on a second-by-second basis, we need to consider a system that works as follows.

The first thing you would do if you felt ill enough to want medical attention would be to call a provincial toll-free phone number. The person on the other end would be a nurse, paramedic, or possibly a physician, supported by a diagnostic computer system. He or she would confirm your identity through voiceprint or similar means, then ask you to describe your symptoms, which would be entered into the computer. Your health records, coupled with a description of your symptoms, should allow the practitioner to make a tentative diagnosis. If the condition is not severe or life-threatening, he or she might prescribe medication, and transmit the prescription to your designated local pharmacy electronically. If you need tests to clarify the diagnosis, the practitioner could send the requisition for such tests electronically, and direct you to the closest testing clinic.

If the practitioner thought that your condition was cause for immediate concern, he or she might direct you to your family doctor, a local health treatment clinic, or, in extreme cases, a hospital. If you had a life-threatening condition, you would be directed to an emergency unit, or an ambulance would be dispatched.

Rudimentary toll-free referral services are already being used by some Health Maintenance Organizations (HMOs) in the United States; in Canada, New Brunswick was first off the mark in this area.

A Two-tiered Health-care System Is Inevitable

One of the most highly prized aspects of being Canadian is our access to a universal health-care system where all are supposedly treated equally. But the reality is that a two-tiered health-care system already exists in Canada. Those who can afford it regularly jump the queue through a variety of dodges and loopholes. I know one wealthy individual, for instance, who was able to jump to the front of the line for heart bypass surgery because he had earlier donated $10,000 to the hospital. Others travel down to the United States and buy any treatment they need, off the shelf, with little or no waiting. Furthermore, Canadian physicians often recommend treatments outside of Canada, or even arrange them. So let's stop being stupidly dogmatic about this issue and tackle it head on.

Instead of pretending that a two-tiered system doesn't exist, let's design one that accomplishes what we want rather than letting our emotions control our actions. Let the rich who want to jump the queue pay extra for their treatments, so that the rest of us can be treated faster. A simple formula might be that if you want to jump the queue for heart bypass surgery, then you can do so by paying for two such operations: one for you and one for the person at the front of the queue. This way, the rich and the poor alike benefit.

By refusing to implement an officially sanctioned two-tiered system, all we do is make everybody equally miserable and reduce overall access to health services. Let me give you a specific, real-life example. A hospital in southern Ontario bought a new CT scan device, but could only operate it eight hours a day, say from 9 a.m. to 5 p.m., because of funding cutbacks. An American HMO with operations in Detroit and Buffalo asked the hospital if they could send their patients into Canada for CT scans because our hospital and technician costs are so much lower than in the United States. The Ontario hospital administrators realized that with this extra money they could amortize the cost of the machine faster, and increase the number of hours they could operate it to 12 a day. Accordingly, they proposed operating the CT scan from 7 a.m. to 7 p.m. for Canadian patients, and renting it to the American HMO from 7 p.m. to 7 a.m. By so doing, they could accommodate more Canadian patients.

The government of the day stepped in and refused to let the hospital do this. The ministry said that if the equipment was going to be used at all, it had to be used for Canadians. As a result, the hospital had to go back to operating it only eight hours a day, leaving it idle the rest of the time. I say that by all means, we should rent out the CT scanner to the Americans, or open the off-hours up for bidding to anyone prepared to pay for faster treatment. With the money generated by such an auction, hospitals could expand the hours of operation for the rest of us.

Access to physicians is another area where we need to consider new options. A doctor could start out her career being required to spend 80 percent of her working hours treating people under the provincial health insurance system. With the remaining 20 percent of her time, she would have the option to see private patients who want immediate access or more hand-holding. For this private service, she could charge any price she wished. None of the cost of those patients would come out of provincial health insurance budgets, leaving more money in government coffers for everyone else. Furthermore, perhaps 25 percent of a physician's fee from private patients might go to subsidize the provincial health insurance system. This would make private consultation distinctly more expensive than public health care, and only those who really wanted it would be willing to pay for it.

As the doctor gained experience, the percentage of her time that she could sell to private patients might go up until it reached 80 percent. By that time, the 25 percent of her fees that she paid to subsidize the provincial health insurance system would be a sizable chunk of her income, but she would still make more than if she dealt only with public patients. The health service could ask the doctor to spend the 20 percent of her time devoted to public patients treating those cases where her greater experience might be most valuable.

One of the biggest problems of our health-care system today is that there are too many doctors in the major centres, and not enough in the smaller towns and cities. To address the problem of under-serviced regions, perhaps we could divide each province into medical areas. At the beginning of each fiscal year, those areas needing physicians would auction off a three-year period. Practitioners would bid for an area by stating their capitation rate, which is a flat fee paid to a doctor for every person served by his or her medical practice, regardless of how often a patient is seen. The provincial government would then select the lowest rates bid for each given area.

The larger, more popular centres might get many bids, but would yield a practitioner much less income per patient than the smaller, less popular centres, which might offer astronomical capitation rates to practitioners who were willing to work there. This would tend to even out the distribution of practitioners while allowing them a way of increasing their incomes. To be sure, practitioners will say that such a system constrains their freedom of choice of where to live and work. But governments are going to constrain that freedom no matter how we manage the health-care system; it's merely a question of how it's constrained. Paying more to doctors who work in outlying areas has already been implemented in a limited way in Quebec and British Columbia. What I'm proposing is a mechanism that lets the market decide who works where, and how much they get paid.

We Will Be Responsible for Our Own Health

Right now, neither you nor I are accountable for our own health. In the future, when health resources will be scarce, we will have to accept at least some of the responsibility for our lifestyles. This is already the case for private insurance. You pay a lower life insurance premium if you are a nonsmoker than if you are a smoker. You pay a higher disability insurance premium if your hobbies include sky-diving and karate than if you collect stamps. This principle will slowly, and with much debate and acrimony, make its way into governmental health coverage as well.

One way this might happen is if governments were to set an insurance premium based on pessimistic assumptions; that is, they will assume that you smoke, don't exercise, and don't watch your weight. Governments could then offer everyone the opportunity to lower their insurance premiums by demonstrating that they are in a lower risk category. Hence, if you do your best to maintain a healthy lifestyle, you might pay little or nothing toward your health care. Since people's lifestyles change, your lower insurance rate would have to be renewed periodically, say every five years. No one would be required to undergo an exam to qualify for a lower insurance rate if they didn't wish to do so.

We might dislike the implicit intrusiveness of this scheme, but one way or another we will eventually be held responsible for the lifestyle choices we make.

The Bottom Line: How Long Can You Afford to Live?

Life expectancy is going to continue to expand as new technologies and new understanding of the workings of the human body improve our ability to keep people alive. It may even be possible, through genetic engineering, to halt or reverse the aging process. But the lengthening of life span is one of the major causes of the financial crisis in health care; what happens if we start tacking on another 30 or 40 years, especially as the new gene therapies are likely to be exorbitantly expensive?

Let's assume that we can solve these problems, financial as well as technical, so that you can live to 120 or more. Do you plan to go out and find a job when you're 90 because you need the money, or merely hope that the money you saved up prior to your retirement will last forever? The final answer to the question "how long will you live?" may come down to this: barring accidents and acts of God, you will live as long as your money holds out.

Is that good news or bad?

Learning: The Most
Important Industry

*"Learning faster than your competitors is the only
sustainable competitive advantage in an environment
of rapid change and innovation."*
– FUTURIST ARIE DE GEUS*

In this chapter I'm going to step outside the narrative "voice" I've used for most of this book. Elsewhere, I've tried to talk almost one-on-one about what the future will mean to you as an individual. However, the most important industry — learning — needs to be discussed in a very broad manner. What happens in education and learning will obviously have a major effect on the lives of your children and grandchildren, but it will also affect you and your ability to stay employed. So permit me, for the moment, to digress while I talk about the changes coming to the field of learning. They will, believe me, become an important part of your future life.

In a world where knowledge workers and knowledge industries are key to the success of our country and our society, learning becomes the strategic industry. Moreover, learning will have to

---

* As quoted in Peter Schwartz, *The Art of the Long View: Planning for the Future in an Uncertain World* (New York: Doubleday Currency Books, 1991), p.187.

become a permanent part of your life if you plan to keep working or stay employed. Anyone who does not relearn their business every three to five years from now on is either in a dead-end job, or is making themselves redundant.

Traditionally we've thought of learning as something kids do while they're in school, and it is certainly true that what happens in our schools is crucial to our future prosperity as a nation. In fact, if we continue to bungle that, we may not even have a future.* But learning has become a very important and fast growing industry in its own right as well. According to Peter Bouffard, president of a Canadian company in the corporate training industry, companies in North America are spending something on the order of $50 billion a year to help their employees sustain that elusive competitive advantage that de Geus talks about.

The process starts with the education of children. But what is education anyway?

The Information Pyramid and the Role of Teachers

Let's begin with a brief discussion about the purpose of libraries, librarians, and teachers. Are they merely keepers and purveyors of information, or are they something more?

One of the clearest indications that libraries are changing radically is the fact that sales of printed encyclopedias have crashed through the floor as the sales of CD-ROM encyclopedias have flourished. Why pay upwards of $1,000 for a set of books that takes up a lot of space, spends most of its time gathering dust, has no more content, and far less sex appeal, than a CD-ROM encyclopedia that costs anywhere from $30 to $100? Although there are some valid answers to this question (such as the inferior quality of the research material that goes into some of these glitzy CD encyclo-

---

* See *Facing the Future*, starting on page 32, "Our Educational System Is a Failure," for an extended discussion of this subject.

pedias), the long-term answer is that the printed reference book is rapidly dying.

But if this is happening to reference books, what does this imply for the ultimate reference centre, a library? As mentioned earlier, technology is making data much more accessible. The two main engines driving this change are CD-ROMs and the Internet, specifically the World Wide Web.

Just to give you a benchmark, a present-day CD-ROM can hold about 600 megabytes of information, which theoretically translates into roughly 100 million words (figuring an average of six characters per word), or about 1,000 books of (text only) material at 100,000 words per book. Within the next ten years, but quite possibly within the next five years, a CD-ROM of the same physical size will be able to hold perhaps ten times that quantity of information, which means you could put most present-day school libraries on a single CD-ROM. Moreover, not only could you put all the books on a single disk, but you will be able to search it much more quickly, find cross-references in a twinkle, and produce a bibliography of great depth with ease.

Turning now to the Internet, using a moderately slow modem of 28.8 kilobits per second I could theoretically download about 3,600 characters a second. This translates into 600 words a second, or a complete book about every 3 minutes. But I don't usually need a whole book at a time. If I'm looking for information of a particular sort, I can use one of the Internet search engines to locate it, then download only the information I need, whether it's in a book or not. Moreover, there are now whole libraries online, including parts of the U.S. Library of Congress, and there are commercial online libraries that you can join for $10 a month that will help you winkle out the information you need.

Libraries and librarians who try to fight against this technology, then, will have about as much success as arguing with the weather. But that doesn't mean books, libraries, and, most importantly, librarians and teachers are going to disappear. Let's start with books.

I'm an author and a futurist. Another author who is also a futurist has been predicting that books are dead, that CD-ROMs are going to take over the world. I beg to differ. I use them both, and it's plain to me that there is a time when CDs are most useful, and a time when books are most useful. For one thing, CDs are not cuddly. Books are. That may sound like a silly reason for the survival of books, but do you really want a cold, hard screen when you're lying on the beach in Hawaii, or would you rather have a soft, plump paperback? Also, not all books are, or will be, available on CD.

True, when I'm working and looking for information, the medium is of less importance than the results. In those circumstances, I'm quite happy to use a CD-ROM, the Internet, or pick up the phone and call someone who knows what I need. But, just as I want to leaf through the morning paper over my morning tea, I want to snuggle up with a book for serious thought or for pleasure. It's a tactile thing, and we are tactile beings. Anyone who doesn't acknowledge this reality is fooling himself.

It may not always be thus. We and our children have grown up with books. But the generations that follow us may not have the same fondness for what is now an increasingly antiquated form. However, for years yet to come there will be books, and they will continue to hold a place of reverence in our hearts and importance in our work.

But what of libraries? And, in particular, what of the non-fiction sections of libraries? They will change, quickly and radically — or people will stop using them, just as print encyclopedias no longer sell. If libraries are places to find information and to be educated, then they must keep up with the state of the art in information.

And, finally, what of librarians and teachers? At a conference of the World Future Society several years ago in Washington, D.C., a teacher-librarian made the point that although there are going to be a lot more needles (meaning useful pieces of information) in the future, the amount of hay (useless information) in the haystacks is rising much faster. Anyone who has spent much time on the Internet knows the truth of this statement. In my mind, the central challenge of the information age is to spin hay into gold. The transformation goes something like this.

Out of the morass of random facts that surrounds us, we must first identify those that are relevant to us, and transform them into data or statistics, depending on what we are doing. We must then interpret the data and give them structure so that they become information. We must then think about the information so that it becomes knowledge. And we must then ponder the knowledge and place it in context so that it becomes understanding, which is also called wisdom. The Book of Proverbs says that wisdom should be more highly prized than gold or jewels. This is the golden rule of the information revolution, and the global economy is enforcing it with a vengeance. It is only with understanding that we can act wisely and well to arrive at the pinnacle of the information pyramid, which is right action.

And where do the librarian and the teacher fit into this? If we see all the facts around us as being equally valuable, then there is no role for them. But if we understand the information pyramid, their role is crucial, and has two parts.

First and most importantly, teachers and librarians must lead their students to realize that there is an enormous difference between collecting random facts and attaining wisdom and right action. Secondly, teachers and librarians must inspire and assist students to move up the pyramid toward understanding and action.

Technology improves the access to facts; it does not help students reach understanding. Climbing this particular pyramid has always been one of the most difficult of human challenges: to create order out of chaos.

Education is not the memorization of facts. It is not the consumption of a defined curriculum. It is not about lectures and classrooms and books and teachers and pedagogy. Nor is it merely about skills or vocational training, although that is the trend many politicians are following. We can now buy and sell information like a commodity, and generally for a very low price. As a result, memo-

rizing facts is of limited value. Skills training will recurringly become obsolete. Education — complete education, which includes such "frills" as music and art — is much more than this.

Education is the quest to understand ourselves, the world around us, and our condition so that we can act wisely. Education is that transformation of ourselves that allows us to move from confusion and anxiety to justifiable confidence and self-esteem. Neither memorization of facts nor mere skills training permits such a transformation.

Computers, technology, and tools like interactive multimedia can be useful in helping a student make this transition, but they cannot engage what I believe is the single most important aspect of the student: his or her spirit. By themselves computers and technology can take a student only as high as the level of information in the information pyramid. Past this level it is difficult to progress toward understanding and wisdom without a guiding intellect.

Over the next 20 years, we will witness and experience the automation of education, just as most other industries have been automated. As we expand the role of technology in education, we must do so wisely. We must find ways of using machines to help teachers become more effective, not merely to replace them.

At the same time, teachers must accept the changes in the educational environment, and their changing roles within it. They must educate themselves for the changes yet to come. If they fail to do this, school systems will either brush them aside, or they will become mere time-servers until their retirement. The choice is: keep up or get out.

One way or another, public school education is going to change radically over the next 20 years — more so, perhaps, than over the last hundred. After the next two vignettes, I'll examine the causes of this change, but for now, let's look at a couple of possible future directions for childhood education.

Kevin is a 55-year-old teacher at the Pealton Board of Education, which has one of the most advanced school systems in North America in the use of technology. When the computer revolution began in education, back in the 1980s, Kevin dabbled with the primitive machines that the Pealton Board occasionally put in his classroom, but never thought much of them. Gradually, though, he became aware that the computer was evolving into a powerful pedagogical tool, so he started using the computer for those of his students who were so inclined.

By the mid-1990s, his students were routinely using the Internet for research, collaborating with their peers all over the world, and creating documents that included video clips, music they had composed themselves, and original graphic arts, as well as text. His students' literacy and numeracy skills flourished as they started to see why such skills were useful, and their abilities to invent and manage projects, singly and in teams, were far beyond those of their less fortunate peers stuck in traditional schools. These skills had been honed through years of schooling that emphasized and encouraged individual initiative and research, required cooperative teamwork on projects, and taught time- and project-management as part of the curriculum.

By the dawning of the new millennium, Kevin was in the vanguard of a new group of teachers who saw the protean potential of computers and who were actively agitating for the Pealton school board to make better use of that potential. Many of his more traditional peers, plus virtually all the union officials in his district, took offense at his activities, with the result that he found his career languishing. The principals of many schools in the region made it clear that he would not be welcome in their classrooms.

But, remarkably, some of the school board trustees started to see the technology's potential both for instruction and for cost effectiveness. Cautiously, they commissioned a number of trials in schools that were receptive to the idea. Kevin spearheaded one of these trials.

After many teething problems, the avant garde trustees finally called in some top-flight commercial trainers. At first the trainers, whose clients were primarily large corporations, didn't really understand how the education system worked, and had a completely different way of judging results than did the educators. Eventually, though, the teachers and the trainers found enough common ground that they started to make some real headway. Over the following ten years, their work swept the district, and the old guard retired, died off, or transferred out.

Today, in 2017, Kevin teaches in one of the schools he helped create. He works with students in the age brackets that used to span grades 10, 11, and 12. He has primary responsibility for about 100 students, whom he sees in rotating groups of 25 every fourth day. His 100 home-form students consider him to be "their" teacher, and he's the first person they usually contact when they have a problem relating to school. In addition, Kevin has responsibility for overseeing a number of student and community volunteer tutors in math, as well as working directly with those students having the greatest difficulty in math. Kevin's tutoring and supervisory responsibilities cover another 250 students over and above his 100 home-form students. Other teachers do nothing but tutor small groups or individual students for enrichment, special needs, or remedial help. Such tutoring is scheduled as needed.

The Pealton students come to one of three regional senior schools for one half-day out of a four-day rotation. On these days, they may receive organized in-class instruction units, or work with other class members in interactive, team-oriented, problem-solving sessions devoted to a major project. In effect, this creates eight groups of students who "time-share" the use of the school buildings. All students do most of their work either at home or at one of the child-care and education resource centres in their neighbourhood.

Each child gets an annual financial credit voucher that gives him or her access to a minimum standard of educational resources. Children who work at home instead of one of the education resource centres can use these vouchers to rent a computer-based workstation for a 12-month period. They also have prepaid access to public facilities for such activities as extracurricular sports, art, music, drama, woodworking, and more.

These facilities and their instructors are also available to the general public on a fee basis, which means that teenaged students often share facilities and classes with adult learners and college students. Parents were concerned about this mixed use of facilities at first. Now, however, everyone in the community realizes that splitting costs between schools and the community at large helps finance facilities that neither would be able to afford on their own. Moreover, adding more mature students to the classes offers students more diversity, makes the classwork more interesting, and offers relevant insights from the outside world to students who will soon be leaving the public school system.

Gina, one of Kevin's students, spends most of her school time working at her own speed at home. Her computer genie, Tik-Tok, monitors the amount of time she spends on her studies, follows her progress, lets her choose from a menu of then-current assignments, and keeps Kevin posted on her progress. In conjunction with John Dewey, the school's central computer system, Tik-Tok makes sure that Gina covers all the necessary core material, and knows it well, before giving her access to more advanced material. Kevin can monitor Gina's performance, both through the results of exercises that Gina does at her workstation, and by witnessing recorded sessions of Gina at work. Gina knows that such recordings take place, and is informed of her teacher's assessments of them. Kevin and Gina see each other in person every fourth day, when she is at the school, talk by videophone frequently, and, of course, Gina can ask Tik-Tok to connect her to Kevin anytime she's having difficulty.

After the preliminary trials proved the underlying concepts, but before the board switched to this system, the Pealton Regional School Board researched the work being done in commercial training. As a result of their trials and research, they reached several conclusions about computer-assisted learning: 1) the large majority of students can work through a given subject curriculum in about two-thirds the time it takes for a normal classroom lecture presentation when they use a well-designed, self-paced, computer-based system; 2) students avoid being labelled as a "brown-nose," a "dummy," or anything else, because each one's path through his or her schooling is unique; and 3) students generally find it more interesting than sitting in class listening to a teacher. The results have been both gratifying and to most traditionalists — especially most teachers — highly surprising.

The first question visitors to a Pealton school usually ask is how the district was able to finance all the equipment, classrooms, and day-care facilities. Many school facilities are shared with outside groups. Corporations, for instance, rent the use of those workstations located in public facilities during evenings and weekends, and use the meeting halls and theatre facilities for conferences and commercial training sessions.

Because the six large regional schools — three junior and three senior — are time-shared by the students, the district incurs much lower costs for maintenance and upkeep than for the 27 small neighbourhood schools it used to operate. Moreover, the district was able to sell off the old land and buildings, and placed the proceeds in a trust fund, the income of which is used to subsidize operations. The district pays an annual fee to the Pealton Regional Transit Commission to provide bussing to and from school for those children under the age of 12 who are not within walking distance. Since the school board is subsidizing existing transit facilities, its costs are far lower than running special school buses.

This dramatic change in school structure is only possible because automation finally came to education, just as it did to every other major industry in the world. As a result, much of the money for courseware purchases and development came from declining staff levels, including fewer teachers.

The number of teachers and the amount of in-class time for each group of students decreases with each grade. Grade 1 students have a lot of direct contact with teachers, spend a lot of time in class, and the student-teacher ratio is generally lower than that of late-twentieth-century schools. Students in their last years of high school, on the other hand, have very high student-teacher ratios, and spend a lot of time in self-directed study, much as university students did in earlier eras. At first, lowering staffing levels was done by a combination of attrition or offering inducements for early retirement. However, teacher attrition has become a major factor now that the baby boom teachers are retiring in great numbers, but is not a problem because the board planned for it well ahead of time. Schools started the switch-over to a computer-based system with the incoming grade 1 class in 2003, following the early field trials. Each year the schools added another grade, so that whichever system the students started with, they stayed with throughout their schooling.

The learners' workstations are one of the highest on-going expenses of the system. The usable life of a workstation is four years. The workstations become obsolete within two, but are still perfectly functional for four years with proper maintenance.

Accordingly, new workstations are always given to the more senior students first as they have the most sophisticated needs, and require more resources than younger students. As the workstations age, they are given to less demanding younger students. At the end of four years, they are sold or scrapped.

However, the school district owns none of the workstations. Instead, it leases them from the manufacturer, which acts as a "hardware publisher," assembling the equipment from standard computer and communications components that it buys in quantity for this contract. The cost of a standard workstation, including the desk, computer, monitor, keyboard, software, and communications equipment, is about $1,450. Amortized over four years, including interest costs and fees for service, maintenance, and support, this works out to about $500 per student per year.

Courseware is not included in this price. The workstations present course material using interactive multimedia (IMM), a combination of text, audio, graphics, photographs, and video that require the student's participation to progress through it. Enrichment materials are always available for those students who want it or show an aptitude for it, as well as remedial or supplementary materials for those who need it. When students need such materials, and contact with a living human being is most appropriate, then the student's genie schedules a videophone connection automatically — usually immediately, but sometimes by appointment.

Students with special needs have all the workstation resources of the regular students, but, depending on their needs, often get much more personal attention from a combination of teachers and specially trained tutors as well. Moreover, when they do use their workstations, the learning materials are tailored to their needs, and provide teaching aids designed with children like them in mind.

Pealton started the development of courseware on its own, but about ten years ago an international conference established a global standard for IMM materials to allow for easy translation from one language to another, and to permit materials to be independent of the hardware that runs it. As a result, the Pealton Board can now pick and choose from a wide variety of courseware available in a global market.

No system is perfect, kids still fall through the cracks, and there are still some problems with student behaviour. But, by and large, the students are happier, more interested, make better progress, and cause fewer problems than in traditional schools. Teachers are carefully selected, form an elite corps, and spend their time doing what they enjoy doing most — mentoring and working intensively, one-on-one, with individual students. Moreover, teachers spend much of their time on enrichment materials, not merely remedial work. They do virtually no paperwork, as their computer genies handle all the administrivia for them. They love their jobs, and find it intensely fulfilling.

The Metro Board
The Metro School Board is still mired in the nineteenth-century model of schooling. They resist the idea of supporting teachers with computers, contending that computers can't teach, only teachers can teach. They ignore the central truth of education: teachers don't teach at all, but rather students learn and teachers help them. It is demonstrably true that computers, properly used, can also help students learn, although not with the flexibility or empathy of a human being.

As they have resisted the trend to automation, the Metro Board schools are now in a bad way because of the aging of the population, and the top-heavy structure of their teaching staff. Payrolls are loaded with aging, soon-to-retire baby boomers at the top of their pay scales, but there is an insufficient number of younger teachers to carry on after them because the board doesn't have enough money to hire new teachers. Class sizes are obscene, with even some grade 1 classes having 50 or more students. Not only are extra resources sparse, but students have to share the aging textbooks, especially in schools where the parents are unwilling or unable to buy textbooks for their own children. There are still a few extracurricular activities, but this is entirely due to the dedication of the teachers involved, and despite the lack of decent resources available.

Community support for the school system is at an all-time low. Not only is the rapidly growing retired population largely unsympathetic to the needs of school-age children — which has generally been true of the elderly through most of recent history — but the poor performance and shabby appearance of the Metro schools have caused those parents who could do so either to move out of the district, or to put their children in private schools. The net result is that voters and elected officials repeatedly deny requests for additional funds to improve the schools.

Hostility, boredom, and hopelessness are the dominant attitudes among the students who are forced to remain. The teachers gave up long ago. Those who could moved to more hospitable schools in other districts. Those who couldn't have turned into time-servers, waiting resignedly until they can collect their pensions, then leaving. The only new teachers willing to enter the system are those who couldn't find employment elsewhere, and the naively idealistic, most of whom leave, burned out, after a couple of years. The situation is bad, and getting progressively worse.

Both of these vignettes are caricatures intended to emphasize the many challenges ahead for our education systems, especially demographics, technology, and declining government funding. I have tried to illustrate both the problems and the possibilities ahead of us, and although it is not my intent, some will choose to infer that I am glorifying technology from my first vignette. Technology is a wild card, a dangerous force we have yet to harness in education, as I will make clear later on. Nor do I believe that mine is the only answer, or even necessarily the best answer; it is merely one possible answer.

In my opinion, the second vignette is the most likely if we continue today's policies, for it merely extrapolates trends that are already firmly in place. Accordingly, we will have to change how we run our schools, whether we want to or not. Since we will be forced to change, why not look for new solutions and new opportunities along the way?

The model we are currently using in education is the mass production system first introduced in 1892 to manufacture watches. We take a batch of raw material — say, 30 children — and move them into the first workstation. There we process them through the grade 1 curriculum. Next we move them to the second workstation, where we process them through the grade 2 curriculum. Then we move them to the grade 3 workstation ... and so on.

But industry is moving away from the mass production model of manufacturing. Instead, it is moving toward a mass customization model, where each product will be unique but produced at a mass production price. Industry can do this by computer-assisted design and automated manufacturing processes.

As a society, we should be moving toward an individually customized model for education. As discussed earlier in the book, the individuals who emerge into the workplace in the future will need to carve their own ways in the world. They will need to be entrepreneurial, creative, innovative, and bring their own unique gifts to work and to life. You cannot instill these qualities in students through mass production education. I believe that we will need a system where each student receives a unique education that coaxes forth their inner talents and creativity. This does not mean that the curriculum won't contain core material that is common to all students. After all, even a mass customization car factory still produces only cars, not airplanes or lollipops. But by seeking out and teaching to the individual talents of students, we are much more likely to engage their interest.

When students are interested and involved in their education, there is no need to drag them through it. Instead, they pull you forward: "My high-end students ... thrive on challenge, want to be pushed, need to know as much as possible,"* said Barbara Ramsay Orr, a veteran English teacher, writing in the *Globe and Mail* in praise of that minority of her students who are not necessarily smarter than past students, but whom she finds to be more willing to work hard because it interests them.

Unfortunately, the percentage of her motivated students represents a declining minority: "I've been teaching secondary school longer than I care to admit. In the past few years, I have had the most inspiring students of my career; also some of the most soul-destroying. And the scary thing is, I think the Luddites are beginning to outnumber the committed learners." She concludes her essay by saying, "We can no longer afford to spend diminishing tax dollars in unproductive ways."

Nor is Ms. Orr alone in thinking that something is wrong. Several commentators have made similar comments, such as Harvard professor Michael Porter in *Canada at the Crossroads: The Reality of a New Competitive Environment*, a special report commissioned by the Government of Canada and the Business Council on National Issues. In this report, Dr. Porter noted that although the Canadian education system is one of the most expensive, per capita, in the world, it does not produce results commensurate with its cost: "Canada's illiteracy rate stands at 24 percent, and more than 30 percent of young people drop out of school before receiving high school

---

* "The growing divide in education," *Globe and Mail*, July 4, 1996, p. A16.

diplomas. The level of advanced skills — critical to sustaining and upgrading sources of competitive advantage for Canadian industry — is inadequate" (page 49).

So our education system is inadequate and we need to change it. **217** Moreover, as I'll describe later in the chapter, there are forces at work that are going to place increasing pressure on the education system to change. But there are a lot of barriers to change. Indeed, our education system is probably the single social institution in our society with the greatest resistance to structural change.

The First Barrier: Our Balkanized System

The first barrier to structural change is the way our education system is organized. At present, education is a provincial responsibility, but local school boards run the schools, with predictable results: some schools are great, some are terrible, and most are in between. And, of course, every school board believes that it is one of the great ones while freely admitting that someone should do something about all those other boards. As a result, education systems are balkanized, and almost impervious to innovation.

This situation may be starting to change. In New Brunswick and Nova Scotia, the provincial governments have abolished local school boards, and Ontario has gutted the local school board system while trying to pretend it hasn't. Is this a good thing or a bad thing? That depends. New Brunswick took control of school boards primarily as part of a provincial government strategy to drag the education system into the twenty-first century, a transition Premier Frank McKenna is trying to encourage the entire province to make. In Ontario, by contrast, it looks as if structural reform in education is being done as part of a provincial tax-grab, with the provincial government swapping responsibilities with municipalities in order to take money out of Toronto schools, and improve the provincial financial position in the process.

Revamping the governance structure of education could go a long way toward breaking the logjam that surrounds education. Progress and useful innovation will happen only if we give more instructional autonomy to principals and teachers within a defined framework. There is a real danger, however, that such reform will merely deliver the education system into the hands of the bureaucrats at the provincial ministries. The reason this is dangerous is that these bureaucrats are long on theory, but do not have to stand up in front of 30 bored and listless kids and make the theory work. As a result, our provincial ministries have a long and sorry history of handing down edicts about how teachers should teach that are pure non-sense. This makes the teachers' already difficult jobs something approaching impossible.

Moreover, moving the authority and responsibility to the provincial level could create real problems for parents. If your son or daughter is having a problem at school, and the principal is not responding to his or her needs, do you go to the Minister of Education for redress? In response, "parent councils" are being proposed to act as local governing bodies. This sounds great, but such councils run the risk of becoming mere rubber stamps for those principals who sweet-talk or baffle them, or turning into witch hunts run by parents who have private agendas and an ax to grind. Worse, many schools will not be able to find enough interest among the parents to produce a governing council. What happens then?

Accordingly, education ministries will have to centralize the functions of school boards carefully and intelligently, or such moves will be an unmitigated disaster.

Teachers' Unions

I write a regular column about the future of education for *Teach* magazine, which is published for Canadian educators. The reason I write this column (which I do essentially for free) is that I am concerned about the future of our education system. What's more, I've said so on several occasions, and in many different ways. In reply, I get letters from teachers who agree or disagree with one point or another of my columns. Virtually all the letters I get agree with my fundamental premise that there are many things wrong with our education system — except for the letters I get from representatives of teachers' unions.

Some teachers' unions put out propaganda to the effect that the Canadian education system is terrific and getting better, that the students love the teachers and vice-versa, and everyone involved in education is doing ground-breaking work. Farmers on the Prairies use that kind of stuff on their fields to ensure good harvests.

Some of the teachers' unions will fight any change in the structure and organization of the education system. They want the status quo. They can't have it, but they can make the road to change a difficult and bumpy one.

In March 1993, I was a guest on CBC-Radio's *Morningside* program, along with a couple of school principals and the president of a teachers' union. The subject was the use of computers in the schools. The researchers at CBC-Radio had asked me to participate because I'm familiar with computers and some of their applications in schools, and because I believe we have used them badly so far. My role was to be the informed skeptic; however, I found myself defending the potential of computers because of the strong anti-technology bias of the head of the teachers' union. Her attitude seemed to be that computers were no good, never could be any good, and those who liked them were just *bad people*. Faced with such an unreasonable attitude, I found myself forced into the contrary view.

Incidentally, the responses *Morningside* subsequently got from listeners pretty uniformly vilified me for my obvious stupidity at suggesting that computers had a place in our schools, which brings me to my next obstacle.

Public Expectations

The general public is largely uninformed about what is and is not happening in the education systems in Canada. What they do know

is that they are not satisfied. As a result, there are calls for reforms, some of which are appropriate, but many of which are dangerous. In particular, many parents — and politicians and commentators — say they want the education system to go "back to basics." What this really means is that they want their kids to learn the same things they learned, and in the same ways.

But the world isn't the place it was 20 or 30 years ago, and what was taught then is not what we should be teaching now. Our schools are still educating students to fit into a mass production world, and we cannot afford to allow this to continue. There are no more time-server jobs out there, so we can no longer afford schools that produce time-serving students. Today's and tomorrow's students need to be actively involved in their own education. Active involvement includes selecting and structuring what they study. Is this possible? I believe it is — because it's being done elsewhere, as we'll see later in the chapter.

But before we leave this point, let me say that one of the structural problems we are going to face is public opinion about education. This means that to move the system forward, we are going to have to educate ourselves.

Computers as Stumbling Blocks

It's common knowledge today that "to err is human, but to really foul things up takes a computer." Making computers work, and making them workable within our schools is going to be a major undertaking. This is especially true as only a fraction — perhaps 20 percent — of teachers are comfortable and educated in the use of computers. Without an informed and enthusiastic teacher population supporting the use of computers, computers in the classroom become a black hole, sucking up money, instruction time, emotional energy, and parental goodwill, and giving little or nothing in return.

The use of computers for "Computer Aided Teaching" (CAT) or "Computer Aided Learning" (CAL) goes back more than 20 years. Almost all such systems fall into the "drill and kill" school, where the computer acts like an automated page-turning and quiz-producing device with the intention of shovelling information into the mind of the student by mindless repetition. This is a bad, boring, soul-destroying use of computers.

More recently, as computers have gained ground in business, and as competition for jobs and incomes has risen, parents have become eager for their kids to learn "computer literacy" to give them a vocational leg-up on their peers. But, as noted in chapter 1, computers are going to change so radically that today's computers will be obsolete long before most of today's kids are in the work force.

Then there are all those cute commercial learning programs, complete with multimedia, sounds, graphics, animation, and quizzes. But most of these are just "drill and kill" exercises with jazzier effects. Sugarcoating a bad idea is worse than a bad idea on its own because it is more seductive. Multimedia does not equal quality.

CD-ROM reference materials have more potential. These are random access materials that can accommodate useful search engines. Children can move through such material at their own pace, and the search engines help them find things that are relevant to their work and interests. Such activity needs to be directed — say, under a teacher's guidance — but CD-ROM reference materials are better than the other alternatives I've talked about so far, and potentially of some value. Of course, the biggest problem is that the text encyclopedias that undergird the most popular CD-ROM reference works, for instance, are often second-rate encyclopedias that have been tarted up with multimedia. At present, form exceeds substance — but it's closer to what will eventually be useful.

The Internet is better still. The Net offers random access to a

221

good chunk of the world's knowledge. The problem is that at least 80 percent of the material that appears on the Net is either garbage (which includes both things like pornography and poorly presented, inaccurate, or useless information), or self-serving commercialism (an ever-increasing percentage of the whole). Still, the remaining 20 percent may be invaluable, and as the total amount of information on the Net continues to rise, so will the quantity of useful information. The ability to access information and resources from your home or school that would otherwise be difficult or impossible to obtain is of tremendous value. Someone researching nanotechnology, for example, will have a hard time finding more than three or four books in any public library in the country. Yet, when I last ran a search on the World Wide Web, I found over 6,600 entries. Most of these were serious discussions about this emerging field.

Being able to "chat" with people all over the world is an even more useful element of the Net. A few schools around the world are starting to exchange information, and the experience is certainly broadening kids' horizons. I know of one grade 7 class in the Toronto area that is working on a joint project with a similar class in Germany. The ability to construct a realistic "world view" improves dramatically when kids can connect with people in other places. This same grade 7 class writes music using computers, which they submit for comment and suggestion to a group of university-level music students via the Net.

The best use of computers today is as tools or enabling technologies that allow students to do work they would be unable to do using traditional means. Students at River Oaks School in Oakville, Ontario, use computers casually and pervasively. Computers are widely available, but are not the focus of study. Instead, they are merely one means of several for pursuing educational ends. At River Oaks, there are a few computers in the lower grades, mostly used to teach writing skills, and many in the higher grades.

In the grade 8 classroom where I worked on a project with the

1995-96 class, there was a MIDI (Musical Instrument Digital Interface) processor hooked to a keyboard that allowed them to create and score their own music, and then use it in presentations. They used ClarisWorks, a combination word processor, graphics program, spreadsheet, and database, to create documents. There was an Ethernet LAN (Local Area Network) running through the school that was tied into the Internet through York University, so they could have immediate, high-speed Internet access. And they used Macromedia Director, the standard program used by multimedia industry professionals, to create multimedia presentations — such as the CD-ROM that I worked on with them.

All the equipment and software used at River Oaks will be obsolete within three years at most, during which time it will be replaced as part of the school's normal operating budget. But the ability to perform sophisticated research, and then turn it into documents of great fluidity, structure, and interest at a level close to that of multimedia professionals, as these grade school students do, instills an enormous sense of accomplishment and self-esteem. It's not the paraphernalia that's of importance. It's the ability to achieve that's important.

Finally, what about IMM — interactive multimedia — the key technology in my "tale of two school systems"? That's a bit like saying, "What about books?" Bad books are bad. Good books are fantastic. IMM is like that, only magnified. The ability to experience a subject using the medium that conveys it best is a great advantage — if it is used well, and not merely to make the lesson sexier. Moreover, IMM allows students to see and experience events and practice skills they might never be able to afford, or have the opportunity to experience in the normal course of their schooling.

"Tactile sense and experiential learning are internalized more rapidly and more permanently than any other method," says Ray Harpell, vice-president and general manager of Performx Inc., a commercial training organization based in New Brunswick.

Translating the technical jargon, this means that letting a student participate actively helps him learn faster, and retain knowledge better, than merely reading about it. Mr. Harpell speaks from his own experience as he used to create such training materials for the military, and now does it for Performx clients. "If a trainee reads about what happens if you do something wrong and winds up crashing your jet plane, that's one thing. But if they try it themselves, and end up causing a crash in a simulation, they sure as hell as are going to remember it." But IMM and the computers to run them are expensive. And that brings us to the ultimate stumbling block to change in the education system.

Money

While the pension and health management systems are being hit because of the aging population, the education system is getting hit with a double whammy. Right now, school-age populations are expanding because the children of the baby boom are flooding the system. This tide will crest sometime around the 1998-99 school year (with local variations) for the entering kindergarten classes, and will then take about 13 years to work its way through the schools — the classic "pig in a snake" image often used to depict the demographic bulge of the baby boomers. Accordingly, costs are rising, class sizes are increasing, and kids are being crammed into classrooms.

At the same time, the baby boom teachers are entering their highest earning years. Ranging in age from 50 at the high end to 30 at the low, boomers form the large majority of teachers in the system. Most teachers in Canada have the option to take early retirement according to a formula, typically where the teacher's age plus years of service add up to about 90 (it can be higher or lower, depending on the school board). If a teacher started teaching at age

24, for example, then she would reach the magic 90 figure at age 57. That means that at age 50 she will be approaching her maximum earnings, two or three times the salary of a new teacher just out of teacher's college.

She may be worth the extra money. Studies have shown that experienced teachers are the single most important factor in determining the success of children's education. But let's leave aside the question of worth for the moment and look only at overall education budgets.

The bulge of baby boomers' children working its way through our schools means that costs will start reaching the maximum at or shortly after the year 2000, and will then start to ease off — just in time for salaries of those teachers at the leading edge of the baby boom to start hitting their maximums around 2003. The average baby boom teacher will reach the age of optional retirement at about 2013, which will create a final, national peak in teacher costs at or before that year. Moreover, both class sizes and total teacher costs will only subside slowly after they hit their peaks.

Now let's look at what's happening in the surrounding society. Because of steadily rising competition from emerging countries, our economic growth is not as high as it was in the decades between 1960 and 1990. More people are falling into the category of unemployables. According to Statistics Canada, real incomes have stagnated over the last 20 years. And the rising number of retirees and elderly people means that government expenditures on health care and pensions are gobbling up budgets.

As a result, school budgets, tight though they may seem right now, are just starting to come under the pressure they will eventually experience. Our schools are going to be in deep trouble if we try to run them the way we have in the past because the money available per student is going to continue to shrink. Something has to change.

The Danger

According to people in the commercial training industry, such as Harpell of Performx, five years ago it took something like 1,200 person-hours to create one hour of computer-based training. Today it takes from 300 to 600 person-hours. The reasons for the drop in cost are the tremendous improvement in the authoring tools that are now available, coupled with the accumulation of knowledge and the expertise of people working in the field. This drop will continue as tools and expertise continue to improve.

To create an entire public school curriculum using IMM would be enormously expensive, and although no one would expect students to spend all their time in front of a computer, let's use that possibility as an illustration. To create enough IMM material for an entire grade 6 curriculum, for example, would take:

- 180 days/school year x 6 instruction hours/day = 1,080 instruction hours
- 1,080 instruction hours x 600 person-hours/instruction hour = 648,000 person-hours.

That's a lot of person-hours, and even more money.

But then again, how many grade 6 teachers are there in Canada? Well, there are approximately 285,000 public school teachers in Canada, which means that there is something on the order of 22,000 grade six teachers, figuring that grade 6 employs approximately one-thirteenth of the total number of teachers. Each grade 6 teacher tries to achieve roughly the same thing with their students over the course of the year as they work through the grade 6 curriculum. Accordingly, to teach the grade 6 curriculum, we currently spend:

- 22,000 teachers x 1,080 instruction hours/year = 23,760,000 person-hours/year.

This means, approximately, that you could afford to finance more than 36 hours of IMM instruction for each hour of teacher instruction you could replace — which could give you an awful lot of choices for each student in a mass customized education system. And that's just for the first year. As long as the curriculum doesn't change radically (and it should change only gradually from one year to the next), in the second year the IMM materials are effectively free, having already been paid for in year one. In contrast, you would have to pay 25,000 teachers all over again to teach the same hours of instruction as they did the year before.

Of course, you would have to have a workstation for each student, but as my first vignette illustrated, this could be financed. Workstations for a class of 30 students, including the costs of maintenance, might cost about $15,000 a year, or less than half the salary of an average teacher.

This spells revolution in education, because sooner or later some education bureaucrat who is more concerned with budget than with children is going to work his way through the arithmetic and clatter down to the office of his boss, the politician. The politician will take 30 minutes to work the arithmetic given above, finally give up and accept her underling's assurances that the numbers are right, and schedule a press conference. In the press conference, the minister of education will rear up and announce a "bold, new initiative" to bring your province into a new era, and wreak absolute havoc on the education system.

There's more to education than budget and curriculum — but I'm not sure that all ministries of education know that, and therein lies the danger. We are facing major budgetary problems in our education system — and a neat, convenient solution pops into view that seems to offer salvation. It even smacks of hi-tech, and feeds into the demand for computer literacy. Just replace teachers with machines and we can start taking money out of education and using it for more important things, like pensions and health care!

You can see why I'm worried. You should be worried, too, because if the bureaucrats go after the schools without proper preparation and consultation, they may well destroy your children's education.

Earlier I seemed to advocate the use of computers and IMM, and fewer teachers and schools. I do advocate these things partly because I don't see any choice, and partly because I don't see any other way to create a system that produces individually customized education (although such alternatives may exist). But I am also aware that this is a dangerous path, and one that we should undertake with extreme care.

However, the path before us has already been travelled by others, and we could save ourselves an enormous amount of pain if we have the wit to ask what they have learned.

Commercial Training

Commercial training people and public education people don't talk to each other. In fact, they don't even want to be in the same room at the same time. Public educators think that commercial trainers are shallow, soulless, money-grubbing hucksters who don't understand the nobility of the profession of teaching, and ultimately don't care about what happens to their students as long as they get paid. Commercial trainers think that educators are wastrels who inhabit a domain of petty politics that operates on emotion instead of reason, and who insist on doing things the same inefficient way teachers have done them for thousands of years because that's the only way they can protect their unionized, featherbedded jobs. There are elements of truth on both sides, but there is also a lot they could teach each other. Having looked at public education and where it's going, let's look at the future of commercial training.

Remember sitting at your desk at school when you were a kid? Remember feeling bored, thinking that the day would never end, and just waiting for the final bell to ring to signal your freedom for the day? This is the way most of us felt through a good part of our school careers. Why should we repeat that experience when there's a better way to learn? Some time in the next 20 years you will need to brush up on some of the skills you need for your work, perhaps in a fashion similar to the following vignette.

229

Benedict looks up from his work as Beatrice, his genie, informs him that co-worker Jane Symmons is calling. It turns out that Jane has been having trouble dealing with difficult customers on the phone, and is not getting the success rate she wants. Since Benedict is one of the most highly rated people in the company for dealing with difficult customers, Jane is calling to ask him for some tutoring on the subject. Benedict readily agrees, remembering how Jane had tutored him on some of the finer points of profit accounting last year.

They arrange for Beatrice to record some of Benedict's conversations when he's dealing with difficult clients, and then transmit them to Jane so that Jane and Benedict can talk about what he did, and why he did it that way. Then they'll arrange for Benedict to audit some of Jane's calls so they can discuss them afterward.

Once their arrangements are complete, Benedict goes back to the courseware he's been working his way through. This module is five hours long, and it deals with the theory and practice of developing corporate strategy, as Benedict wants to start taking on more managerial tasks within the company.

This process of peer mentoring is one part of ThinkStart Software's Virtual University program. The Virtual University only exists in cyberspace; it has no physical existence. ThinkStart has more than 500 employees spread over four time zones, and could not afford to provide the level of training it does if they had to pull each employee away from his work, fly him to another city, and house and feed him in a hotel. Instead, employees can take courses whenever they choose right from their workstations at home or in their regional offices.

The company enrolls each employee in Virtual U. when they join the company, and puts them through an orientation course at their workstations. They learn that there are more than 200 course modules available to them, ranging from half-hour refresher courses, to 23-hour courses that they can take over a series of days. They are free to choose whichever course they want from the corporate menu, and to take it whenever it would be most useful for them. Typically, an employee will choose a course right after he realizes that he needs the knowledge the course provides. Because employees study a subject right after they've had a problem with it, their retention rates are sky high.

Management developed the original menu in conjunction with HighPer Training, a professional training company, but has since added new courses suggested by the employees themselves. Employees can take up to 40 hours of training a year at no charge, and can have as much additional training as they wish to pay for at a cost of $75 an hour, which merely recoups the cost of the courseware development.

The courses are linked to the company's performance measurement system. When ThinkStart originally hired HighPer, the training firm scheduled a two-day, online conference with management and as many employees as could attend. At this conference, they got management to articulate what they wanted to see the company achieve, their strategic reasons for wanting these things, and what they would need to achieve them. They were candid about their financial position, limitations, and expectations, and made available their entire thinking about the direction the industry was going, their concerns about their competitors, and what they thought was going on with their clients and the marketplace. They also revealed all the inner workings of the company so that the employees knew how sales were made, how the company made its profits, and how employee compensation fit into the picture. HighPer had made it clear that the days of restricted disclosure of information were over; every employee who was worthy of working for the company needed to know exactly what was going on, and what it meant. It's only in this way that the people who make up the company can move forward together.

After management had their say, the employees were asked to set overall performance targets. When management felt that the targets were not high enough to allow the company to achieve its goals, they said so, and asked the employees to consider whether there was some way they could raise the targets, and if there were some resources or support that would allow them to do so. If targets seemed unrealistically high, HighPer broke them down to average daily work performance goals for each employee, then compared them to current performance goals. If employees still felt they wanted to aim for those targets, management accepted the targets. Otherwise, they revised them. Eventually everyone reached a consensus about how much each person was going to do and when.

Next, HighPer Training worked with employees to identify the competencies they needed in skills, knowledge, and attitude, and determined how they could measure their level of competency in every area. The training system measures each employee in every task relevant to his or her job, and delivers the results to each employee every day. If performance starts to fall below the targets the employees have set for themselves, their performance charts tell them where.

They can then either take IMM courses or refreshers to build up their skills, learn from the experiences of their peers in online video chat groups devoted to that competency, ask for mentoring help, as Jane just did with Benedict, or take part in an online video conference course that is scheduled according to demand,

and which includes a live instructor as well as IMM materials.

If an employee does not correct a problem on his own initiative, management will intervene and ask if there is something they can do to help. This is rare, however; it typically happens when an employee is experiencing personal problems outside of work. Then management arranges counselling or other support if the employee wishes. If the employee doesn't improve his performance, the work group will eventually be the one to ask him to leave, not management.

Employees get a relatively low base salary, about enough to pay for groceries and the mortgage, but they also participate in two bonus pools: one tied to overall company profitability and the other tied to their work group's performance. Management pays bonuses monthly based on the average results of the last six months. Management and employees have agreed on a schedule of bonuses for the specified targets. If they exceed targets and profits increase, the bonus pools grow larger, too. Theoretically, there is no ceiling on bonuses.

Although the money is nice, it is the mutually supportive, collegial atmosphere of working for the company, coupled with each employee feeling in control of his or her own destiny and the ability to achieve satisfying results that makes them as enthusiastic as they are. Their training is not separate from their work, it's an integral part of their jobs. They call it "just-in-time learning," and it makes a big difference to their working lives.

Imagine being able to learn what you need to know, when you need it. Imagine working on your own with a computer, comparing notes with other people to learn from their experiences, and getting more traditional instruction when you think you need it, all without leaving your home or office. Do you think you'd find it easier and more interesting to learn new things?

Although this is only one possible future scenario for commercial training, much of it comes not from tomorrow, but from what some of the firms at the leading edge of the field are working on today.

Learning in the workplace is big business today, but the learning business itself hasn't changed much since the days of Aristotle. "Most corporate learning still takes place with an instructor lecturing a room full of employees," says Peter Bouffard, president of Fredericton-based Performx Inc. "This can be an expensive and inefficient way of delivering information."

When Air Canada pilots go for refresher courses on flight operations relating to the exterior inspection of an Airbus A320, Boeing 767, or any of three other aircraft, they now do it sitting at a computer terminal rather than out on the tarmac, because of work done by Performx. Performx is working on a $13-million contract for Air Canada to produce a series of learning systems using interactive multimedia, including pilot refresher courses.

IMM delivers course material through a multimedia computer that might cost $3,000 — less than the cost to fly a single student to another city and feed and house him for the duration of a single course. Individuals can work their way through new material at their own pace, and at a convenient location. Plus, for the flight operations course described above, Air Canada doesn't have to keep an expensive aircraft on the ground for instruction purposes. As a bonus, almost all the material gathered for the pilots' course can be reused in courseware for external inspections by mechanics. This dramatically cuts the course production costs.

Although it can be hard to get precise measurements, a variety of corporate applications shows that computer-based training (CBT) can cut instruction time by at least 25 percent over comparable classroom instruction. Executives with their eyes firmly on the bottom line are convinced that computer-based training is a good investment. As an article in the *Journal of the American Management Association (JAMA)* points out:

Ernst & Young conducted its own test to rate the effectiveness of interactive multimedia over classroom learning. To judge both types of training, it gave the same test to students who completed its one-day auditing class as it did to those taking its three-and-a-half-hour desktop program. The results? [The] students taking the interactive course scored 20 percent to 25 percent higher than those having classroom training. (February 1995, page 17)

I've sat next to people on planes who spent the flight working on multimedia course materials, accomplishing something interesting and worthwhile with time that they might otherwise have felt was of marginal value.

IMM can also select the best media to convey information. This means a technician can hear the sound of a properly tuned jet engine, see a 3-D diagram of its construction, manipulate the parts on the screen, scroll through the maintenance procedures, and watch a video of the engine being serviced, either step-by-step in stop-action, or at normal speeds, all without leaving his workstation. The computer can also present supplementary materials if the student needs them, or call a human instructor for help if the problem is beyond the system's capabilities. Aside from straight instruction, IMM can also involve the student in simulations of real-life situations and let them learn experientially as well as theoretically. American retailer JCPenney found that by being able to simulate customer encounters, they were able to help their customer service representatives reach peak proficiencies in a third less time than classroom training would have taken, according to the previously cited article in *JAMA*.

Some critics describe CBT as little more than "electronic page turning," effectively just an expensive way of putting a printed manual on a computer screen. Indeed, many companies that have tried computer-based instruction tools in the past have been left with a bad taste in their mouths. But CBT has changed dramatically since 1990. First, costs and the time it takes to develop CBT materials have dropped dramatically. Next, multimedia are far more adaptable than text-based materials. Printed texts take a long time to produce, print, and distribute, and can cost thousands of dollars to replace. Multimedia can be downloaded immediately by modem to a recordable CD or network server, and reproduced at a cost of about $1 per disk. This facility allows corporations to update all or any part of their instruction materials quickly and easily. Plus it's easy to keep materials up-to-date by corporate Intranet.

Not all is rosy in IMM, though, and IMM is not necessarily suited to every learning application. "It's easy to create multimedia courseware that looks snazzy," comments George Doherty, Performx's vice-president of business development. "But without the underlying instructional design, the knowledge of *how*, *what*, and *when* to teach, all you have is a flashy, expensive video. It's like when desktop publishing first came out, there was a rash of horrible newsletters produced by people who had no background in graphic design or editing."

Moreover, because the overhead costs in developing IMM courseware can be high, the best situations for IMM are those where there is a large number of geographically dispersed students, a complex or high-risk work environment, or a continuously changing market. Bob Blalock, director of learning technologies at AMR, parent corporation of American Airlines, estimates that producing courseware in multimedia format is more cost-effective than classroom training whenever there are more than 300 students (*JAMA*, February 1995, page 19).

The Virtual University

As well as working with Air Canada's pilots and other personnel, New Brunswick's Performx Inc. is also creating a virtual university for a San Diego software developer. This California company has 500 people spread over a wide geographic region, and believes that continuing education is crucial to its ability to compete in the fast-paced, cutthroat software business. They wanted to set up a university-like environment where their employees could study the materials they needed when it was convenient.

"There are three factors in establishing a virtual university," says Bouffard of Performx. "Content, pedagogy, and community. The content is straightforward and identified by the client. The pedagogy is important, but we know how to do that from our years of experience in other commercial projects. The interesting part has been to foster a sense of community. Some of the most important learning comes from shooting the breeze with people who do the same things you do, and getting their angle on how to tackle a particular problem."

The best way to learn one kind of competency may not be the best way to learn another, and different people learn best in different ways. As a result, Performx, using their client's Intranet to transmit the materials, is offering a range of learning opportunities to their client's employees. These include:

- straight IMM courseware;
- online chat rooms, either where people just drop in when they want, or where regularly scheduled discussions among peers can take place. The company supports these chat rooms with video-conferencing equipment and online whiteboards.
- mentoring arrangements, where one employee with a high skill level can tutor another employee, with or without video-conferencing; and
- prearranged classes that use a combination of IMM materials and a live instructor. These, too, are supported using online whiteboards and video-conferencing equipment.

Because Performx has depth of experience as a technology-based learning company, they are building in performance management tools to gauge the task-specific skills gained through each training module for every student. As a result, the client will know how well their people are learning, and managers will be able to tell what benefits they are deriving from each dollar invested in training.

Better yet, if you as an employee use this kind of system, you will be able to tell how well you are doing at all times — and what steps you could take to do even better. All the management studies are unanimous in concluding that people enjoy doing good work, and that the best way to motivate people is to help them perform their jobs well. A virtual university gives workers a tool box they can flip open and use at any time to improve how well they do their jobs.

Although Performx may have a jump on many other training organizations, it is not alone in this field. Indeed, commercial training that produces bottom-line results that are measurable and definable is going to be a major growth industry over the next 20 years.

Take a Step Back

Now step back a moment. Think about a learning system that can reach people over widely dispersed geographic areas; that can deliver measurable, cost-effective learning to predetermined standards; that can offer the best use of all available resources, including human instructors in distant locations, computer-based training systems that increase comprehension and decrease instruction time, peer mentoring, and subject discussions; and that employs the best medium for each explanation or presentation. Add a customized learning path for each learner created in consultation with the learner herself. Sounds like what we'd need for individually customized public school education, doesn't it?

Why don't we decide to manage the important transition that we have ahead of us in education, instead of just letting it happen by accident? We could establish a national working group to consider the possibilities, and set up trial projects devoted to discovering what works and how best to use it. We could fund this group by moneys from one or more levels of government, corporate sponsorships, or getting school boards to pay a modest annual subscription to have access to the findings. Members of this working group would include the best people we can find among active teachers, principals, school board administrators, union representatives, parents, ministry of education officials, representatives from colleges and universities, commercial trainers, and industry. Their primary objective would be to produce the best possible education model for our children. Secondary priorities would be to find ways of using technology intelligently to improve educational results, manage the financial problems of education, and to make the transition as painless and equitable as possible for all concerned. I'd love to see this happen — but I don't expect it.

Instead, I expect that over the next 20 years, we will spend billions of public education dollars reinventing technologies piecemeal that commercial training firms could provide off-the-shelf right now. It seems to me that there's an obvious fit here — but I'll bet that the public sector will work hard at ignoring it.

We face major challenges in the funding, priorities, and structure of education over the next 20 years. We can't continue stretching diminishing resources to cover an expanding student population, or we risk losing the many good things that our education system does achieve. At the same time, automation is inevitably going to come to education, just as it has to every other industry. Managing this transition will be crucial to the future prosperity of our country. The potential is there for interesting new opportunities as well as tragic disaster. It's up to us to choose which we experience.

11
The Soul Under Siege

I've predicted changes in our society in other chapters, but I'd like to draw these threads together into a unified narrative here. What will it be like to live in the online, wired society of tomorrow? How will people relate to each other? How will the relationships between men and women change? What will happen to families? Will our world be a safe, caring place, or a lonely, dangerous one?

There is no one answer for these questions, because our society is going to exhibit much greater variations in social patterns than it does now. The highs will be higher, and the lows will be lower. Some people will experience a more interesting, more supportive, and more comforting world, and others will fall into a living hell. How our society, as a whole, develops is going to depend on the actions that we, as individuals, choose to take.

Having said this, there are going to be aspects of the future that will try our collective endurance and our souls. Indeed, I believe several factors will conspire to place the soul — the core of our humanity — under siege. Let me start by looking down into the pit, visiting the worst of our tomorrows, before talking about some of the better things that could happen.

The Global Village

"It takes a village to raise a child" is an African aphorism that became popular in the 1980s with social workers, and is widely quoted in the popular media of the 1990s. This saying expresses the reality that young Homo sapiens are taught how to become civilized human beings by many people, not just their parents, and that the responsibility for this task is shared by all members of the community. Community, then, is of vital importance to the preservation of culture, the functioning of society, and the conduct of interpersonal relationships.

But it isn't only children that need a "village." Anyone who deems themselves human needs one as well, for it is in the ways we relate to each other that our humanity is exercised and illuminated. Unless we are solitary renegades, like the Unabomber, our humanity depends on relations with others and participation in some form of community, whether it's a church choir or a street gang. So let's look at how our ideas of community could change over the next 20 years.

In any discussion of the future, Marshall McLuhan's "global village" concept from his 1962 book *The Gutenberg Galaxy* inevitably pops up. McLuhan believed that improvements in communications technology meant that the world was becoming smaller. He thought that our growing ability to communicate with each other, know each other's business, and participate in each other's lives no matter where we lived was bringing us closer together. As a futurist, I'm often asked how the global village is doing.

It's true that it's getting progressively easier to become acquainted with people anywhere in the world, and to stay in touch. Technology, most notably the Internet, is having a dramatic effect on the rich elite of humanity. Combine this technological capacity with cheaper and faster travel, greater economic interdependency (courtesy of the global economy), and ceaseless news coverage by a proliferating number of news sellers, and McLuhan's image of a global village becomes easy to believe.

But a village of 5.8 billion people — the world's current population — is not a village at all. It is impossible to know the names, the
needs, and the backgrounds of more than a tiny fraction of this
number. There are too many conflicting values for us to share a code   241
of conduct, ethics, or morality, and the responsibility for community
is spread too thinly for it to have any meaning. A global village
cannot raise a child, nor can it offer succor and support to a mature
human being.

Indeed, the growth of global communications has as much capacity to divide people as to unite them. For example, religious,
spiritual, and ethical differences both rise and fall with global awareness. On the positive side, heightened awareness of common
problems and of the great teachings of spiritual leaders produces
areas of agreement among ethical leaders and movements, and
furthers the acceptance of shared goals. But this same heightened
awareness produces friction and xenophobia as well, and the news
media compound the problem with shallow portrayals of foreigners
as cardboard cut-outs. Hence, many Western news consumers
think of Arab Muslims as crazed religious fanatics armed with
sub-machine guns, while many Arab Muslims think of Westerners as
corrupt purveyors of sin and violence. The exposure of these two
groups to each other, each carrying values that seem mutually exclusive, heightens xenophobia, lack of understanding, and conflict.
Try, for instance, to hold a dispassionate discussion of female
circumcision/female genital mutilation between those who see it as
a necessary aspect of their culture, and those who view it as physical and sexual abuse of women, and you will quickly see the triumph
of passion over reason. Neither side can imagine that the other has
any possible justification for its views.

Nor do we need to wander far from home to reach such emotional
sticking points. Consider, for instance, the "debate" (if one can call
it that) on the issue of abortion in the developed world. Any debate
that can, at one extreme, include the shooting of your opponents as

the only moral course of action to preserve innocent life, or the taking of innocent (although not yet truly human) life as an inalienable right, obviously carries deep emotional roots that are hard to reconcile.

But religion, culture, and ethics are not the only areas that produce conflict. One of the largest areas of dissension over the next 20 years will revolve around economics, specifically jobs and incomes. Indeed, the battle lines are already forming. In developed countries like Canada, people are losing their jobs because much of the work we do can be done by people in developing countries for a small fraction of our wages. While a worker in a factory in Canada might cost his employer something in excess of $10 an hour, plus benefits, a worker in a factory producing much the same kind of product in Vietnam might make less than 20 cents an hour. A software engineer in India will receive perhaps one-fifth of his Canadian counterpart for the same work.

Throughout history, work with a high labour content has migrated to places where labour costs are low. The difference today is the breathtaking speed at which this is happening. Inevitably and not unreasonably, people get upset when their livelihoods disappear. In the words of Buzz Hargrove, head of the Canadian Auto Workers' union, following the strike against General Motors in October 1996, "We aren't going to let GM give our jobs to people somewhere else in the world just because they're willing to do them for less money."

Clearly, people in developed countries who are used to receiving an honest day's wage for an honest day's work will resent being undercut by cheap labour somewhere else in the world. Likewise, the governments of foreign workers are going to resent any measures taken by the fat cat governments of the rich countries to keep their jobs at home. Are the rich countries, they will ask, somehow entitled to these jobs that they should keep them at the expense of the rest of the world?

Does all this mean the global village will become a war zone? Not necessarily. Most human interaction today, be it global or local, is peaceful and largely without conflict, and this pattern will continue. As information becomes more widely available, and we start building our world views based on common facts, thoughts, and discussions, the vast majority of us will be able to co-exist in relative harmony, just as we do now. Most of us have no reason to threaten others because what we really want to do is get on with our lives. However, when basic beliefs, language rights, cultural practices, or lifestyles are threatened, then tribal anger will flare, and hostility will come to the fore.

I suggest that Marshall McLuhan was wrong, and that his now-venerable phrase should be changed to "global villages." The world population is being sliced and diced into all sorts of splinter groups, not necessarily tied to nationality. For example, there is now a global village of gays and lesbians who provide each other with mutual support, information, and tactics. "Without the Internet," said one lesbian recently in Zimbabwe, where homosexuals were under attack by the government, "we would probably have just quickly faded back into oblivion" (*Economist*, January 6, 1996). Instead, the gay-lesbian global village offered advice and tactics, and organized local protests that embarrassed President Robert Mugabe when he visited places as widespread as South Africa, New Zealand, and Holland.

Over the next 20 years, all kinds of global villages will emerge: netheads, Deadheads, butterfly watchers, Esperanto-speakers, pro-lifers, survivalist militia members, proponents of gun control, right-wing wackos, left-wing wackos, terrorists, pedophile pornographers, poets, futurists — in short, just about any grouping of humanity possible, all independent of geographical location. McLuhan's vision of a unifying world, while true in some ways, will be proven wrong in one important respect: because there are going to be more splinter groups coming into contact with each other than ever before, there will be more disagreement, more violence, and more hatred over more issues than ever, even as the majority of humanity remains indifferent to these disagreements. We may be headed into a more dangerous world, where grievances abound and

the friction between groups will act as a whetstone that sharpens the cutting edge of violence. Few of us will feel safe; just ask the residents of Oklahoma City, Belfast, or Israel; or consider the rise of white supremacists and neo-fascists; or ponder the actions of a lone gunman like Marc Lépine at Montreal's Ecole Polytechnique.

The Addicted Society

We have become addicted to consumption and to our own amusement, and this addiction is gradually shredding the fabric of our society. History shows that populations that have access to a ready supply of sugar gradually increase their consumption of sugar. Similarly, our addiction to consumption and entertainment has crept up on us gradually as advances in technology have allowed us to improve our standard of living. Nor is this surprising; people would rather live in greater comfort and with greater convenience, if they can.

The Western world's standard of living rose gradually throughout the nineteenth and twentieth centuries, but accelerated dramatically in the 1960s and 1970s. The consistent rise of affluence following the Second World War, coupled with the discovery by advertisers of the selling power of television, produced a new, spend-thrift mindset in young and old alike. As Canadian sociologist and pollster Angus Reid says in his recent book, *Shakedown: How the New Economy Is Changing Our Lives*:

After 20 years of prudence, older Canadians were ready for a fling, and neither romanticized poverty nor revolutionary wars were what they had in mind. They had suffered more than their share of poverty and more than their share of war. Now, they wanted something more consistent with the dreams that had sustained them through all the hard times. And young people, who had placed such a premium on freedom of expression and individuality, were beginning to discover that consumption could satisfy both needs. (page 56)

We have reached the stage where it is difficult for us to imagine a lifestyle that does not revolve around procuring more and more goods and services. Our economy is viewed as being "sick" if people are not spending in a persistent, nationwide feeding frenzy. Ministries of finance around the country worry if consumers sit on their hands. Economists solemnly talk about waiting for consumers to open their pocketbooks and lead us out of a recession.

Business, naturally, has done everything possible to coddle, cajole, support, encourage, and foster our addiction to buying things. The credit card, the easy car loan, the layaway plan, the shopping centre, the shop-at-home catalogue, the Home Shopping Channel, the "satisfaction guaranteed or your money back, try-it-you'll-like-it" offer, and the slick direct-mail campaign that promises that "you may already have won" are all enticements to spend, but few of the goods we buy are actually necessary. We often spend without knowing precisely why we do so.

As we worked our way deeper into this addiction, we dragged our governments with us. Not only did governments become boosters for consumption, but they invented new ways for us to spend money we didn't have. Government programs poured money into the economy to plump up our pay cheques. They gave us money directly in the form of pensions and welfare. They saved us from reaching into our pockets and spending our own money for things like health care and prescriptions. They created new jobs and new salaries for new government workers with programs for job creation and infrastructure, for multiculturalism and language training, and for just about every other purpose imaginable.

Because we liked all this "free" money so much, to keep the process going governments invented new ways of financing this spending. They plundered the work of economist John Maynard Keynes, citing his government spending theories as justification for running up deficits in bad times, but ignoring his countervailing theory that governments need to create offsetting surpluses in good times. Program spending stopped growing in the mid-1970s when the costs of servicing the rising debt load started to eat up revenues. Instead of trying to rectify the situation by reducing debt levels, governments borrowed more money to pay interest on their debts. By the time governments began to take back money by reducing program spending and raising taxes in the 1980s, higher interest rates defeated their efforts and perpetuated the deficit cycle. In more recent, more desperate times, governments have started pretending that they can pull money out of thin air by running lotteries and skimming the profits from legalized gambling, conveniently forgetting that profits they make on gambling are not only extracted from the economy, but typically come from those Canadians who can least afford it.

Of course, it's not just Canada that has been caught up in this frenzy, it's the entire Western world — and increasingly the developing world, too. There people watch Western-produced television and conclude that this addiction to consumption is the key to progress and happiness.

Here in Canada our federal and provincial governments, with our approval and connivance, have run up debts and incurred unfunded liabilities amounting to about $1.8 *trillion* as the legacy of our addiction to be handed on to our children, according to the January 1995 policy paper of the Canadian Institute of Actuaries entitled *Troubled Tomorrows — The Report of the Canadian Institute of Actuaries' Task Force on Retirement Savings* (page 24). That amounts to more than $60,000 for every man, woman, and child in Canada, or almost a quarter of a million dollars for a four-person household, on top of the personal debts we have run up for ourselves.

During most of the 1990s governments have attempted to back away from a financial abyss by cutting back on all the programs they invented to give us money and services in the first place. What they don't say, and what most people don't realize, is that the purpose of all this slashing goes to pay the ever-burgeoning interest on accumulated debts. Federal and provincial governments have actually been running operating surpluses, on average, since 1961, as tax revenues have exceeded program spending. The burden of debt will be eased enormously by lower interest rates, and a balanced budget is certainly a step in the right direction, but a balanced budget does not pay off our debts; it merely keeps those debts from getting bigger.

The social price we pay for our consumption addiction is the necessity of working harder to earn more income to feed our habit. Indeed, another interpretation of the success of women entering the labour force, as they have in increasing numbers since the Sixties, is that as families have become addicted to consumption, they've needed to boost household income to finance their expanding habit. I am not suggesting that it's a bad thing for women to establish their own lives and careers, nor am I advocating that women be relegated to staying home with the kids. I am merely observing that some of the impetus for women to work originally came from the desire for a better home, a nicer car, fancier clothes, more exotic vacations — in short, from the consumption addiction.

Regardless of how you view the development of the two-income household, we have now reached the stage where for many people it is no longer a luxury, but a necessity, and one that carries an enormous cost in human terms. We have become too busy and too tired to do anything useful beyond work and resting up to work some more. Today, when you ask someone how he or she is, their answer will almost invariably include some comment that they are either "very busy" or "really tired." This pressure on our time and energies is compounded by the higher levels of competition produced by the emergence of the global economy, by the downsizing of corporations, and by the rampant fear that unless we work harder, we won't be able to hold on to our jobs. We are now going through a transition between a high consumption addiction supported by dual-income families, and a consumption addiction we can no longer quite support because of reduced incomes and fears about job security.

"Amusing Ourselves to Death"

If you ask someone who is "tired" and "busy" what they do with their downtime, they will often tell you that they just plunk themselves in front of the television and vegetate to recover from the day's stresses. "It's mindless; I don't have to think about anything," they explain.

In itself, relaxing in front of the tube isn't a bad thing, but it does have two negative effects. First, it consumes time that could be used for other activities. Time spent watching television is time that is not spent creating, thinking, studying, exercising, or visiting with other people. This last point is particularly significant, because our most vital relationships flourish only through shared time and activities. While people can be companionable while watching television, the experience they share is typically both trivial and not of their own creation. I believe television does not re-energize people, but rather saps their energy and initiative.

Which brings us inevitably to the question of content and of television's second negative effect. While watching high-quality documentaries, news, and arts programming may enhance a viewer's experience of the world and provide solid, thoughtful material they can share and discuss, viewing the latest episodes of *The X-Files* or *The Simpsons* leads to little more than a rehashing of cultural drivel. American social critic Neil Postman calls this addiction to meaningless content "amusing ourselves to death."

It is increasingly apparent that what we view on television affects how we think, how we behave, and, ultimately, who we are. This issue most frequently comes up in relation to children, and what effect TV has on them. Some social scientists and media analysts deny that television has any effect on the minds of children. I disagree. You need look no further than the tens of billions of dollars spent on television advertising each year. If television didn't affect thinking and behaviour, then television advertising would never have evolved to its present sophistication. Indeed, it would disappear overnight.

The *Economist* recently reported on the differences in attitudes and school performances between the children of immigrants and the children of natural-born Americans. The study cited, titled "Children of Immigrants: the Adoption of the Second Generation," is by Alejandro Portes and Ruben G. Rumbaut, sociologists at Johns Hopkins University in Baltimore, and they found, among other things, that:

> The longer children have lived in America, the less homework they do, the worse their performance in school and the lower their academic aspirations. Also, they watch more television. Indeed, just as the length of time spent doing homework is a good predictor of academic success, so time spent watching television is an accurate predictor of academic failure. (February 17, 1996, page 77)

To borrow a phrase from pollster Angus Reid, television connects "directly with the central nervous system," providing a conduit to the subconscious. A program may or may not have a stated message to sell (although more and more propaganda is appearing on television as infomercials or even as straight news), but the viewers receive messages, even when none is intended. These messages typically advocate values we might not wish to promote if we thought about them, such as that consumption leads to happiness, or that violence is a good way of resolving conflict. This last message, delivered by just about every cop, lawyer, and detective show on the air, is hitting home: public concern about crime continues to rise even though crime statistics have been falling for several years.

Television is the unblinking eye, a subconscious purveyor of unspoken values. It devours our time and attention and excretes trivia and harmful propaganda. It was, for four decades, the biggest and most potent intrusion into our homes and psyches, but its domination is now being rivalled — by computers. Computers are different from television — more complex, harder to dismiss — and of greater potential value and power. But they, too, devour time, both inside and outside of work, and disconnect us from each other.

I make my living using a computer. I have a degree in computer science. I'm probably one of the youngest people in the world with more than 35 years of experience in using computers, having programmed my first computer when I was nine years old in 1959. I like and enjoy them, but I'm not blind to the cost they exact.

It is precisely because computers are so powerful and so flexible that they are also so fascinating and potentially so destructive. Computer games are not passive entertainments, like television; they interact with the player. The best games are addictive. Some people play them into the early hours of the morning, and even sneak them into the office to play at work. They are true marvels of technological sophistication, but they are still time wasters, and often the time wasted is not spare time.

The Internet has been called by some the equivalent of a second brain for anyone who knows how to use it well. It offers enormous potential for thought, discussion, research, interaction, and intellectual cross-fertilization. But how many people actually use it in this way, compared with those who surf from one amusing but trivial topic to another? Like TV, the Net and computer games distract us from worthier pursuits and devalue our relationships with each other. Advice columnists regularly get letters from people whose spouses never spend time with them because they're playing computer games, or who have developed an online relationship with someone who is more interesting. The state of California now accepts compulsive computer-game playing as legitimate grounds for divorce.

All in all, the addicted society is creating large numbers of people who are driven to consume, exhausted because they have to work long hours to pay for their lifestyles, and disconnected from each other. The effects are being felt in our homes and workplaces, with consequences that are ominous.

The Fall of Home and Family

In a world where consumption is a supreme virtue, families are a liability. Families cost money and cut down on choices. A family house requires a mortgage and lots of invested capital. To keep a healthy relationship with a spouse and children takes time, and such time can't be spent in the pursuit of purely individual pleasure. Creating and maintaining a successful family takes sustained, patient, self-denying effort — which is horribly out of tune with our instant gratification, television-watching, cyber-speed society.

Moreover, the economics of family life have shifted dramatically from the early twentieth century. Children, who were an asset in a labour-intensive, mainly rural society, are now a liability and an expensive luxury in a mechanized, largely urban society. Women, who were once effectively chained to their husbands by lack of economic alternatives, are now much freer to seek their own careers and their own lives. Fathers are discovering that if they break the bonds of family and escape, either back to being single or into another relationship, their incomes go up, often dramatically, even as the incomes of mothers, who are usually left with the children, drop dramatically.

Government policies have, overall, increased the financial pressure on families and accelerated their demise. Take, for example, tax policy. An Ontario family with two dependent children and two working parents who each made $30,000 a year, paid a combined total of $12,612.71 in 1995 income taxes. The same family would have paid almost $4,600 more, or a total of $17,208.38 if the entire household income of $60,000 had been made by one parent while the other stayed at home with the children.

Family life is under pressure from all sides, but does the demise of the conventional family really matter? There have been many arrangements between men and women and their offspring in the history of humanity. Is this merely a new variation suitable to a new era? The short answer is "no." We are discarding the structures of the past before we have new structures to replace them, and the results are devastating.

One of the primary purposes of families of any type is to nurture and civilize children, and how well or poorly we accomplish this will determine the future of our society. Unfortunately, my interpretation of the evidence indicates that Western society, including Canada, has not been doing well at raising children. The *Economist* magazine, in a survey published September 9, 1995, of studies done in Sweden, Germany, the United States, France, and Great Britain, drew a number of conclusions regarding families in the Western world. The survey drew together the following points:

- In every country surveyed, and in studies done over multiple generations, children of single-parent families don't do as well in school, get into more trouble more often, are not as healthy, have more emotional problems, and are more likely to become single parents themselves than children from similar socio-economic backgrounds who live in two-parent households.
- The absence of fathers is a major contributing factor in the

impoverishment of children. A family that splits in two is quite likely to produce at least one household below the poverty level.

- In households where money is tight, parental discipline   253
tends to become harsher and more arbitrary. Harsh and arbitrary discipline is not the way to raise responsible, self-disciplined adults.

- The absence of a father in a household tends to produce boys who are more aggressive, and may become casual, even predatory about sex and violence. The absence of a father also tends to produce girls with low self-esteem who are more likely to be young and unmarried when they first get pregnant.

- Although there are obviously many exceptions, stepfathers and boyfriends are, on average, a poor substitute for biological fathers, offering less emotional and financial support, and being more likely to abuse the children they live with.

So "broken homes," as we used to call them, frequently mean bad news for children. And the incidence of broken homes is rising. American economic analyst Ed Rubenstein, writing in *Imprimis* magazine, identified two principal factors leading to an increase in crime: single motherhood and poverty. In 1960, 22 percent of American black children were born to single mothers. In 1995 this rose to 68 percent overall, and exceeds 80 percent in American inner cities. Meanwhile, white illegitimacy, which was 2 percent in 1960, has reached 22 percent today — exactly where black illegitimacy was in 1960. Worse, Rubenstein traces a connection between the increase of births to single mothers and an increase in violent crime:

Using sophisticated statistical models, economists have at last begun to measure the impact of family dissolution on crime. In

1994, William Niskanen, chairman of the Cato Institute [an American think-tank], reported that a 1 percentage point increase in births to single mothers appears to increase the violent crime rate by 1.7 percent. ... The U.S. differs from the permissive welfare states of Western Europe in having an underclass that is not merely poor, but has few chances of escaping poverty. (August 1995, page 2)

Turning to Canada, in the survey mentioned earlier, the *Economist* noted that in 1960 about 4 percent of Canadian births were to unmarried mothers. According to Statistics Canada, the figure for births out of wedlock stood at about 23 percent in 1991, including single-parent families and common-law births, which is about the same as for white Americans. And about 20 percent — one out of five — of all Canadian households with dependent children are now single-parent households.

Dr. Robert Glossop of the Ottawa-based Vanier Institute of the Family was cited by the *Toronto Star* as pointing out that youth violence is rising, our teen suicide rate is the third highest in the world, having doubled since 1979, and teen pregnancies in Canada are up 20 percent since 1987. He attributes these things to, "quite frankly a lack of morality, a lack of attention to the moral dimensions of our lives" (October 24, 1996, page B1). In the same *Star* article, Bill Damon, director of the Centre for Human Development at Brown University in Rhode Island, is quoted as saying that the teaching of shared standards of behaviour is being neglected in children in Europe, North America, and Australia: "When we tell children that their first goal should be self-love, we are suggesting to them that they are the centre of the universe." The result is children who are "self-centred, irresponsible and ultimately demoralized." This lack of moral guidance and emphasis on the self has a detrimental effect on all kids, regardless of family structure.

I phoned Dr. Glossop to ask what he thought lay ahead for the structure and stability of Canadian families. He indicated that many of the births out of wedlock in Canada are taking place in common-law relationships, which resemble traditional family structures. This is especially true in Quebec, where about half of couples today do without the confirmation of church or state of their commitment to each other. Does this mean that all is well? Not necessarily.

Dr. Glossop noted that common-law relationships are statistically less stable than traditional marriages, and that second and third marriages are less stable than first marriages. As a result, he estimated that perhaps as many as 40 to 45 percent of today's children will experience at least one divorce, separation, or recombined family before they reach the age of 18. Children who have gone through this kind of experience have more emotional and social problems than children who have not, and are more likely to experience marital break-ups in their own relationships when they become adults. "The experience of childhood is far less stable than it once was," he concludes.

Now think ahead to what these trends might mean 20 years from now if they remain unchanged. Yesterday's insecure, aggressive 18-year-old boy could become an amoral, neurotic 38-year-old businessman who beats his wife and abuses his kids. His spiritual sister, who today might be a shy and withdrawn 8-year-old, could become a 28-year-old young woman who skips from relationship to relationship, never settling, never contributing to the society in which she lives, never finding satisfying work or a way to be comfortable in her own skin. These two are dispossessed, alienated, full of self-loathing, anger, and frustration — and they could be your neighbours, the future citizens of your community. And people like them will multiply if unstable families produce more instability and a rising number of insecure and unhappy children.

Is a society with insecure and angry people walking the streets the kind of place you want to live? It may turn out that way. You could wake up 20 years from now in a Canada where more than half of all children are born in unstable families. You might walk the streets of your community in an uncomfortable state of constant wariness, much as you would in parts of New York City today, because you know that some of the people around you are walking time bombs, waiting to explode. Or you could find yourself forced to retire behind the walls of a gated community, living in a prison of your own making because the real prisons can't hold all the people who are dangerous. Certainly this is what is happening in many parts of the United States today, and although we are not as far down this road as our American cousins, this is the direction we seem to be headed.

"Sometimes," said American sociologist Charles Murray, referring to the crumbling of American families, "the sky really is falling."

The Decline of Male Domination

The bleak scenario I've just outlined is an extrapolation of trends currently in place. If they are left undisturbed, this is the future we will experience. But trends rarely remain undisturbed, and there are other things happening in the world that could help turn society in a more positive direction.

One such trend is the gradual decline of the male domination of Western society. At first I dismissed this idea as wishful thinking on the part of feminists, but the more I look at it, the more likely it seems to be.

Think back to when you were a kid. Unless you are quite young right now, chances are you lived in a world where Daddy went to work and Mommy stayed home; where Mommy was called "the little woman" and was told "not to worry your pretty little head about such things"; where "man's work" and "woman's work" were mutually exclusive; where the idea of a female prime minister or president was dismissed as fanciful nonsense; where a boss pinching his secretary's bum and then chasing her around his desk was considered somewhat undignified, but ultimately just comical.

It is just 80 years ago that women first got the right to vote in Canada, starting provincially in Manitoba, Saskatchewan, and Alberta in 1916, and federally with the Women's Franchise Act of 1918. Before this, women's legal status in many respects was that of chattel slaves or children. While not yet fully equal to men economically, women today have seen dramatic improvements in their legal status and social roles. This is another way of saying that the masculine domination of society is giving way — and will continue to do so for several reasons.

The first is awareness. It is no longer considered cute or funny for a man to sexually harass a woman; it is a crime. As more women achieve senior positions in corporations and governments, it will become more natural for people to see women as suited to such roles. As more role models emerge for young women, they will become more willing to put themselves forward for opportunity and advancement.

The next reason that women's advancement will continue is the change in the nature of work. In an agrarian society big muscles were the most important job qualification. In an industrial society, muscles became progressively less important as machines did more and more of the work, and a greater proportion of total economic activity became white-collar paper pushing. The barriers to women doing work equal to that of men began to fall.

Today in a world where the key industries process and sell information, and where creativity and innovation are the crucial strategic skills, people are prized for their brains, and whether the body that houses a given brain is male or female, black or white, poor or privileged, is largely irrelevant. In a world that is moving toward a true meritocracy, women will be on equal footing with men, whether men like it or not. In addition, more and more people will be self-employed entrepreneurs whose clients care more about results than the old-school tie. These trends remove many of the barriers that hold women back today, including the very real "glass ceiling" that has prevented them from being promoted to the upper levels of major corporations.

The increasing financial clout of women as investors will also lead to their advancement. As women make more, they will save more. As they save more, they will invest more. As they invest more, they will take a greater interest in how their money is invested — and they are unlikely to invest in those institutions that oppose the advancement of women or hinder healthy family relationships. Many people today are more sophisticated about the inner workings of finance, which were once considered an arcane science knowable by only a few. As a result, there is a growing population of women capable of exerting considerable influence in the financial world.

One impediment to women's financial equality persists: the outdated thinking of our financial institutions, particularly the chartered banks. These institutions are still male dominated and still, in general, discriminate against women. According to Catherine Swift of the Canadian Federation of Independent Business, it is still more difficult for a woman to get a loan for a small business than it is for a man, even though businesses started by women are statistically more likely to survive than those started by men. Over time, however, even the banks will fall into line.

Finally, women will advance through the sheer force of superior numbers. Women already outnumber men in our society, and they live longer. As life expectancy overall rises, the proportion of the total population that is female will rise as well. This will be especially telling starting around 2007, as the baby boomers start reaching their sixties, and boomer men start dying off more quickly than women. Because the boomers were the first generation of women to fight, as a group, for equality on all fronts, the survivors will have both the awareness and the political will to push for an end to male domination in all areas.

A major signal of things to come occurred in the 1996 U.S. presidential election. The majority of men voted for Republican Bob Dole; the majority of women voted for Democrat Bill Clinton. Clinton won despite threatening some major power groups, like tobacco growers and corporations, and despite running against the apparent tide of fiscal restraint that calls for the slashing of government programs. For the first time in the history of American politics, the "gender gap" was a key factor in the outcome of a presidential election.

The implications of this trend should not be lost on Canadian politicians who wish to see their parties victorious in the next 20 years. Today, the white male "suits" of the Ralph Klein government of Alberta and the Mike Harris government of Ontario emphasize financial matters like deficits and tax cuts above and at the expense of social issues, such as health care, welfare, and child care. Both of these governments represent the dying culture of male-dominated politics; women will demand more compassion from government — and will vote for those parties and candidates who offer it.

The effects of this shift will be widespread and diverse. To give one small example, trade policy may be affected, with governments being elected on platforms to impose trade embargoes on countries that have inadequate child labour laws and unsafe industrial codes, even if this policy limits Canada's economic growth. And because Canada and the United States are not alone in experiencing the growth in women's political clout, the governments of other developed countries may be forced to respond with policies that appeal to women voters. This change in emphasis may jeopardize the hard-won financial stability that governments in Canada have sought through the deficit-reducing 1990s, depending on how well politicians elected with women's support can balance conflicting demands on the public purse.

Governments, following an already established trend toward group rights as opposed to individual rights, may even begin to reserve a percentage of seats in parliaments and local councils for women in proportion to their numbers on the rolls of registered voters. It may turn out, in 20 years' time, that men will find themselves accorded the lesser voice and the lesser share of society's wealth.

A society that becomes more accommodating toward women will also become more accommodating toward women who are lesbians and, by extension, more accepting of gay men. By 2017, lesbians and gays will be largely accepted with all the rights and protections they now seek. Only a minority of hard-core homophobes will hold out against the tide of change. Homosexual couples will routinely raise children, perhaps even their own genetic children. Genetic engineering, in combination with artificial insemination for lesbians, or with a host mother to bring a fetus to term for gays, may allow two men or two women to produce a child that is genetically "theirs."

As women's power grows, technology for technology's sake will lose its glamorous appeal. Bill Gates may be viewed as an antisocial freak, not a billionaire hero. Scientific and technological developments will be valued for their utility and ethical effect on society, not just in terms of how much fun geeks can have in developing them, or how much money companies can make by exploiting them.

Men may not like these changes. Who, after all, enjoys giving up perks, power, and influence? But the smart ones will recognize the changes to come, and ride the wave of women's emerging power.

The Flight to Community

History tells us that humanity is endlessly adaptive. As a result, people will respond to some of the more negative trends I have outlined in this chapter, and start to fashion their lives in a more livable, more humane way. I call this the "flight to community." Instead of standing where we are and fighting against the forces working to degrade our lives, we may move to someplace where a sense of community is easier and more natural, where our neighbours, and not a TV or computer screen, are our chief source of news and entertainment.

Humanity's 200-year migration from village to city may be about to reverse itself, at least in the developed world. We may now flock from large urban areas to smaller cities and small towns. Indeed, there is preliminary evidence that this trend is already happening. There are several reasons for this reversal. First, that it is becoming possible to engage in big-city activities without living in one. You can play the New York Stock Exchange without being in New York. You can make a bet on a horse race in Hong Kong from Wawa, Ontario. You can communicate by fax, phone, and e-mail with people in just about any country in the world. And the communications revolution talked about in chapters 2 and 3 is only going to increase the possibilities. Accordingly, 20 years from now, most of us will be able to live wherever we want. Our work will no longer dictate our residence.

Does this mean that we will all decamp to live in the boonies, hip deep in snow drifts from November to April? Probably not, although remote communities will get some urban exiles. The first take on this flight from the cities seems to indicate that people will settle somewhere within a radius of about one and a half to two hours' drive from a major international airport. This radius encompasses a lot of territory, and opens the way for small towns and cities to see a renaissance of growth and development.

One of the major reasons why people will move to small towns is because they offer, well, a small-town attitude. Life's more relaxed. People tend to be friendlier and more concerned about their neighbours. There is, in short, more of a community feel in a small town than in the bedroom districts of big cities.

As this trend starts to grab hold, the major urban centres of this continent will be the losers. Tax bases will erode. As people spread out, urban transit systems are going to come under pressure; it will take more miles to reach fewer paying riders. As a result, services will decline, which will only encourage people to leave urban areas at an ever higher rate. The decay of the American inner cities may repeat itself in Canada, unless municipal governments think about what they are doing, and tailor their strategies accordingly. When you no longer need to visit Bay Street or Burrard Street to conduct business, what's the point in coming to Toronto or Vancouver? What has Calgary got to offer that Red Deer doesn't in an age where electronic communications can bring to your home almost any information, entertainment, or service you need?

Well, live theatre for one thing. And live sporting events, particularly at a major league level. Arts and entertainment, culture and museums. Sophisticated restaurants, and nifty little stores selling stuff you can't get in catalogues. Culture and ambiance may replace business and paper pushing as the *raison d'être* for cities. Cities impair their cultural offerings at their peril — and so-called "bottom-line" municipal politicians may be cutting their own throats.

One response to the diminishing appeal of big cities is the development of so-called "lifestyle communities." A lifestyle community is built around the concept of a village, comprising people living together in a low-density, human-scale, landscaped setting, sharing basic communal facilities for recreation, restaurants, and shopping. Automobile traffic flows around the community, not through it, furthering the sense of shared living. Community events are organized, such as lectures, films, small-scale dramatic productions, and local sporting events. Basic health-care facilities are available. Indeed, most of the amenities necessary for everyday life are close at hand, keeping people in the community and in close proximity with each other. In effect, such developments recreate the environment of a small town or city, but with the added advantage of being close to the greater resources of a larger urban setting.

Such communities differ from the gated communities I mentioned earlier in one major way. There are no gates and no guards. The purpose is not to hunker down in a safe bunker, but to encourage people to socialize. The attitude is also different. The intent is not to pull up the drawbridge but rather to create a humane setting. Some of these positive attributes can be found in the better gated communities, but their primary purpose is always safety and the exclusion of undesirables.

Lifestyle communities are now starting to emerge for retirees. Retired couples or individuals buy lifetime tenancy in an apartment or small house. They have their own living, cooking, and eating quarters, but a cleaning and security staff takes over the more physically demanding jobs. A nurse is on call 24 hours a day to deal with medical problems. Everyone is entitled to (and pays for) one meal a day in a communal dining centre, which is run as a restaurant. They can buy as many more meals as they wish so that people who do not wish to cook for themselves or eat alone don't have to. Developers are starting to see the appeal of this kind of community for the elderly, and I believe that younger people will also start to see the attraction of such communities, perhaps even within a big city.

What a concept: being with people and enjoying their company. Could it ever catch on in Toronto?

The Patchwork Society

In March 1992, at a conference of the Association for Investment Management and Research in Chicago, Richard F. Hokenson, a vice-president and research analyst for the brokerage firm of Donaldson, Lufkin & Jenrette, was asked about the implications of the aging baby boomers for the retailing industry. The questioner was looking for a smooth, simple generalization based on demographics. What he got was something much more complicated:

People are not conforming to the traditional age patterns. Retailers look at the age charts and say, "Isn't this great for industry, because [baby boomers] are the traditional heavy buyers of our product or service. We can put our feet up on the desk and watch the orders flow in as this baby boom gets older." It has not worked that way. The trends toward non-marriage and divorce introduce interruptions in the life cycle. People of the same age behave differently. That is why all of the conclusions based on age and income data are misleading. They are basically based on looking at the parents of the baby boomers, who are a socially homogeneous group. Baby boomers are not a socially homogeneous group, and they will not behave as their predecessors did.

We are entering an era where people and societies are becoming more idiosyncratic. This means that there are going to be inner-city ghettos and nice, safe, small towns. It means that some people are going to live hard-driving, type A, yuppie lifestyles, and others are going to retreat to a quieter, gentler way of living. It means some people will become serial spouses, and others will stick to traditional monogamy. Broad-spectrum generalizations about Canadians' behaviours and attitudes are going to be less useful than they have been in the past.

Our future lies in a patchwork society, with lots of diversity and more extremes. The point to remember is that *you* can have a lot of influence on what parts of it happen in *your* life. You can work to prevent the erosion of the social values you cherish, the isolation of individuals, the marginalization of a permanent underclass, the addictive enslavement of our minds, and the danger to our souls. What it takes is thought, action, commitment — and compassion, the greatest virtue.

It's your life. It's your society. It's your future.

12 Tomorrow Morning

I njoy being a futurist. I like reading about and researching what's happening in the world, and pondering over what might happen next. I enjoy the consulting challenges of my clients, the retreats and brainstorming sessions I'm asked to conduct, and the keynote speeches I'm commissioned to deliver. But occasionally I stop and wonder if all this stuff that I expect to happen can really be true. It all seems so strange.

The world I've described in this book is substantially different from the world around you today. Emotionally it's hard for us to accept that so much could change, and in such a relatively short time. It's difficult for me, and I work with these concepts every day. Yet look back at how much the world has changed over the last 20 years. Among the many events we've witnessed are:

- The collapse of the Soviet Union and its Eastern European empire, the crumbling of the Berlin Wall, the reunification of Germany, and the demise of communism and socialism as credible economic theories.
- The emergence of Japan as not only the second largest economy in the world, but as the originator of many of the

world's major manufacturing trends, and an established leader in the production of high-quality products. Remember that little more than 20 years ago "Made in Japan" still meant shoddy, inexpensive goods.

- The emergence of RDCs — Rapidly Developing Countries — such as Taiwan, Hong Kong, Singapore, and South Korea, and, more recently, countries such as Malaysia, Indonesia, and Chile. These countries, which we formerly thought of as inconsequential, are now giving the rich, developed countries a run for our money, providing both serious competition and significant opportunity.

- South Africa has made a peaceful transition out of apartheid under the guidance of Nelson Mandela, a former political prisoner who would have had every reason to be bitter toward the white supremacists who had imprisoned him, rather than working with them for change.

- The real incomes of the North American middle class, instead of continuing the steady upward march of the 1950s and 1960s, have stagnated since the late 1970s. No longer are parents confident that their children will live a better life than they have.

- We have gone from a world that was on the verge of running out of oil, where line-ups grew like mushrooms around gas stations, and where people were expecting oil prices to rise to $100 a barrel and $3 a litre at the pump, to one where oil prices are lower, in real terms, than they have been in 30 years. Few people today worry about where tomorrow's oil will come from. Indeed, it is a global coalition of *consuming* nations that is preventing one of the major oil producers, Iraq, from driving down prices by selling oil on the world market.

- Smoking tobacco has gone from being socially acceptable to being universally stigmatized. Twenty years ago, fathers still took their sons to a local tobacco shop to help them choose what brand of tobacco they would smoke. Today we treat smokers like lepers.

- The consumption of large amounts of alcohol has gone from being a cool thing to do to being unhealthy and dangerous. Business lunches today are more likely to feature mineral water than martinis.

- Standards of acceptable discipline used in child-rearing have changed dramatically. Twenty years ago, few people would have commented upon spanking your child in public, much less have you arrested for doing so, as happened in London, Ontario, in 1995. As for the possibility of a 6-year-old boy being suspended from school for giving a 6-year-old girl a kiss that she had asked for, as happened to Johnathan Prevette of North Carolina in September of 1996 — that would have been beyond belief.

- Computers have gone from being million-dollar mainframes supporting batch processing or time-sharing, to being hand-held devices that have substantially more power than those mainframes, yet that weigh less than a kilogram, can communicate by radio or infrared light beams, and cost less than $1,000. Twenty years ago, IBM was thought to be impregnable, and capable of growing forever, and no one had ever heard of Microsoft, Apple, Intel, Dell, or Corel.

- Today you can have hundreds of television signals delivered to your living room by satellite instead of three to five networks dominating the airwaves.

- Twenty years ago, phones were hard-wired into the wall, and belonged to The Phone Company (there was only one in your area). Today, cellular companies give away hand-held portable telephones to new subscribers, and you can call almost anyone, anywhere in the world while walking along the street.

There are lots of other examples of how much, and how fast, the world has changed. The rate of change is also accelerating, so that our lives are going to change even more radically during the next 20 years than they did during the preceding two decades.

I said at the outset of this book that your future life is going to be more like surfing a series of waves than treading a predictable path. The variety of changes I've tried to portray in this book should illustrate what I meant, and should reinforce my point that your future will hold more opportunity and less security than ever before.

Spider Robinson, a Canadian science fiction writer of international repute, once commented that success comes from continually doing the next thing. Let me, then, suggest some ways in which you can figure out what your "next thing" should be.

The Next Thing

Throughout this book, behind the scenes I've balanced an interesting contradiction: individuals are becoming meaningless, yet the individual is more important than ever. Both parts of this statement are true.

Individuals are becoming meaningless because, with 5.8 billion of us crowding the globe today, perhaps 8 billion 20 years from now and maybe 20 billion before the year 2100, one person "don't amount to a hill of beans," as Bogie remarked in *Casablanca*. This is one reason why we feel disconnected from and discontented with our governments: our voices don't seem to matter.

Yet, at the same time, technology and all that it implies is creating a world where one person can influence thousands, millions, or billions of others. Terrorists take hostages and blow up a plane, so millions of people must endure security checks to screen out that tiny fraction of one percent who are dangerous. A scientist discovers the meaning of a particular segment of the human genetic code, and thousands or millions of lives are saved or improved. A techno-weenie beavering away at 3 a.m. in his basement finishes a new piece of software, the world falls in love with it, and an entire new industry appears and eventually employs millions of people. An aborigine eats a newly killed animal in the jungles of Africa, as his forebears did for millennia, but his kill carries a mutated virus that unleashes a devastating new plague that is carried around the world before anyone even knows it exists.

We are leaving an era where governments and institutions determine the shape of the future, and entering an era where the future will largely be shaped by individuals. We may not be able to affect events on the world stage, and that's not necessarily where I would suggest you look. In trying to decide what your next thing is, start from where you are. Look at the people around you, and the tasks close at hand. Pick a task that fits your talents and abilities, and that will affect you, your friends, family, and your community, then start with that. And, when you've found that thing, do it, then do the next thing, and the next, and the next . . . You may eventually wind up doing your next thing on the world stage. If so, it will fit with who you are and where you came from, because you built your way up to it.

Courage

Occasionally people respond with anger and hostility to something I've written or said about the future. At first I couldn't understand why they were reacting to me this way. After all, they merely had to disagree with what I'd said, and ignore it. Why, instead, should they react so strongly to what is, after all, merely one man's opinion?

As I reflected on this over time, I reached the conclusion that I'm merely a convenient focus for their hostility. Their real motivation is fear, and specifically fear of the strange and uncomfortable future that lies ahead of us. They know, consciously or unconsciously, that there will be events and changes that threaten them and their lives, and it is really this knowledge that they are responding to. How do we deal with this fear, and not let it paralyze us?

Viktor Frankl was a Viennese psychiatrist at the outbreak of the Second World War. Because he was a *Jewish* Viennese psychiatrist, he wound up in Auschwitz, the Nazi death camp in Poland. In his horrifying and inspiring book, *Man's Search for Meaning*, Frankl talks about how the human spirit responds to terror and despair. He witnessed it every day in himself and among the other prisoners, and what he found was that most of the men in the camp became passive, merely existing from one day to the next, turning themselves off from life and reality. A few, though, used adversity as a stepping stone to becoming human beings in the fullest sense, turning the bitter experience into a challenge. These men sought ways to change the terror and horror of the concentration camp to inner triumph by retaining their humanity in the face of inhuman treatment.

Frankl describes the despair that drained men's will to live, causing some to cease responding to the beatings of the guards or the entreaties of their friends, who simply gave up and decided to die. "I have nothing to expect of life any more," they would say, and no one knew how to answer them. From these experiences, Frankl reached a profound insight:

> What was really needed was a fundamental change in our attitude toward life. We had to learn ... that *it did not really matter what we expected from life, but rather what life expected from us*. We needed to stop asking about the meaning of life, and instead to think of ourselves as those who were being questioned by life — daily and hourly. Our answer must consist, not in talk and meditation, but in right action and in right conduct. Life ultimately means taking the responsibility to find the right answer to its problems and to fulfill the tasks which it constantly sets for each individual.*

---

* Viktor E. Frankl, *Man's Search for Meaning* (New York: Washington Square Press, 1985), p.98. Emphasis is Frankl's.

We don't need to be in such dire straits to benefit from this advice. Life challenges us to come up with answers to its problems, to fulfil its tasks, and to accept the responsibilities that fall upon us. The answer to our fears must come in right action and right conduct. Our future offers both more opportunity and less security than we have had in the past. How we respond is up to us.

What Did I Miss?

I make no claims to being right about everything. In fact, anybody who talks about the future is giving you their opinions, and necessarily will be wrong some of the time. That's why I say that I don't predict the future, but, instead, try to help people plan intelligently for the future.

I'm sure I've made mistakes, overlooked some factors or events, and made too much out of others. If you know of something I've gotten wrong or overlooked, let me know by writing to me at the following address:

Richard Worzel
c/o Stoddart Publishing Co. Limited
34 Lesmill Road
Toronto, Canada
M3B 2T6

I will reply, if I can. If you want to discuss my speaking, consulting, brainstorming, or other futurist-related activities on a commercial basis, please contact my agent:

The David Lavin Agency
24 Duncan Street, 4th floor
Toronto, Canada
M5V 2B8
Phone: 416-979-7979 or 800-265-4870
Fax: 416-979-7987

Thank you for your interest. I do appreciate it.

Suggested Reading

People ask me how I keep up with all the stuff that goes on in the world, and with what might happen in future, and the simple answer is that I can't. At least in theory, I need to know everything about everything, and neither I nor anyone else can do that. However, *trying* to keep up is a lot of fun, if somewhat frustrating at times. As one way of helping you keep up, here are some publications that might be of interest:

Future Studies
- **Facing the Future: The Seven Forces Revolutionizing Our Lives**, Richard Worzel (Toronto: Stoddart Publishing, 1994). As mentioned earlier, *Facing the Future* complements this book.
- **The Art of the Long View: Planning for the Future in an Uncertain World**, Peter Schwartz (New York: Doubleday Currency, 1991). An eminently readable book that can serve as a text on scenario planning. Based in part on the very successful work of the group of futurists who work for Royal Dutch Shell.

- **Future Search: An Action Guide to Finding Common Ground in Organizations and Communities**, Marvin R. Weisbord and Sandra Janoff (San Francisco: Berrett-Koehler Publishers, 1995). Weisbord and Janoff detail how an organization or a community can come up with a plan that involves everyone, including those people you don't want to include, to accomplish mutual goals that you thought were impossible. This approach will not work with those who are impatient and insist on having their own way, but it is a powerful tool for those who can manage it.

The Economy and Employment

- **The Future of Capitalism: How Today's Economic Forces Shape Tomorrow's World**, Lester C. Thurow (New York: William Morrow, 1996). Thurow is a professor of economics, a former dean of MIT's Sloan School of Management, and an articulate pessimist. His book is well written, well documented, and explains much of what's going on around us.

- **Boom, Bust and Echo: How to Profit from the Coming Demographic Shift**, David Foot with Daniel Stoffman (Toronto: Macfarlane, Walter & Ross, 1996). Foot is a professor of economics at the University of Toronto, which surprises a lot of people who think he's a demographer. He has studied demographics for more than 20 years because he believes it can be helpful in explaining some of the things going on in Canada today. However, much as I respect his work, his explanations are one-dimensional; two-thirds of the future cannot be predicted by demographics, as he contends. Nevertheless, a good, readable introduction to the field.

- **The End of Work: The Decline of the Global Labor Force and the Dawn of the Post-Market Era**, Jeremy Rifkin

(New York: G.P. Putnam's Sons, 1995). This book is two-thirds brilliant and one-third wastepaper. Rifkin's analysis of what is happening to the labour force is excellent, but his suggestions are lame, unworkable, and a disappointing end to an otherwise terrific book.

- **Job Shock: Four New Principles Transforming Our Work and Business**, Harry S. Dent, Jr. (New York: St. Martin's Press, 1995). Dent, like Rifkin, looks at what is happening in the job market these days. Unlike Rifkin, he comes up with specific proposals for companies and individuals to deal with the changes ahead. His proposals are intended for individual action, though, rather than institutional action, which is Rifkin's preference.
- **The Economist**. This weekly British publication (which calls itself a newspaper) is, for my money, the best news magazine of its kind in the English language. It is fiscally conservative, socially liberal, highly opinionated, well reasoned, well written, and thoughtful.

Society and Government

- **Reinventing Government: How the Entrepreneurial Spirit Is Transforming the Public Sector**, David Osborne and Ted Gaebler (Reading, Mass.: Addison-Wesley, 1992). This book has become a bible among officials who are trying to continue delivering services on reduced budgets by making government more responsive and entrepreneurial.
- **Shakedown: How the New Economy Is Changing Our Lives**, Angus Reid (Toronto: Doubleday, 1996). Reid is best known as one of Canada's leading pollsters, but he was trained as a sociologist. He has a keen eye for what's happening in our society, as well as a deep concern for his compatriots and country.

- **The World in 2020—Power, Culture and Prosperity: A Vision of the Future**, Hamish McRae (London: Harper-Collins, 1994). How will global power shift over the next 25 years? Which countries will dominate the global market-place? Will America rise or fall? Hamish McRae, a former reporter with the *Manchester Guardian*, undertakes the task of answering these questions in prose that is crisp, clear, and free of jargon. His only significant omission (other than largely ignoring Canada) is that he hardly mentions Africa.

Health

- **The Coming Plague: Newly Emerging Diseases in a World Out of Balance**, Laurie Garrett (New York: Farrar, Straus and Giroux, 1994). This book reads like a thriller, but its story line is all too real.
- **The Hot Zone**, Richard Preston (Rockland, Mass.: Wheeler, 1994). Similar to *The Coming Plague*, but focuses on the Ebola virus. Forewarned is forearmed.
- **Altered Fates: Gene Therapy and the Retooling of Human Life**, Jeff Lyon and Peter Gorner (New York: W.W. Norton, 1995). Lyon and Gorner, journalists for the *Chicago Tribune*, won the Pulitzer Prize for their reportage on genetic research. This book reminds me of *The Double Helix*, the story of the discovery of the structure of DNA, in that it is readable as a human interest story and informative about an important emerging technology. It also discusses some of the practical and ethical dilemmas we'll face in employing these techniques. The good news flipside of *The Coming Plague*.

Technology

- **Nano — The Emerging Science of Nanotechnology: Remaking the World — Molecule by Molecule**, Ed Regis

(Boston: Little, Brown, 1995). This eminently readable account of Eric Drexler's life and work will surprise you with the possibilities of this largely unrecognized technology. For current information, you'll need to go to the Internet. Try *http://www.foresight.org/index.html* as a starting point.

- **Metaman: The Merging of Humans and Machines into a New Global Superorganism**, Gregory Stock (Toronto: Doubleday Canada, 1993). Stock's fascinating thesis is that humanity today forms a single, collective organism more powerful than any collection of individuals. For instance, he points out that no one individual, starting with only raw materials, could manufacture a modern computer. Computers, therefore, are a product of the human race, not of individual human beings.

- **The Millennial Project: Colonizing the Galaxy in Eight Easy Steps**, Marshall T. Savage (Boston: Little, Brown, 1994). This fascinating book is *not* intended as science fiction; it is a completely serious proposal to do exactly what the title says. Along the way, it offers simple solutions to such problems as energy supply, pollution, overpopulation, and disease. Whether you believe Savage or not, this book will make you look at the cosmos in a different light. Maybe our problems are the result of thinking too *small*!

Acknowledgments

No book is the work of one person alone, even though the author carries final responsibility for it. Let me then thank all those who made this work possible:

My wife, assistant, and first editor, Jacky Simmons. My literary agent, Beverley Slopen. My speaker's agents, David Lavin, Kelly MacDonald, Gisele Robert, Heather Muir, and Cathy Hirst of the David Lavin Agency. Donald Bastian, Angel Guerra, and the helpful folks at Stoddart Publishing. Bob Shoniker of R.G. Shoniker & Associates/Courage Capital. Lee Sobel and Bill Worzel of Arroyo Software. Wilson Markle of Telesat Canada. Francis McInherney of North River Ventures Inc. in New York City. Lewis Jackson, portfolio manager for McLean Budden. Dr. Uri Sagman, oncologist. Don Black, president of Child Health Corporation of America of Kansas City. A senior bureaucrat in a provincial ministry of health who does not wish to be named, but who deserves my thanks anyway. Peter Bouffard, president of Performx Inc. Wili Liberman, editor of *Teach* magazine. Brian Alger, teacher. Tony Redpath of the Ontario Centre for Materials Research. Adrian Browne of Fieldworker Inc., for the idea of changing "global village" to "global villages."

Since I set up shop as a futurist in 1989, I've been fortunate to have worked with a wide range of interesting clients, and organizations that have taken an interest in my work. I'd like to publicly thank them for their support. The list is by no means complete.

Amoco Canada
Bell Canada
British Columbia School Superintendents' Association
Burnaby (B.C.) School District #41
Canadian Association of Broadcasters
Canadian Association of Credit Union Executives

ACKNOWLEDGMENTS

Canadian Association of Financial Planners
Canadian College of Health Service Executives
Canadian Direct Marketing Association
Canadian Gas Association
Canadian Home Builders' Association
Canadian Life & Health Insurance Association
Canadian Paperbox Manufacturers Association
Canadian Parks and Recreation Association
Canadian Produce Marketing Association
Canadian Ski Council
Canadian Standards Association
Canon Equipment Canada
Certified General Accountants Association of Ontario
CIBC Wood Gundy
Credit Union Managers' Association
Crop Protection Institute
Deloitte and Touche
Delta (B.C.) School District
Faultless Starch / Bon Ami Company
Florida A&M University
Grocery Products Manufacturers of Canada
Humber College
IMAX Corporation
International Business Machines
Kansas City Young Presidents' Organization
Manulife Securities International
Marshall Macklin Monaghan
Microsoft Corporation
Mobility Canada
National Research Council of Canada
Nissan Canada
Ontario Association of School Board Officials
Ontario Food Processors Association
Ontario Hospitals Association
Ontario Landscape Architects
Price Waterhouse
Purchasing Management Association
Queen's University
Richardson Greenshields
Stentor Resource Centre, Inc.
Surrey (B.C.) School District
Toronto Law Office Management Association

Index

284

293